FEMINISM A...
MOVEMENT...

PERSPECTIVES ON GENDER

Pleasure, Power, and Technology: Some Tales of Gender, Engineering, and the Cooperative Workplace

Sally Hacker

Black Feminist Thought: Knowledge, Consciousness, and the Politics of Empowerment

Patricia Hill Collins

Understanding Sexual Violence: A Study of Convicted Rapists

Diana Scully

Maid in the U.S.A.

Mary Romero

Black Women and White Women in the Professions: Occupational Segregation by Race and Gender, 1960–1980

Natalie J. Sokoloff

FEMINISM AND THE WOMEN'S MOVEMENT

DYNAMICS OF CHANGE IN SOCIAL MOVEMENT, IDEOLOGY AND ACTIVISM

Barbara Ryan

Routledge
New York ● London

Published in 1992 by
Routledge
An imprint of Routledge, Chapman and Hall, Inc.
29 West 35 Street
New York, NY 10001

Published in Great Britain by
Routledge
11 New Fetter Lane
London EC4P 4EE

Library of Congress Cataloging in Publication Data

Ryan, Barbara,
   Feminism and the women's movement: dynamics of change in social
movement ideology and activism / Barbara Ryan.
     p. cm.—(Perspectives on gender)
   Includes bibliographical references and index.
   ISBN 0–415–90598–2.—ISBN 0–415–90599–0 (pbk.)
    1. Feminism—United States—History—19th century. 2. Feminism—
United States—History—20th century. I. Title. II. Series:
Perspectives on gender (New York, N.Y.)
HQ1426.R93 1992
305.42′0973—dc20
                                                           92–91
                                                            CIP

British Library Cataloguing in Publication data also available
ISBN 0-415-90598-2 (HB)
ISBN 0-415-90599-0 (PB)

To my mother,
Edith Eileen Dougherty Ryan

and children,
David, Paul, and Jeanne Harris

CONTENTS

Acknowledgments   ix

Abbreviations   xi

Introduction   1

Chapter 1
THE EARLY WOMAN'S MOVEMENT: FROM EQUAL
RIGHTS TO SUFFRAGE   9

Chapter 2
THE WOMAN'S SUFFRAGE MOVEMENT AND THE
AFTERMATH OF VICTORY   21

Chapter 3
RESURGENCE OF FEMINISM: THE CONTEMPORARY
WOMEN'S MOVEMENT   39

Chapter 4
IDEOLOGICAL PURITY: DIVISIONS, SPLITS, AND
TRASHING   53

Chapter 5
SOCIAL MOVEMENT TRANSFORMATION: THE WOMEN'S
MOVEMENT FROM 1975 TO 1982   65

Chapter 6
CHANGING ORIENTATIONS IN IDEOLOGY AND
ACTIVISM   79

Chapter 7
AMERICAN WOMEN AND THE WOMEN'S MOVEMENT
DURING THE REAGAN/BUSH YEARS   99

Chapter 8
DIVISIONS REVISITED: PORNOGRAPHY, ESSENTIALISM/
NOMINALISM, CLASS AND RACE   113

Chapter 9
THE SEARCH FOR A NEW MOBILIZING ISSUE: THE
WOMEN'S MOVEMENT AFTER THE ERA   135

Chapter 10
CONCLUSION   153

Notes   163
Bibliography   177
Index   197

ACKNOWLEDGMENTS

There are many people who have contributed to this research. For productive discussions and continuous encouragement I thank Norma Mendoza, Donna Theis, Geneie Williamson, Chris Guerrero, Mary Ann Randell, Judy McNeilly, and the members of the Thursday on Friday Discussion Group, most notably Jan Whitaker, and Eric Plutzer.

Bill Berg, Sylvia Pedraza-Bailey, David Pittman, Don Strickland, Marvin Cummins, and Henry Berger provided needed assistance in the early years of formulating and defending my dissertation topic, which began this work. Rebecca Klatch added to my thinking about women's activism in general; and Joyce Trebilcot deserves my deep gratitude for broadening my understanding of feminism in countless ways. As the chair of my dissertation committee, John Zipp provided me with strong support from the beginning of my thinking about doing this research. It is difficult for me to find the right words which will express how much he contributed to this work. Without doubt, his impact can be found in a project which increasingly became more focused and analytical.

The people mentioned above were living in the St Louis area when I began this research, most were students or faculty at Washington University. It saddens me to think how a university that provided so many of us with an environment to meet and develop our ideas no longer has a sociology department. For all my negative feelings about that administrative decision, I remember the years I spent there fondly and I appreciate the research funds Washington University provided for the early stage of this study. In addition, faculty development awards which contributed to my ability to complete this work came from Widener University, for which I am very appreciative.

Input from other social movement scholars, particularly those involved with research on the women's movement, have sharpened my thinking and impacted in critical ways the final analysis developed in this book. For sharing their insights, criticisms, and suggestions I thank Myra Marx Ferree, Verta Taylor, Judith Lorber, Clarence Lo, Pamela Oliver, Steven Buechler and Janet Saltzman Chafetz. I particularly want to thank Myra Marx Ferree for encouraging me to publish this work and then providing me with guidance on how to do that.

Lisa Freeman, before she left Allen and Unwin was my first editor, and her enthusiasm for this book is appreciated. When Allen and Unwin became Unwin Hyman, Loren Osborne became my new editor and she provided encouragement until Unwin Hyman became a part of HarperCollins where the fine editorial skills of Sarah Dann at HarperCollins contributed to this book. While editing the final copy of this work, I was notified that HarperCollins had sold the Unwin Hyman Academic program to Routledge, Chapman and Hall. Thanks to Max Zutty and James Geronimo, this fourth and last transition was accomplished smoothly with Routledge in getting this book to press.

I am indebted to Scott Graczyk, Judy McNeilly, and Suzanne Wells for volunteering their time to transcribe interviews, Karen Zimmerman for arranging to have interviews transcribed by work study students in the Women's Studies Program at Washington University, and Valorie Perry for translating my editing notes into readable form. Students in my social movement class engaged me in lively discussions on feminism and the women's movement; I particularly want to acknowledge Davida Karol Craig, Joanne Halley, and Christine Lee for conducting four of the interviews that were used in this project.

Those others who also suffered through the process of this research and writing deserve special recognition. To this end I have dedicated this book to my mother and my children for providing me with love and care, and for giving me their understanding and patience through these years; and to Standford Snyder I acknowledge my deepest appreciation for his continuing support in the midst of my distractions over finishing this work.

Finally, I want to thank the feminist activists who generated the data this research is based on. It is these activists, and the many who came before them, that have created an environment in which women's generalized discontent could be organized into a vibrant and long lasting social movement. I thank them for their commitment to improving women's lives and for sharing their knowledge with me. Without their efforts this book would not have been possible.

ABBREVIATIONS

AAUW	American Association of University Women
ASA	American Sociological Association
AT&T	American Telephone and Telegraph
AWSA	American Woman's Suffrage Association
BPW	Business and Professional Women
CARASA	Committee for Abortion Rights and Against Sterilization Abuse
CD	Civil Disobedience
CIA	Central Intelligence Agency
CR	Consciousness Raising
CU	Congressional Union
CWLU	Chicago Women's Liberation Union
DOB	Daughters of Bilitis
DSA	Democratic Socialists of America
DSOC	Democratic Socialist Organizing Committee
EEOC	Equal Employment Opportunity Commission
ERA	Equal Rights Amendment
FACT	Feminist Anti-Censorship Taskforce
HOTDOG	Humanitarians Opposed to Degrading Our Girls
HOW	Happiness of Womanhood
IWY	International Women's Year
LDEF	Legal Defense and Education Fund

NAACP	National Association for the Advancement of Colored People
NAM	New American Movement
NARAL	National Abortion Rights Action League
NAWSA	National American Woman's Suffrage Association
NOW	National Organization for Women
NWP	National Woman's Party
NWPC	National Women's Political Caucus
NWSA	National Women's Studies Association
NWSA	National Woman's Suffrage Association
NYRW	New York Radical Women
PAC	Political Action Committee; Progressive Action Caucus
PCSW	President's Commission on the Status of Women
RCERA	Religious Committee for the Equal Rights Amendment
SCLC	Southern Christian Leadership Conference
SDS	Students for a Democratic Society
SM	Social Movement
SMO	Social Movement Organization
SNNC	Student Nonviolent Coordinating Committee
S-R	Stimulus Response
SWP	Socialist Workers' Party
UAW	United Auto Workers
UFAC	United Feminist Action Campaign
WAP	Women Against Pornography
WCTU	Women's Christian Temperance Union
WEAL	Women's Equity Action League
WILPF	Women's International League for Peace and Freedom
WITCH	Women's International Terrorist Conspiracy from Hell
WRAP	Women's Radical Action Project
WTUL	Women's Trade Union League
YSA	Young Socialist Alliance

Knowledge and experience have to be gathered
by wide and prolonged study;
they do not come by an infinite repetition
of the same private experiments.
Charlotte Perkins Gilman, *The Home,* 1903

The content of education itself validates men
even as it invalidates women.
Its very message is that men have been
the shapers and thinkers of the world.
Adrienne Rich, *On Lies, Secrets
and Silence,* 1979

Let us never cease from thinking—what is this
"civilization" in which we find ourselves?
What are these ceremonies
and why should we take part in them?
What are these professions
and why should we make money out of them?
Where in short is it leading us,
the procession of the sons of educated men?
Virginia Woolf, *Three Guineas,* 1938

INTRODUCTION

The origins of sociology can be traced to the social upheavals of the nineteenth century when the desire to understand social change led to the development of a study of society.[1] Within this framework a central interest has been social movements, those groups of people intent upon having a say in how social relations are organized.[2]

Historically, social movement research has centered on personality characteristics of participants and retrospective analyses of the factors leading to the origin or demise of a movement.[3] The ongoing process of change within the movement, while it is occurring, has received little attention.[4] Consistent with most research on social movements, studies of the contemporary women's movement have focused on the organizing stage and the differences between various groups of feminist activists.[5] Far less attention has been given to movement transformation, including changing group relations related to constituent pressure, shifting social conditions, and societal resistance.

Organized activity on behalf of women's rights began in the United States in the mid-1800s. The U.S. women's movement is, in essence, a movement that is nearly a century and a half old. The contemporary movement is connected to the early movement through the basic desire to bring about equality for women in the social structure. Although there have been differences in defining exactly what constitutes women's equality, the fundamental desire for improvement in women's condition underlies the history of feminist organizing.

This book is a study of feminist group relations and social movement change in the contemporary women's movement in the United States. The woman's rights movement and the suffrage movement are included in order to examine effects of earlier activism on the present, and to establish the continuity of thought and process in women's organized efforts to change social systems and gender relations. The contemporary movement, now a quarter of a century old, has existed under two contrasting social environments. It is a movement consisting of distinct sectors and diverse groups, some of which no longer exist and others of which have undergone substantial alteration. These characteristics of the contemporary movement, plus the historical connection of earlier feminist activism, make the U.S. women's movement a good case study for examining social movement change.

Much of the literature on the contemporary movement adopted a description of movement sectors developed in the early 1970s which analytically divided activists by group and ideology into alternative feminist perspectives. Distinctions were drawn between a "women's rights" and "women's liberation" sector, with further ideological classifications identified as socialist, radical, and liberal feminism. Because contemporary theoretical analyses of feminist ideology were originally formulated within either a Marxist or radical feminist perspective, liberal feminism was generally viewed negatively in terms of both ideology and activist method. Yet, it is this segment of the movement which constitutes the majority of participants in the United States, and it is largely liberal feminists who can be found in rape crisis centers, abortion clinics, monthly strategy meetings, pickets, marches, state legislative sessions, and congressional hearings. Liberals, it appears, are short on theory but long on activism.

The actual work of the movement, and who does it, raises questions about the use of feminist identifications which divide activists into competing ideological camps. Moreover, because these divisions are not constant, that is, they sometimes rise to the fore and other times fade into the background, understanding how and why these "toleration" shifts occur is central to the study of social movement change. For instance, a fluctuating pattern of solidarity and fragmentation began in the latter part of the 1970s when feminist ideological divisions became more ambiguous and a "rights" vs. "liberation" distinction was no longer clearly evident. Indeed, by the early 1980s theoretical consistency appeared to be developing among activist groups, with strategies moving primarily towards political engagement. However, after the defeat of the Equal Rights Amendment (ERA) in 1982, divisions once again arose, although these divisions were not replications of the earlier period.

Despite these dramatic shifts, very little work has been done on analyzing change in activist direction and feminist relations within the contemporary women's movement. Thus, there is a need for research which both describes current movement characteristics and analyzes the social forces, structures, and processes which facilitate social movement change.

This research was instituted to study the women's movement as a social movement in order to delineate the forces of change operating from both within the movement and outside the movement. For the purpose of this study the contemporary movement is divided into three time periods: the organizing stage (1966 to the mid-1970s), the unity mobilization period (1975–1982), and the post-feminist[6] era (1982–1990). The first period, initially characterized by the excitement of discovery, represents the culmination of a transition process throughout the early part of the 1970s. By 1975 many of the original groups had disbanded, even as the movement experienced substantial growth in numbers and new organizations. Disarray spread, reassessments were made, and new leadership emerged. By the end of the 1970s a growing anti-feminist backlash encouraged internal movement realignment leading to a concerted ERA drive by diverse feminist groups. Yet, in the post-ERA period, amidst a decade of resistance from outside forces, a loss of unity is reflected in the re-emergence of intra-movement hostilities.

ANALYTICAL FRAMEWORK

The theoretical perspective used for this research is resource mobilization. A resource mobilization approach is useful in studying the life history of specific movements (Zald and McCarthy 1979), for examining the level of societal support and constraint on movement organizing (Oberschall 1973; Tilly 1978), and to connect social movements to the central political processes of society (Skocpol 1979).

A resource mobilization framework focuses on the ways a movement creates interest and support for its goals. Resources refer to assets such as money, expertise, media attention, power, and votes; however the primary resource is the people around which the movement is organized. Mobilization refers to the control and use of assets, particularly how people get together and what they do. Mobilization is defined in two ways: activation of commitment and creation of commitment (Gamson 1975). Mobilization as activation involves the already committed members and the forms of organization and activism they undertake. Mobilization for the creation of commitment concerns the actions implemented by the movement to increase the base of potential participants, i.e. developing raised consciousness to that part of the constituent group which is not yet active.

By using the basic tenets of resource mobilization theory, social movements can be examined on a number of different levels; for example, to explain why different segments of a movement initiate different types of social change strategies (Freeman 1979), what types of outcomes are related to variant tactics (Tilly 1978), and how movements become transformed from dormancy into action

(Lofland 1979). An important component of resource mobilization theory, therefore, is the variability of research questions that can be explored. A second positive aspect is the range of questions that can be omitted. For instance, this theory takes as evident that there is deprivation, that there is awareness of it, and that there is discontent because of it. The question changes from why people join a social movement to how people attempt to change their condition.

Using this theoretical framework a centrality of analysis is the ongoing problems and strategic dilemmas which contribute to the dynamic of growth, decline, and change within a social movement. Typically, these areas of interest are examined by focusing on the structure and working of social movement organizations. This analysis has led to a critique of resource mobilization based on the lack of this perspective's incorporation of ideology and symbolic meaning in the mobilization and commitment process (McPhail 1983; Tilly 1983; Zurcher and Snow 1981). Because resource mobilization was developed with the intention of replacing analyses of movement participants with an analysis of movement organizations (McCarthy and Zald 1977), it is not surprising that this framework is now being criticized for too much emphasis on structure (Turner 1983).

When emotional response is left out, the documentation of mobilization strategies is incomplete because ideology and symbolization are used by social movements as effective strategies for mobilization. Previous resource mobilization research has relegated ideology to an unimportant position since it has been considered a "given" with a consistent agreed upon meaning. But ideology has multiple meanings and those meanings are subject to change over time. Thus, a central feature of this book is an analysis of the impact of ideology and symbolic meaning for feminist activism and feminist group relations.

METHODOLOGY

Most books and studies on the women's movement have been done by either academics, who are usually not activists, or activists who write about what they know from their personal experience in one particular group.[7] Given the desire to find out how change in the broad-based movement came about, I gathered data on feminist groups and activists that represented both the small group sector and the mass movement sector of the movement. The research methods employed were primary and secondary literature review, participant observation and oral history interviews.[8]

Questionnaires of large numbers of people would not provide answers to questions requiring insider knowledge. Select people, literature, and events offer the possibility of learning the interactive process of social movement transformation. In viewing the world through the eyes of feminist activists, the aim is to understand activism in participants' own terms in order to interpret the meaning of diverse forms of feminist groups and the changes that evolve over time within and between groups.

Although not inclusive, the following constitute the major groups studied for this research. Representative of liberal feminism is the National Organization for Women (NOW), the oldest and largest of the contemporary women's rights organizations; and the National Women's Political Caucus (NWPC), founded in the early 1970s to promote women in politics. Included are a variety of radical feminist groups, most of which no longer exist, such as New York Radical Feminists and The Redstockings from the origin stage; and others, such as A Group of Women and A Grassroots Group of Second Class Citizens, representing groups which arose to introduce civil disobedience into the ERA campaign. Socialist feminist groups are represented by the Chicago Women's Liberation Union, one of the most enduring of the women's unions, finally disbanding in the late 1970s; and the New American Movement (NAM), organized specifically to be a socialist feminist organization, merging in 1982 with the Democratic Socialist Organizing Committee (DSOC) to become the Democratic Socialists of America (DSA). Also included in this study are a variety of service-oriented organizations,[9] academic feminists involved in women's studies, non-aligned feminists, and participants in different aspects of the women's culture.

The primary documents consist of leaflets, flyers, newsletters, position papers, organizational newspapers, and feminist networking publications. Some of these publications were collected during my participant observation studies, some were given to me by activists who had started archival collections in their localities,[10] and some were found in the women's section of the Special Collection Department at Northwestern University, the Library of Congress, and the Schlesinger Library on the History of Women in America, Radcliffe College.[11] Publications were examined for (a) similarities and differences between groups, (b) changes over time in definitions of problems/solutions, and (c) the use of ideology and symbols for creating meaning in issues and actions.

Participant observation for this study officially began in Fall 1980. I participated in movement activities of the National Organization for Women, including state council meetings, state and regional conventions, and five national conferences, the last in 1987. In 1980 I joined the New American Movement (NAM), attended local meetings, a national interim committee meeting, one national convention, and the formal merger meeting resulting in the new organization of Democratic Socialists of America (DSA). In 1982 I joined the Congressional Union (CU) and in 1983 I became a member of a splinter group called A Group of Women.[12] In 1983 and 1984 I attended national "Women's Gatherings," participating in the particular kind of activism they specialize in: civil disobedience.

Interviews of feminist activists provided the major source of data for this research project. These interviews furnish information on current movement ideology and actions from the perspective of involved participants. The structure of the interview was open-ended and informal; the purpose was to gain factual information and experiential insights from varied perspectives. For questions related to ideology, I asked respondents their personal definition of feminism, what ideological label they applied to themselves, how they acquired their feminist beliefs, and how these beliefs changed over time. For questions related to activism, I asked why they were members of a particular organization(s), how they felt the kind of activism they did affected the generalized goals of women's liberation, and if/why their group's method of goal attainment changed from the early years of involvement to the present. These interviews were oral history interviews which included background information of respondents and their personal life experiences.

INTERVIEW SELECTION

Forty-four interviews were done on feminist activists located in various parts of the country. Three criteria were used in the selection of those to be interviewed: long-term activism, individuals who were leaders or well-known theorists, and participants who would jointly represent the broad spectrum of ideological perspectives and activist strategies.

I felt participants who became active in the movement after the mid-1970s would not be aware of what the movement was like before that time and would not be in a position to give an accurate comparison. Therefore, I decided to interview people who had been involved at least since the early 1970s. Leaders and theorists were the people who would know not only what changes took place, but also how and why, since many of them would have been intimately involved in the process. For the third criterion, I wanted to be sure I had representatives of liberal, socialist, and radical feminism as well as activists who were involved in political work, civil disobedience, theoretical development, and the women's culture.

Even though I had a clear idea of who I wanted to interview and how I would proceed, some modifications were adopted during the course of the research. One of the first was a loosening of my selection criteria. This change was based on interviews of non-aligned feminists and activists who had only recently become involved, and a growing recognition on my part that feminism and the women's movement consists of more than organizations specifically stating their goal as that of women's liberation.[13]

Through my participant observations, I learned about individual activists and different types of involvement. Based on this information, I actively sought out either particular people or particular types of people. For the most part, I wanted representatives of groups or issues rather than specific individuals per se. The major exceptions to this were Eleanor (Ellie) Smeal, a long-time leader of the

National Organization for Women, and Sonia Johnson, organizer of a number of feminist groups involved in civil disobedience. In the case of these two activists, I felt they each represented particular orientations which developed within the movement out of their leadership.

There was nothing random about my selections although in most cases individuals could be replaced by another person representing their position. Aside from Smeal and Johnson, there were also some activists I was particularly interested in because of their unique backgrounds. An example of this type of feminist activist is Chris Riddeough who has a history of activism in the Chicago Women's Liberation Union, New American Movement, Democratic Socialists of America, and the National Organization for Women.

I used three methods to get the broadest spectrum of feminist activists without expending inordinate amounts of travel time and money. First, I did interviews of people within a short travel range, i.e. from St. Louis to Chicago. This area was accessible to me and happened to be a major area of feminist activism. Illinois was a highly activist state for a sustained period of time during the ERA drive. Springfield, the state capital, hosted political organizing, frequent marches, a fast, a vigil, and numerous acts of civil disobedience. Moreover, Chicago had been the home of the first Women's Liberation Union and the former national headquarters of both the National Organization for Women and the New American Movement.

This contact method brought me in touch with diverse types of activists, but still left me without representation from activists in other parts of the country in national leadership positions. Because I had limited external funds for this research, I narrowed my vision to one area of the country which was a repository of organizations and activist events—Washington, D.C. The national offices of NOW, the National Women's Political Caucus, and A Group of Women were all located there. In addition, the year I traveled to D.C. to do interviews there was a three-day "Women's Gathering" for feminists interested in taking part in a civil disobedience demonstration on Women's Equality Day,[14] one day before the Civil Rights 20th Anniversary March. By planning my trip when there would be an influx of feminist and civil rights supporters into the City, I was able to connect with people from the upstate New York area and extend my travel to include a visit to the Seneca Falls Women's Peace Encampment.

A final method of accessibility to desired respondents was to go to feminist conferences where activists I was interested in interviewing were scheduled to speak. This setting offered a cluster of people from around the country in one location, and I successfully used this method on a number of occasions.[15]

My major criterion in selecting interviewees was to reach feminist activists with diverse orientations. An interesting finding in my research is that the activists I interviewed revealed a high level of cross membership, congruent ideology, and dual activism roles. This finding becomes important in later chapters for understanding problems in current definitions of "types" of feminism.

OUTLINE OF THE BOOK

Following this introduction is an overview of the nineteenth-century woman's rights movement, the factors which led to the transformation of this movement into a movement for women's suffrage, and the decline of feminist activism after the achievement of the 19th Amendment. Chapters 3–5 detail the resurgence of feminism in the 1960s, analyze the process of change leading to the noticeably altered mid-1970s period, and examine the ERA drive and the 1982 defeat of this amendment. Since the ERA had been a major goal throughout the 1970s, this was a significant point in the history of the movement. Chapters 6–9, on the post-ERA period, examine how a social movement responds to a defeat of this proportion, and discuss the promise and problems of a new mobilizing issue for the 1990s. The conclusion draws together the previous chapters and presents an analysis of change in the women's movement.

PERSONAL REFLECTIONS

I need to conclude with a more personal note. Over the last century, the concept of women's rights has led feminist activists to embark on many paths in attempting to achieve a more equitable society. Feminism in its many diverse forms does not appear to be an inconsequential passing phenomenon; there is every indication that it is an instrument for fundamental social change processes of significant proportion. For this reason, a study of the U.S. women's movement is central to understanding American society. However, my decision to study feminism and the women's movement was not made for this reason alone. Quite simply, I wanted to study this movement because I believe in the importance of women organizing to change themselves, their lives, and the social environment. By researching feminist activism, I had the opportunity to interact with history making people and events; to become, quite literally, intimately connected to one of the most impactful social movements of this century and to contribute to the expansion of knowledge about feminist women's experiences and achievements.

Chapter 1

THE EARLY WOMAN'S MOVEMENT: FROM EQUAL RIGHTS TO SUFFRAGE

> But I ask no favors for my sex, surrender not our claim to equality. All I ask of our brethren is, that they take their feet from off our necks, and permit us to stand upright on that ground which God designed us to occupy.
>
> (Sarah Grimke, 1837)[1]

Early women's rights advocates began their activism by thinking that women's secondary position in society was the result of some mistake, an oversight, carried on through ignorance and custom, to be righted by bringing the matter to public attention. In the nineteenth century, women's rights advocates embarked on a mission to inform the public of the need for change in women's status in the social system. They undertook a variety of issues, eventually focusing on the vote as a necessary step in the process of having a say in the social and political decisions over their lives. A simple enough demand in a democracy premised on citizenship participation. But the history of the early woman's movement reveals another story altogether.

Beginning with the first call for the franchise in 1848, over 500 separate campaigns were launched in the years it took to achieve women's suffrage. These included 56 state referendum campaigns, 277 separate efforts to persuade state party conventions to add women's suffrage to their planks, 19 congressional battles, and the ratification campaign in 1919 and 1920 (Kraditor 1981; Papachristou 1976; Blatch and Lutz 1940; Catt and Shuler 1923). Susan B. Anthony traveled the country speaking on women's rights and suffrage for over 40 years

(Barry 1988). Elizabeth Cady Stanton engaged in lyceum trips, those "long weary pilgrimages from Maine to Texas, that lasted twelve years; speaking steadily for eight months—from October to June" (Stanton and Blatch 1922: 218). More than 200 suffragists were arrested, eventually to be vindicated by an appeals court which ruled their arrests and imprisonment illegal, but not before many had suffered imprisonment and forced feedings. Yet, a century later we are informed that:

> One of the easiest victories of the democratic cause in American history has been the struggle for the extension of the suffrage. . . . The struggle for the ballot was almost bloodless, almost completely peaceful and astonishingly easy. Indeed the bulk of the newly enfranchised, including Negroes and nearly all women, won battles they never fought. (Schattschneider 1960: 100)

That the denial of suffrage was only one of many wrongs women set out to right, and that this one issue took 72 years to win, is lost in Schattschneider's description. In calling the achievement of women's suffrage "astonishingly easy," whole generations of women's lives are negated. In addition, the resistance to women changing conceptions of themselves and their place in society is obscured.

In actuality, the first U.S. woman's movement had a long and varied history involving many aspects of social movement change. Indeed, the fact that this first wave of the women's movement had a markable beginning and end makes it readily assessible for examining issues pertaining to the origin, spread, and decline of a social movement.

THE ORIGINS OF THE WOMAN'S RIGHTS MOVEMENT

When the woman's movement began many people had never seriously entertained the thought that women's role might be differently arranged than it was. But the idea of women's rights was not new. Preceding the rise of an organized women's movement, debates on the equality of the sexes can be traced back to much earlier historical periods. For instance, written protests are found in the eighteenth century, most notably with the publication of Mary Wollstonecraft's *Vindication of the Rights of Women*. Published in England in 1792, Wollstonecraft was about 50 years ahead of her time, and this publication was generally met with ridicule by women and men alike. However, she did find readers in the United States as two editions were published and a synopsis of her work was printed in 1792 in *The Lady's Magazine and Repository of Entertaining Knowledge*.

The first tract on women's equality to be taken seriously, and to gain widespread recognition, was by John Stuart Mill. In 1861 he published *The Subjection of Women* (see Mill 1970), an intellectual analysis of women's position in society, developed over a 28-year working relationship with Harriet Taylor. Through this publication Mill is often credited with providing the liberal philosophy which spawned the ideology of the woman's rights movement. However, this assertion fails to take into consideration the collaboration of Mill with Taylor, and, in particular, the influence of Taylor's more feminist views.[2]

In addition, the development of the woman's movement precedes the publication of Mill's article. An organized woman's movement began in the United States in 1848 when the first women's rights conference was held in Seneca Falls, New York. Although this conference is considered the beginning of the U.S. woman's rights movement, the roots of 1848 go back to the turn of the century and are found in a number of parallel developments, beginning with women's activism in moral reform causes.

Philanthropy and feminist consciousness raising

In the early 1800s, women began working for reform in the areas of prostitution and prisons. Women's involvement in these issues almost always began through church auxiliaries and, in accordance with the dictates of the times, were separate from male reform organizations. Over time this church-related activity developed into an accepted role for women outside the home: benevolent philanthropy.

There were two important outcomes for women working in moral reform societies. First, they were able to develop confidence in their ability to organize and get things done. In recognizing their own capabilities, women began to cultivate "both a sense of personal worth and a pride in their sex" (Berg 1978: 193). And second, they developed a conscious awareness of themselves and other women as a sex category.

Throughout the nineteenth century, the spread of industrialization and urbanization created both misery and affluence side by side. Middle-class women, being beneficiaries of the latter, had time for outside activities. Through their charity work they became aware of class inequalities; but even more starkly, they were confronted with the negative effects of gender differentiation. Women, they knew, were a group separate from men. Still, as they could see when they began associating with those less fortunate than themselves, women did not constitute a unified group equally affected by their sex classification. Early philanthropy was centered on poor widows, unmarried mothers, and prostitutes; the mission for the middle-class woman was to help these lost souls convert to a better way of life (Hogeland 1976). However, interactions with prostitutes and poor women led reformers to feel that the problem was not deviant women; rather it was a social problem created by an unfair system. Deviant women were, after all, only

women who did not have a male protector. Indeed, without the men who supported them, what would their own situation be?

Rather than instilling a feeling of superiority, reform work left middle-class
women feeling vulnerable. In a remarkable turn of events, philanthropist women
identified with "deviant" women, emphasizing the similarities of women rather
than the differences (Berg 1978). Here then was a germ of feminist thinking, a
reversal of de Beauvoir's conception of women as "other"—that "moment in
woman's self-perception, when she begins to see man as 'the other' . . . when
her feminist self-consciousness begins" (Lerner 1977: xxiii).

Philosophical and religious influences

Women had been influenced as much as men by the libertarian sentiments generated by the Enlightenment and the French Revolution (O'Neill 1969). Closer
to home, the American Revolution provided an ideology which, at least in
theory, legitimized the idea of sex equality. Nevertheless, when applied to
women, there were other material and ideological beliefs overriding the philosophy of the new democracy. During much of the 1800s, both by law and by
custom, women were considered "non-persons." African-American women who
were slaves had no rights at all, while other women were restricted in their
opportunities for self-support through poverty wages. Married women were prevented by English Common Law from inheriting property, controlling their own
earnings, or retaining custody of their children upon divorce. No woman could
serve on a jury or vote on the laws that governed them (Bjorkman and Porritt
1917).

The law was a powerful restraining force on the emancipation of women, but
an equally strong restraint was the religious principles which maintained wives'
rightful subordination to their husbands. On the other hand, the power of religious ideology was a motivating factor for some women. Many of the early
activists were first initiated into a consideration of women's equality through the
practices of their Quaker religion. Another religious support was the evangelist
revival begun in the late 1700s.

The new evangelism was a refutation of fundamental beliefs found in Calvinism, most importantly the belief in predestination. The puritan work ethic, derived from Calvinism's ethos of hard work and frugality, was based on a belief
in having been chosen by God at birth for a heavenly afterlife. The way one
knew they had been chosen was revealed in their success in their present life
through clean living, equated with hard work. Such beliefs set the stage for the
accumulation of surplus, a necessary precondition for the growth of a capitalist
economic system in the new society. Over time, as capital accumulated, the
proof of one's chosen state was displayed through ornate homes and leisure
consumption. Symbolically, non-employed and elaborately adorned wives be-

came part of this display, described by Thorstein Veblen (1899) as conspicuous consumption and conspicuous leisure.

In opposition to the increasingly distorted beliefs and practices of Calvinism, the wellspring of revivalism was that good works, not predestination, were your passage to heaven. One could earn their way in.

The evangelist revival presented a doctrine of perfectionism in which there was an "acceptance of an obligation to perfect oneself and one's community" (Griffith 1984: 20). Thus began a spirit of reform which influenced the spread of most early nineteenth-century social movements. The major contribution evangelism made to women's advance was to encourage activist participation in church work. Many women were attracted to this revivalism, and "Congregational Presbyterian women began to do in the late 1820s what only Quaker women had been able to do up to this juncture—to speak in public" (Rossi 1973: 257).

The educated woman

Aside from a Quaker or revivalist background, the most common feature women activists shared was an educated background. Education for slaves was non-existent and for non-salve women suppressed. Before an organized woman's movement began, middle-class women were agitating for the right to higher education. Arguments were put forth in terms of the benefits to be accrued to the husband and children of educated mothers and wives. Believing this to be true, Emma Willard petitioned New York legislators for funding to open a female seminary which would offer courses in the tradition of men's colleges. The state refused her request, but in 1821 she opened Troy Female Seminary with local tax money. Even as Willard espoused a traditional role for women, Elizabeth Cady Stanton, a student at Troy, found a role model in Willard as a person with self-respect and dignity. Given the liberating effects of education, it is not surprising to learn that women who graduated from Troy did not follow traditional gender role expectations. In spite of the fact that Willard's goal was to make better wives and mothers, "her pupils were less likely to marry than women in general and, if married, they bore fewer children than their contemporaries" (Scott 1984: 80).

In 1833 Oberlin College opened its doors to all races, creeds, and sexes. Initially women were admitted so that they might be trained for their future role as proper minister's wives and for the calming influence they might exert on boisterous male students (Hogeland 1976). Overriding the known subversive elements of an educated mind, women were allowed to slip into the universities. This mistake was explicitly discovered when some of the first Oberlin graduates, instead of being cultured appendages of their husbands, began breaking down gender barriers. Early graduates included Lucy Stone, soon to become a leader in the woman's suffrage movement, and her sister-in-law Antoinette Brown, first woman to become an ordained minister.

For activist women, education was seen as a chance for women to improve their own lives, as well as a vehicle for changing traditional views of women held by the rest of society. The Enlightenment conviction that reason paves the way to progress lay at the base of most progressive social movements of this period. Rational principles generated in women an "enthusiastic, if naive, belief in education as the cure-all for human ignorance and corruption" (Rossi 1973: 3). Thus, it was educated women who began the woman's rights movement, convinced that, by educating the populace about the injustice of women's position, equitable laws and practices would follow.

Temperance and abolition work

An important reform movement which moved women into the public arena was temperance. In the 1830s hundreds of church-related temperance societies with women's auxiliaries were formed. Unlike early philanthropists, women who joined the temperance movement did not do so solely for altruistic reasons. Although temperance began as a campaign based on moralistic and ethical standards of behavior, a husband's consumption of alcohol could be destructive to his wife's life because married women were dependent on and subject to their husband. Women temperance workers did not generally believe in women's equality; they wanted restrictions on alcohol use in order to maintain a secure "moral" family life. Nevertheless, they were involved in an attempt to change gender relations since it was men's behavior they were trying to regulate.

Elizabeth Cady Stanton publicly connected temperance and women's rights by advocating divorce when alcoholism was present. Shocking as this was to most reformers at the time, within a few years they began to feel that "temperance was a matter of women's rights as well as a religious and humanitarian reform" (Papachristou 1976: 19). In 1849 Amelia Bloomer established *The Lily*, a temperance newspaper, which also became a voice for women's suffrage when Stanton began contributing articles under the pseudonym "Sunflower" (Griffith 1984: 64).

Social reformers tended to be involved with multiple issues: temperance, moral reform and, the cause which was most likely to lead women into activism in their own behalf, abolition. Lucretia Mott, Elizabeth Cady Stanton, Susan B. Anthony, Lucy Stone, Antoinette Brown, and the Grimke sisters were all involved in efforts to eliminate slavery. In the early 1830s when anti-slavery societies were formed, Lucretia Mott was present at the organizing meeting of the American Anti-Slavery Society. None of the women in attendance were allowed to sign the founding document, but Mott asked for and was given permission to speak. A short time later she helped found the Philadelphia Female Anti-Slavery

Society (Papachristou 1976: 3–4) and later was one of the organizers of the Seneca Falls Women's Rights Conference.

In the course of speaking against slavery and the criticism they received for this activity, female abolition workers became self-consciously aware of women's subordinate position. Frances Wright, a British-born activist, publicly attacked the idea of an "appropriate sphere of woman" and shocked audiences when she lectured on the combined issues of anti-slavery, social reform, and women's rights. Two American speakers to confront criticism were Angelina and Sarah Grimke, who studied under Theodore Weld, an advocate of women's participation in the evangelism movement. In their lecture tours with the American Anti-Slavery Society, the Grimke sisters often received a negative reception—not on the content of their abolition talk, but because they were women speaking in public. As a result, they began including the issue of women's rights in their lectures. Talk of women's rights, though, antagonized many of the clergy and abolitionist supporters. Lucy Stone attempted to solve the dilemma by speaking about abolition on weekends and about women's rights during the week (Hole and Levine 1971); however, resistance among abolitionists persisted. In 1837 Angelina Grimke wrote that she and her sister had found themselves, unexpectedly, "in the forefront of an entirely new contest—a contest for the rights of women as moral, intelligent and responsible human beings."[3] This experience led the two sisters, in their speeches and writing, to draw women's rights and abolition together theoretically.

After three years of lecturing and writing, Angelina Grimke married Theodore Weld, symbolizing "the joining of the two reform movements of antislavery and woman's rights" (Rossi 1973: 262). The marriage of Grimke and Weld was only one of a number of such intimate connections between the two social movements. Lucretia Mott was married to abolitionist James Mott, Elizabeth Cady Stanton to Henry Stanton, also an abolitionist leader. Lucy Stone married Henry Blackwell, who was influential in the abolition movement and later in the movement for women's suffrage, and Antoinette Brown became Lucy Stone's sister-in-law when she married Blackwell's equally active brother Samuel (Flexner 1975; Rossi 1973). In spite of these activist unions, the "woman question" remained a controversial debate in anti-slavery circles.

Although women and men worked together in abolition societies, in the mixed-sex groups women had their place. Indeed, it was at the 1840 World Anti-Slavery Convention in London, where women were refused recognition as delegates, that Lucretia Mott and Elizabeth Cady Stanton first discussed the idea of organizing a women's rights convention.

Much has been made of women's recognition of their own position in society through working in abolition. Drawing a connection between the slave's condition and women's status did occur; however, other factors, including denigrating treatment from male abolitionists, contributed to this process. As Carol Ellen

DuBois argues, women did not discover their secondary status through abolition work:

> [T]heir discontent was as much cause as effect of their involvement with the anti-slavery movement. What American women learned from abolition was less that they were oppressed than what to do with that perception, how to turn it into a political movement. (1978: 32)

ORGANIZING A MOVEMENT

It took eight years for Mott and Stanton to meet again to plan the first women's rights convention. Given only a few days' notice of a meeting to be held in a small rural area in upstate New York, the significance of the event was demonstrated by the fact that over 100 people attended the 1848 Seneca Falls Woman's Rights Convention. Paraphrasing the Declaration of Independence, the tone of the convention was set by the opening remarks: "We hold these truths to be self-evident, that all men and women are created equal." Resolutions were passed calling for women's equality in education, inheritance, property rights, divorce, and child custody. Only one resolution did not pass unanimously: a call for the franchise. This radical demand eventually became the rallying cry for millions of women, but for those in attendance in 1848 only one 19 year old lived long enough to vote (Flexner 1975).

Within a month another convention was held in Rochester, New York. Through her mother and sister, who had attended the Rochester convention, Susan B. Anthony learned of this beginning organizing effort for women's rights. However, Anthony, a Quaker heavily involved in abolition and temperance work, did not become involved initially. It was three years after the first women's rights convention before Anthony and Stanton met, beginning a long-term friendship and collaboration as leaders of the radical wing of the woman's rights movement (Barry 1988; Dubois 1978).

The reaction of these early meetings was immediate. A barrage of negative press helped publicize and call attention to women's rights and, as a result, local small groups formed in the Northern states. Larger geographical linkages were forged by holding annual national conventions. Within a short time the women grew bold as their numbers increased and they gained confidence in themselves. In the spring of 1850, the Salem Ohio Women's Rights Convention had the first, and only, all female cast of officials and presenters. Men were not allowed to speak, even as part of the audience, a format which was a fundamental change from previous time. For example, education advocate Emma Willard always asked a male to speak for her on the podium or, if she had to speak, she would do so while sitting in a chair. Even the Seneca Falls Convention had been chaired by Lucretia's Mott's husband as none of the women felt equal to the task (Hole and Levine 1971; Rossi 1973; Flexner 1975; Scott 1984).

A convention in Worcester, Massachusetts in 1850 had an international effect. Harriet Taylor wrote about the organized agitation of American women and made a plea that the example set in America be followed in England. Before the year was up a petition was presented to the House of Lords calling for the franchise for English women.

In 1851 at an Akron, Ohio convention, male participants tried to take over the meeting, proclaiming that women's inferior physical abilities allowed them to involve themselves only in home activities. Sojourner Truth, a former slave, stepped forward and gave her historic "Ain't I a Woman" oratory debunking this argument.

> But what's all did her talkin 'bout? Dat man ober dar say dat women needs to be helped into carriages, and lifted ober ditches, and to have de best place every whar. Nobody eber help me into carriages, or ober mud puddles, or gives me any best place and ain't I a woman? . . . Look at me! Look at my arm! I have plowed, and planted, and gathered into barns, and no man could head me—and ain't I a woman? (Martin 1972: 103)

Because there was no mass media or rapid transportation system, the spread of the movement was slow, mainly by word of mouth. There was no organized national movement; women in attendance at one meeting chaired the next in another location. The substance of the meetings reflected the participants, nearly all of whom shared similar backgrounds and concerns. The movement, therefore, consisted of a scattering of groups with an agreed upon women's rights agenda. There was no conflict over ideology or theory, as almost none was articulated. The early woman's movement was simply seen as an extension of natural rights to women than men already possessed.

Dress reform as an early challenge to feminine restrictions

From the beginning of organized women's rights activity, the press had belittled activists; but the first major defeat was suffered in the dress reform movement of 1851–54. The new style of clothing feminist introduced consisted of a knee-length skirt with pantaloons. The costume became known as the Bloomer after Amelia Bloomer publicly advocated the "short dress" in *The Lily*. Dress reform was eagerly adopted by early feminists as a release from uncomfortable and unhealthy clothing. In addition, dress reform was seen as a way to change perceptions, both personal and social, about women's role. The excitement of the experiment with freedom quickly cooled, however, when unabated ridicule was heaped on Bloomer women. As a result, most gave the costume up after a short time.

The Bloomer had been designed and initiated by Elizabeth Smith Miller, cousin of Elizabeth Cady Stanton and only daughter of abolitionist leader Gerrit Smith. After Stanton stopped wearing the Bloomer, Smith scolded her for not being able to sustain the dress reform goal. Women's dress style, he wrote in an 1855 letter, has been one which "imprisons and cripples," much like the cramped foot and degradation Chinese women have been forced to bear. He went on to declare that women's voluntary imprisonment indicated a contentment with their helplessness (Smith 1968 [1855]: 125).

In Stanton's reply she argued that attaining equal relations between women and men went far beyond style of clothing. Slaves, she reasoned, are kept in simple uninhabited garb, but slaves they are still. Thanking him for his concern, she insisted that it was women alone who would decide what needed to be done to allow them to be their own person. As to the frequently heard charge that women feared the loss of chivalry with the wearing of the Bloomer, she cynically remarked:

> In social life, true, a man in love will jump to pick up a glove or bouquet for a silly girl of sixteen, while at home he will permit his aged mother to carry pails of water and an armful of wood, or his wife to lug a twenty-pound baby, hour after hour, without ever offering to relieve her. . . . If a short dress is to make the men less gallant than they now are, I beg the women at our next convention to add at least two yards more to every skirt they wear. (Stanton 1968 [1855]: 131)

Stanton, along with other women's rights activists, wore the Bloomer only about two years, although Elizabeth Smith Miller prevailed for seven. When Susan B. Anthony expressed concern that abandoning the costume might be taken as a sign of a lack of commitment, Stanton replied:

> We put the dress on for greater freedom, but what is physical freedom compared with mental bondage? . . . It is not wise Susan, to use up so much energy and feeling that way. You can put them to better use.[4]

Pragmatism, and occasional timidity, were found in the early woman's right movement. Yet, even as many of the changes activists sought seem mild to twentieth-century sensibilities, the woman's rights movement was radical. Feminists were asking for "simple justice," an appeal which actually called for vast changes in women's social and economic position, as well as in traditional gender attitudes. In departing from the prevailing belief of separate natures for the sexes, these early advocates argued for egalitarian relations premised on similar capabilities. The feminist foundation of their ideology was a view of women as autonomous human beings.

The Civil War years and post-war schisms

From the 1850s until the Civil War, the movement was mainly concerned with grassroots organizing. Activism consisted of meetings, conventions, and petitions to state and national legislative bodies. Women's rights was closely tied to antislavery, so much so that the woman's movement depended on the abolition movement for much of its constituency. With the onset of the Civil War in 1861, all activity for women's rights was suspended.

Northern women became active in gathering food and bandages for the war effort. In less than two months, the government officially authorized a Sanitary Commission based on the organizational work already being done by women's groups. The Sanitary Commission provided the supplies and labor needed for the care of the wounded, work that brought Northern women out of their homes and into the war effort. Although no organization such as the Sanitary Commission developed in the South, Southern white women also experienced a changed role, from "belle" to overseer of plantations and businesses.

In 1863, after a number of Southern victories, Susan B. Anthony and Elizabeth Cady Stanton called a convention of women to form a Loyalty League. President Lincoln had issued the Emancipation Proclamation, but it freed slaves only in the Rebel states. They proposed the need for a constitutional amendment (the 13th) that would also free slaves in the border states and that would prohibit slavery permanently. In addition, they wanted this amendment to provide "liberty to all; national protection for every citizen under our flag; universal suffrage, and universal amnesty" (Stanton and Blatch 1922: 197). Ironically, in forming the Women's Loyal National League, a division between abolition and women's rights emerged. Of the resolutions presented at the convention, only one provoked controversy: the inclusion of the franchise for both the freed slaves and women. Those in attendance were split on whether to include women as this might cause the amendment to fail. Stanton, Anthony, and Lucy Stone were the most outspoken supporters in favor of keeping the two issues together. Stone, who chaired the convention, argued that "if the right of one single human being is to be disregarded by us, we fail in our loyalty to the country" (quoted in Stanton, Anthony, and Gage 1881: 65).[5]

The 13th Amendment outlawing slavery passed without mentioning suffrage for blacks or white women. Immediately afterwards, a 14th Amendment was proposed with the intent of granting citizenship rights to freed slaves and, by inference, suffrage. The 14th Amendment was significant because it contained the word male, the first time this designation had been used in the Constitution. In 1866 at the first Woman's Rights Convention held since the war, a coalition abolition and women's rights organization, the American Equal Rights Association, was founded. The question of whether to support the 14th Amendment as it was written in order to at least get citizenship rights for black males, or reject it in favor of an amendment which also included women, was debated. Women's rights activists raised the question of black women being left out of this amendment, but it was clear from the resistance this issue created within abolition circles that, in this case, black women were to be classified into a sex category.

The 14th Amendment with the words "male citizen" left intact was passed. In 1869 a 15th Amendment was introduced to grant black males the right to vote. Once again, women's efforts to have sex included in this amendment were rebuffed by abolitionists who feared this inclusion would jeopardize passage. Undesirably, the forces for abolition and women's rights, instead of working together, were now pitted against each other.[6]

Anthony and Stanton organized the National Woman Suffrage Association (National) to work for the inclusion of women in the 15th Amendment. The National was the first independent organization formed for women that was defined and controlled solely by women. In association with the National, Stanton and Anthony published *The Revolution,* a journal covering an array of issues meant to address a broad spectrum of women's concerns.

Six months after the founding of the National, the American Woman Suffrage Association (American) was formed to work for passage of the 15th Amendment as it was worded with the intention of working for a 16th Amendment for women's suffrage after passage of the 15th. This organization, led by Lucy Stone and her husband Henry Blackwell, tended to represent civic and professional women and placed its efforts on state referendums for women's suffrage. Stone and Blackwell published *The Woman's Journal,* which focused on the sole issue of suffrage.

Before the war, the woman's rights movement had made progress on a number of issues raised at the 1848 conference. For instance, the activists had made significant gains in two of their most sought after goals: inheritance rights and entrance into educational institutions. However, passage of the 14th and 15th Amendments constituted a political setback for white women as they were now, for the first time, explicitly excluded from politics. For more than five years, activists for abolition and women's rights had been intensely involved with the issue of suffrage. The result of these efforts, the 15th Amendment granting black males the vote, showed women they had no power to influence the content of laws. Moreover, the extensive effort expended by abolitionists to secure suffrage for African American males helped to strengthen the view that suffrage was the key to altering the legal position of women as well (DuBois 1978). It is not surprising, then, that by the end of the 1860s the primary goal of the woman's movement was to obtain equal status through the vote; and thus, the woman's rights movement became the woman's suffrage movement.

Chapter 2

THE WOMAN'S SUFFRAGE MOVEMENT AND THE AFTERMATH OF VICTORY

[I]f woman would fulfill her traditional responsibility to her own children; if she would educate and protect from danger factory children who must find their recreation on the street; if she would bring the cultural forces to bear upon our materialistic civilization; and if she would do it all with the dignity and directness fitting one who carries on her immemorial duties, then she must bring herself to the use of the ballot—that latest implement for self-government. May we not fairly say that American women need this implement in order to preserve the home?

(Jane Addams, *Why Women Should Vote*, 1917)

Feminism is as broad and definite as we make it. . . . Political freedom—simple permission to vote—is a very tiny part of freedom, and we want all there is.

(Alice Park, *The Suffragist*, 1920)[1]

The split in the early woman's movement originated over a strategic dispute, but also resulted from antagonistic feelings which had developed on the part of the leaders. When a social movement divides into contending factions, the result can be beneficial or destructive. The possible negative effects are the amount of time spent on intra-movement sectarian quarrels and internal attack. The possible benefits are increased numbers and types of participants, and the creation of new ideas, issues, and methods. The National Woman Suffrage Association and the American Woman Suffrage Association attempted to represented different segments of the population; but, because this schism was not primarily an ideological division, it was incapable of producing a significant contrast in goals or organizing efforts. Both groups were committed to the principle of equal rights for women, and both felt the vote represented that principle. As Eleanor Flexner has argued, the two groups clashed "not on whether women should vote, but on *how* that goal could be won" (1975: 156).

From 1870 to 1890 the movement consisted of the American and the National working separately at educating the populace through speaking tours and the distribution of printed materials. The American worked almost solely on state referendums for women's suffrage. The National worked for a federal suffrage amendment and on state referendum campaigns; they also ventured into other issues,[2] unsuccessfully in some, such as trade unionism for women,[3] and embarrassingly into others, such as free love.[4]

Although little advance was made in achieving the vote, the speaking tours were laying a foundation for new attitudes to develop, if not about suffrage, at least about women assuming more public roles. The process of gaining suffrage provided inspiration to women throughout the country to see themselves in a broader enlightened context. Jessie Harver Butler, an activist in the Consumers' League in the 1920s and in the women's liberation movement in the 1960s, remembers how such activism influenced her mother's commitment to woman suffrage:

> I remember vividly when the campaign for women's suffrage was going on in Colorado, how she climbed into that spring wagon. I can see her yet doing it. She toured that valley to get the men to vote for woman's suffrage. And this wasn't something that a good little housewife, even in Colorado, in those days was supposed to do. Of course, this is when that great woman's suffrage leader, Susan B. Anthony, had been all over the state for months. (Butler 1976: 65)

When women moved out of the home into public arenas, they established a role model for other women to follow. Even the late nineteenth-century club woman's movement contributed to this emancipatory trend, since club meetings were set up solely for women's pleasure and engagement beyond their family role.

CONSERVATISM IN THE PROGRESSIVE ERA

In 1890 the two suffrage organizations reunited into the National American Woman's Suffrage Association (NAWSA). Both the National and the American had spent 20 years working for a cause in which neither had been successful. With this truce, the movement began extensive mobilizing efforts. Coalitions were forged with other women's groups and local suffrage organizations sprang up throughout the country. Elizabeth Cady Stanton was voted the first president; the following year Lucy Stone died and two years later Stanton was discredited when her book *The Woman's Bible,* a non-sexist reinterpretation of Christian doctrine, was published. Anthony took over the leadership, holding it until 1900, but she found it difficult to maintain a progressive direction with the influx of more moderate activists brought in through the organization's coalition and mobilization efforts.

Support for suffrage was now being drawn from a wave of Christian reform sweeping the nation. New groups and associations were formed in unprecedented numbers during the period 1890–1920, known as the Progressive Era. Local laws were being enacted for the enforcement of Sunday closings, censorship, and social purity legislation.[5] Christian feminism, found predominantly among women temperance workers, was part of a developing coercive approach to reform. The Progressive Years saw the Women's Christian Temperance Union (WCTU) develop into the largest and most influential women's organization in the country. By the mid-1890s the WCTU had half a million members while NAWSA had fewer than 10,000 (DuBois 1981: 178).

The WCTU was organized as a religious experience and the work its members promoted was considered a moral crusade. Yet, in 1879 the WCTU experienced a progressive impulse under the leadership of Frances Willard. A dynamic organizer and speaker with far-reaching interests, Willard expanded the issues of the temperance movement from an isolated concern with alcohol to a broad-based set of social concerns. She moved the WCTU from saloons to the political arena, and overcame opposition to women's suffrage by arguing that the ballot was the best means to secure protection of the home and family (Flexner 1975; Gusfield 1970b; Papachristou 1976). At Willard's death in the late 1890s the WCTU concentrated on temperance again; however, the commitment and interlocking interest of temperance with suffrage remained.

Another new force, the settlement house movement, also became interested in women's suffrage. Hull House in Chicago, founded by Jane Addams in 1889, was the first and most famous of the settlement houses. Settlement houses were places where middle-class reformers lived in the middle of city slums in order to more completely work with the residents in the area. Rather than finding an unfortunate underclass, settlement residents found their services being used by working-class women who could not earn enough money to provide for their children. This led settlement workers to become involved in the campaign for women's suffrage in order to affect labor laws. Thus, Jane Addams became a frequent speaker at NAWSA meetings, serving on the board and publishing in *The Woman's Journal*.

More women were attending universities during this period and, as had occurred earlier, educated women challenged traditional ideology about women's place. In the latter part of the 1800s, as new universities were built in the Midwest and Western regions of the country, administrators found themselves in a situation similar to the Civil War years when many colleges formerly admitting only male students began to enroll women so that they might maintain tuition figures. By 1892 when the University of Chicago opened, 40 percent of the entering students were women. Ten years later there were more female than male students, as was the case at other schools in this part of the country. Increasing female enrollment provided both economic relief and academic concern to university officials.

> If the great fear among educators in the post-Civil War years was of declining enrollments and bankruptcy, the fear of the 1900s was that the universities might become female academies. Schools that had welcomed women when they represented economic salvation now worried that American universities had only been saved from the fate of insolvency to be subjected to the much worse fate of feminization. (Rosenberg 1982: 44)

At the University of Chicago the first department of sociology was established and the first sociological journal, the *American Journal of Sociology (AJS),* was published. Social interaction theory was developed there in what is now called The Chicago School of thought. Biological theory of sex behavioral differences was displaced by a sociological theory based on the dichotomous social worlds that female and male children enter at birth (Rosenberg 1982).

Jane Addams lectured at the University of Chicago and published in the *American Journal of Sociology.* Conversely, university social scientists frequented Hull House and used it as a laboratory for study (Whitaker 1984). Both the social action of women and the research milieu at the Chicago School supported the study of gender roles as legitimate areas of inquiry. For instance, Jessie Taft's thesis, *The Woman's Movement from the Point of View of Social Consciousness* (1916), argued that "emancipation was not simply an economic or a political problem; it was a psychological one as well" (Rosenberg 1982: 141).

Charlotte Perkins Gilman also published frequently in *AJS,* espousing the need for women's economic independence and a reorganized family arrangement, issues echoed by others such as anarchist Emma Goldman, socialist Chrystal Eastman, and birth control crusader Margaret Sanger. New scientific thought and "radical" ideas added additional support to the belief that women need not be excluded from the public domain.

Activists were interested in improving women's lives, but they did not agree on what was needed to accomplish this task. Some argued for equal treatment of the sexes, others believed that women needed special protections. An example of women's involvement in social reform favoring the need for protection was the Consumer League. Local leagues were organized in the 1890s for the purpose of involving consumers in the conditions of workers. In 1899 the National Consumers' League was formed in order to investigate the labor conditions of women and children. Florence Kelley, a former resident at two settlement houses (Hull House in Chicago and Henry Street in New York), was elected president. She led the League to take a position supportive of women's suffrage based on her belief that women possessed stronger reform tendencies than men and, with political power, could create humanitarian social conditions. Later she became one of the staunchest opponents of the Equal Rights Amendment because of her desire to obtain protective labor legislation for women and children.

There had been attempts to unionize women since the mid-1800s. Most were short lived because of the lack of support from male unions and the difficulties women had in finding time for union activism. In 1881 the Knights of Labor invited women to join their ranks, and at one time 50,000 women were members. But by the 1890s the Knights declined in influence and the American Federation of Labor (AFL) became the rising union organization. The AFL, however, did not welcome women into its fold. On the contrary, the AFL was pivotal in dividing workers along gender lines. Without the assistance of the organized labor movement, women workers turned to middle-class reformers and political legislation to improve their working conditions (Kessler-Harris 1975).

By the early 1900s 20 percent of the workforce was female; yet working women earned only 53 percent of what men earned in the same jobs (Papachristou 1976). Women's lower pay was well known, but a sex wage differential was justified on the premise that men were breadwinners, and thus there was a need for a male family wage. Indeed, union leaders and legislators continued to advocate women's place as the home and to warn of the dangers to the loss of femininity if women moved out of their "protected" sphere. There is a sense of *déja vu* when, some 50 years after Sojourner Truth made her "Ain't I a Woman" plea on behalf of slave women, Rose Schneiderman, a union member and suffrage activist, made a similar plea on behalf of working women:

> We have women working in the foundries, stripped to the waist if you please because of the heat. Yet the Senator says nothing about these women losing their charm. . . . Of course you know the reasons they are employed in foundries is that they are cheaper and work longer hours than men. Women in the laundries for instance, stand for thirteen or fourteen hours in the terrible steam and heat with their hands in hot starch. Surely these women won't lose any more of their beauty and charm by putting a ballot in a ballot box once a year than they are likely to lose standing in foundries or laundries all year round. (Quoted in Flexner 1975: 267)

The comforts of femininity and a male head-of-household ideology held little salience for single, working-class, and equal rights women. Indeed, persistent efforts to improve women's wages led women organizers to talk of sex oppression as early as the 1830s (Taylor 1979).

In 1903 Lillian Wald, founder of the Henry Street Settlement in New York, and Jane Addams were among those present at the founding of the Women's Trade Union League (Addams [1910] 1960). Middle-class and working-class women worked together in the WTUL to improve working women's lives; interest in suffrage was based on the usefulness of the vote for changing their working conditions. The WTUL successfully promoted both feminism and trade unionism; a dual commitment which theoretically, and in actuality, revealed a desire for female solidarity across class lines (Fish 1988).

Women were gathering in various associations during the last two decades of the nineteenth century. The Club Woman's Movement was the most widespread, with groups forming in rural and urban areas alike. Women's clubs were basically literary and social groups in origin, but even these gatherings were held in suspicion by those afraid of change in women's roles. For instance Grover Cleveland, in a May 1905 issue of *The Ladies' Home Journal* argued that:

[T]his particular movement is so aggressive, and so extreme in its insistence, that those whom it has fully enlisted may well be considered as incorrigible. . . . I believe that it should be boldly declared that the best and safest club for a woman to patronize is her home. (Quoted in Gluck 1976: 9–10)

In 1890 the club movement federated into the General Federation of Women's Clubs, and by the turn of the century the Federation was actively supporting women's suffrage. Black women formed separate clubs similar to white women's clubs, although their clubs included the political goal of improving racial conditions. Indeed, it was out of the black women's club movement that Mary Church Terrell in 1896 helped organize the National Association of Colored Women and from which Ida B. Wells Barnett led the anti-lynching movement. Black women's clubs worked for suffrage either through their club associations or by forming autonomous suffrage organizations (Flexner 1975).

Southern white women were among the last to organize. When NAWSA held their annual convention in New Orleans in 1903 the spread of southern white women's participation increased noticeably; however, in order to maintain their involvement, questionable policies within NAWSA were allowed to be adopted. The organization agreed to a "states rights" concept, allowing individual states to decide organizational structure and suffrage provisions, such as education and property qualifications. In this way racially segregated suffrage groups could be organized and, if woman suffrage passed, black voting rights could still be restricted. Reminiscent of an earlier period, the organization nearly split in two when NAWSA took the previous abolitionist position that the race question and the woman question were separate issues. Unlike the earlier period when abolitionists classified African American women by sex, suffragists were now classifying African American women by race.

SOCIAL MOVEMENT EFFECTS OF COALITION BUILDING

A critical social movement task is gaining new adherents, particularly those who become activists. Implicitly, then, an increasing base of support has constituted a major indicator of social movement advance. However, this assumption, when applied to the early woman's movement, raises questions about the effect large numbers of new recruits have on the ideological foundation of a movement.[6]

For instance, at the same time Elizabeth Cady Stanton was holding established religion responsible for maintaining women's inferior position, the WCTU was using religion to draw adherents to its cause. The tone of lectures at WCTU meetings and NAWSA meetings revealed different perceptions of women's role in society. One position, often called social feminist,[7] claimed for women a higher moral calling based on the differences between the sexes, while the other position, self-defined as the feminist position, argued for sex equality based on the similarities between women and men. Yet, in the campaign for the vote, NAWSA and the WCTU became allies, forging a coalition and establishing joint memberships for many participants.

Enlarged support through coalition ties can also affect a movement because of the opposition new groups may bring with them. Even though the woman's movement was now pursuing a single goal, this one issue was related to many others. The more suffrage was seen as a tool rather than a principle, the more concrete the opposition became. For instance, when activists argued for the vote to combat women's problems in the workplace, manufacturing interests took notice.

In a like manner, the Women's Christian Temperance Union brought to the suffrage movement committed workers but also committed enemies. In the minds of those interested in preventing the passage of either the 18th Amendment (Prohibition) or referendums for establishing dry states, votes for women was equated with the passage of Prohibition. Suffragists reported many fraudulent election practices, such as the buying of new immigrant votes by the "wet" forces. Throughout the 1800s there was a steady migration of new immigrants, with the largest numbers entering the country during the Progressive Era—at the peak more than 10,000 a day. All referendum questions were limited to the voting population, meaning only men could vote on whether women should be allowed the same privilege. Many times the immigrants did not understand English, but the suffrage question was put on a separate ballot, often colored pink, to make it easier to vote according to instructions (Catt and Schuler 1923; Blatch and Lutz 1940).[8]

When women in the South began joining NAWSA, southern legislators banded together to block women's suffrage in their states. The ten states that failed to ratify the 19th Amendment were the heart of the former Southern Confederacy.

They defended their position by arguing for a state's rights position even though the South had given the Prohibition campaign some of its strongest support. In the first year the 18th Amendment was introduced to the states, 11 Southern States passed it. Indeed, "every state that failed to ratify the women suffrage amendment on the alleged ground of federal interference ratified the federal prohibition amendment" (Catt and Shuler 1923: 487). In contrast to the rest of the nation, the South was in favor of dry status but not in favor of women's votes. This apparent contradiction was based on a fear that extending suffrage to women would reaffirm the 15th Amendment and therefore, end voter qualification laws which kept black males from voting.[9]

This brief history reveals that after 1890 the suffrage movement gained support from diverse groups and experienced an ever-increasing and overlapping membership base. However, along with additional proponents came additional opposition. Thus, the more interests that mobilized for suffrage, the broader the implications of women voting, and the wider the resistance.

NEW FORCES AND NEW METHODS

In spite of new sources of support, by the end of the first decade of the twentieth century NAWSA's membership was less than 100,000 and no state had passed suffrage for 14 years.[10] The English suffrage movement, under the influence of Emmeline Pankhurst, had introduced the use of militant tactics in their campaign. Three American women, Harriot Stanton Blatch, Alice Paul, and Lucy Burns, gained experience with this method through their participation in the English movement. Upon returning to the United States, Harriot Stanton Blatch, daughter of Elizabeth Cady Stanton, formed a New York suffrage association, introducing street speaking and parades. Within NAWSA, Alice Paul and Lucy Burns attempted to mobilize a federal amendment strategy, rather than the state-by-state campaign that had been pursued since the 1890s. In 1912 the board of NAWSA appointed Alice Paul, Lucy Burns, and Crystal Eastman to a Congressional Committee to investigate the possibility of a federal suffrage amendment. The plan was given so little support that NAWSA allowed them a budget of only $10 per year.

In 1914, leaving the constraints of NAWSA behind, Alice Paul organized the Congressional Union (CU) and embarked on an energetic, newsworthy, and militant campaign for suffrage (see Blatch and Lutz 1940; Gluck 1976; Irwin 1921; Stevens 1920). She "staged scenes," introducing tactics and splash not found in the movement since its inception. Always calling newspapers ahead of time, she organized demonstrations on a grand scale with stirring songs and pageantry. The Union adopted colors—purple, white, and gold—held parades with women dressed in white carrying tri-colored banners, and established a weekly publication, *The Suffragist*.

Congressional Union members engaged in actions to call attention to the issue of suffrage, thereby keeping it in the minds of the President, Congress, and public. Innovative strategies were introduced, including a 1915 caravan from California to Washington in which CU members collected over 500,000 signatures petitioning for women's suffrage. They applied pressure to President Wilson by arranging delegations to visit the White House from the Women's Trade Union League and the General Federation of Women's Clubs. In 1916, in the states where women could vote, the CU formed a Woman's Party to divert women's votes from the Democratic Party. This campaign did not prevent Wilson from getting re-elected; however, the Woman's Party was able to claim a woman's protest vote (Irwin 1921; Stevens 1920).

In 1917, the United States declared war on Germany. Ignoring the war, the Congressional Union officially became the National Woman's Party (NWP). The NWP initiated picketing at the White House and held "Watchfires of Freedom" in which they burned newspaper clippings of President Wilson's words. The first picket lines appeared in January, and for the next year and a half, on most days that Congress was in session, women carrying purple, white and gold banners were to be found in front of either the White House gates or the Capitol. Delegations representing different states or organizations took turns on the picket line, thereby insuring a constant reminder to the President and legislators of women's demand for suffrage. The effect of the new militant tactics on the Woman's Party was both the defection of large numbers of members and even larger numbers of new recruits. By the end of the campaign the membership had grown to about 25,000 activists (Irwin 1921).

Seen as unpatriotic for continuing to picket during the war years, the NWP went even further when they co-opted war messages for their cause. Using President Wilson's own words, they displayed a banner declaring "we shall fight for the things which we have always held nearest our hearts—for democracy, for the right of those who submit to authority to have a voice in their own government" (Irwin 1921: 207).

The NWP hoped to embarrass the government by calling attention to the "inconsistency between a crusade for world democracy and the denial of democracy at home" (Stevens 1920: 84). Another banner read: "Kaiser Wilson, have you forgotten your sympathy with the poor Germans because they were not self-governed? Twenty million American women are not self-governed. Take the beam out of your own eye."

After six months of uneventful picketing, the first of a series of arrests began, which extended over a year. Attacks by heckling crowds became a frequent occurrence. Each time banners were ripped away, new processions of women with banners appeared. On one day 148 banners were destroyed. Arrests continued and always the women refused to pay their fines.

Increasing penalties were invoked, resulting in prison terms of 30–60 days at the Occoquan Workhouse. Eventually some suffragists, including Alice Paul, were sentenced to seven months in prison. Calling themselves political prisoners, 17 imprisoned suffragists went on a hunger strike. The response from authorities was to force feed them through a tube in their nose. The jail itself was filthy, overrun with rats, and the food was "loaded with worms" (Kettler 1976: 244). Under public pressure the government released the suffragists early, and upon their release they toured the country in prison garb telling of their experience. The NWP honored 81 former prisoners with silver "prisoner of freedom" pins at a mass meeting which raised over $86,000 to continue the picketing (Stevens 1920). This process of arrest, refusal to pay fines, jailing, hunger strikes, forced feeding, and eventual release continued throughout the remainder of the suffrage campaign. With the constant coverage provided by the press, women's suffrage became a household word.

At the same time that the National Woman's Party was engaged in dramatic protest, there were changes going on within the National American Woman's Suffrage Association. In 1915 Carrie Chapman Catt, who had been president of NAWSA from 1900 to 1904, once again resumed leadership. Catt, an experienced organizer, immediately set about increasing membership. In addition, she introduced a "winning plan" to accomplish the goal of suffrage by 1920 on the federal level. This plan represented a change in strategy from a sole emphasis on state referendums to immediate passage of the federal amendment. With both major suffrage organizations utilizing different tactics to achieve the same goal, the amount of suffrage activity in the nation's capital was greatly increased.

Based on a belief that antagonizing the Democratic Party would be harmful rather than beneficial, NAWSA participated in the parades organized by NWP but not the picketing. Throughout those last years NAWSA remained on cordial terms with President Wilson and, after the U.S. entry into World War I, when the NWP displayed banners declaring America undemocratic, NAWSA publicly denounced those tactics. Even when Woman's Party members were being jailed and force-fed, NAWSA remained silent and did nothing to help secure their release. Both organizations were fervently committed to attaining suffrage for women, both felt the time for succeeding was upon them, and both felt the tactics employed by the other were an impediment to achieving their mutual goal.

As the suffrage movement gained strength, important changes were occurring in the social and political climate. In 1913, when Alice Paul began mobilizing a militant wing of the movement, the 16th and 17th Amendments were passing Congress. Both of these amendments reflected progressive impulses: the authorization of a federal income tax (called a communist measure by those opposing it), and the election of U.S. senators by citizens rather than state legislative bodies. A period of social change brought on by World War I and the reconstructive mood at the war's end (November 1918) left an opening for new directions. It was during this period that other countries were granting suffrage to women—26 in all between 1915 and 1920 (Blatch and Lutz 1940). Importantly, in the United States 30 states had already passed presidential suffrage for their female residents by the end of 1919. Moreover, the 18th Amendment, having passed Congress, was ratified by the states in January 1919. With the passage of Prohibition, much of the fierce resistance from the liquor interests collapsed and within six months Congress passed women's suffrage.

In the final years of the suffrage campaign NAWSA claimed a membership of 2 million, an astounding number for a social movement.[11] Even as NAWSA pushed for a federal amendment, the organization continued to work at the state level, first by having state constituencies pressure their representatives in congress, and, second, by building state organizations to pass referendums allowing women to vote in those states. Once Congress passed the amendment, the highly organized state affiliates began their work. Finally, on August 26, 1920, the state ratification process was accomplished and the 19th Amendment, allowing women to vote, became part of the United States Constitution.[12]

SOCIAL CHANGE AND SOCIAL MOVEMENT CHANGE

Social movement change does not occur in a vacuum. It is an ongoing process of responding to other forces in society. By integrating the study of social movement transformation with social history we can see the interactive effects of change in the larger society with change in a social movement.

The demands of the early movement were bold, certainly out of step with the social environment of the times. This phase of the movement was a time for creating an idea and spreading it. Introducing new ideas or behavior is risky (even if in later years it is seen as mild); yet, caught up in the fervor of the moment, activists tend to scorn public opinion. For instance, years after the dress reform movement many feminists wondered how they had summoned enough nerve to wear the short dress (Stanton and Blatch 1922). This early phase, whether activists actually do something purposely to shock the public or their actions are simply seen as shocking, serves the purpose of gaining attention. As Elizabeth Cady Stanton argued: "It will start women thinking, and men, too, and when men and women think about a new question, the first step in progress is taken" (quoted in Griffith 1984: 58).

Later, in the attempt to create a mass movement, an aura of legitimacy is needed. When the early woman's movement split it was not simply over a different strategy related to the 15th Amendment; it was also over whom the National and American associated with and what issues they took up. The name and content of their respective publications reveal they were addressing different segments of the population. As women's suffrage became more acceptable over time, the National and the American were able to merge and begin forming coalitions with other groups around the issue of suffrage. Having settled on one goal, and one that had become legitimate, the organization was moderate enough for greater numbers of women to join.

The interacting process of social movement activism and the social environment also operates in the relationship between the various organizational components making up the movement. Thus, the introduction of alternative tactics is part of a developing social movement ambience which serves the purpose of simultaneously sustaining the movement and charging it with new energy. Through the development of new, even oppositional social movement groups, the movement introduces different methods, which both increases awareness and broadens the base of support. For instance, when the movement became stale, even while growing in numbers, the formation of the Congressional Union/National Woman's Party provided innovative tactics and strategies. Militancy arose because woman's suffrage had become so acceptable no one noticed it.

The introduction of militancy created more publicity, which in turn increased the possibility of greater concern for the passage of the 19th Amendment. Indeed, with the increased awareness created by the picketing and subsequent arrests of NWP members, NAWSA was assisted in mobilizing new members across the country in its state organizing campaign, a direct result of a more extreme group helping a more moderate group become more socially acceptable to join.

During the last phase of the suffrage movement, the NWP and NAWSA each claimed that the other was harming the progress of women's suffrage. The National Woman's Party believed that the tactics of NAWSA placated President Wilson and the Democratic Party, and as such exerted no pressure on them to change. NAWSA believed that the picketing of the NWP was insulting to the President and would set the campaign back 50 years. The Woman's Party called NAWSA conservative and credited their own militant activism with the achievement of the 19th Amendment; NAWSA thought the picketers were fanatics and credited their own state-by-state work with the ratification of the federal amendment. But each group, in actuality, played a vital role in achieving suffrage. Where NAWSA was involved in the organizational work, the Woman's Party filled in with the shock and drama that elicited the emotional response necessary to focus attention on the issue. Even the arrests of NWP members served to create a sympathetic audience against a boorish governmental response. Both groups and both methods were necessary to fulfill the social movement mission.

Regardless of how many types of groups develop or the outcome of their

efforts, the process involved in social movement activism has effects on established ways of thinking. Movements which achieve no gains tend to be ignored;
however, success will almost certainly cause oppositional movements to arise.
Challenges to the status quo activate those opposed to changing the way things
are and frequently lead to greater restrictions. For instance, after women started
speaking out in their own behalf, restrictive laws began appearing on abortion
and contraceptive materials. By the end of the 1800s even the dissemination of
contraceptive information was banned through the Comstock Laws.[13]

Reacting to these new restrictions, the birth control movement organized in
earnest during the latter stage of the suffrage campaign. While NWP members
were being arrested in Washington, Margaret Sanger was being arrested in New
York for opening information clinics. In general, suffragists supported the notion
of women controlling their reproductive functioning but, eying the reprisals
being dealt birth control crusaders, they feared the outcome of introducing another controversial issue into the suffrage campaign. Their literature rarely mentioned birth control, yet in many localities the two issues were promoted side by
side. Still, without more active feminist engagement, Margaret Sanger "increasingly had to turn to the eugenics movement for support, using its arguments in
her own propaganda and de-emphasizing the earlier feminist ones" (Gluck
1976: 28).

There are few guidelines to the mobilization task all social movements must
address. This is because of the many variables connected to both the internal
workings of the movement and the ongoing changes in the social structure.
Often tactics which are successful during one period may fail in another. The
last years of the suffrage campaign demonstrate the importance of timing for the
introduction of tactical strategies. Unlike the earlier period with dress reform,
where the shock value of the short dress was merely shocking, the NWP was
successful in its militant efforts. Although dress reform served the purpose of
drawing attention to the issue, it did not draw public support. In contrast, by the
time the Woman's Party used militant tactics, there was significant support for
woman's suffrage.

The heart of the resistance to women voting was the view that women were
not autonomous beings. Consistently throughout the suffrage campaign opposition was expressed in terms of women's position in the family and the incom-
patibility of this role with the public role of politics. Women were seen as being
in the protection of men, a view expressed by one segment of the English suffrage movement in attempting to obtain the vote for single women and widows,
but not for married women (Stanton and Blatch 1922).

The anti-suffrage movement, which began appearing in legislative hearings in
the early 1900s, openly argued for women's subordination to family interests.
Anti-suffrage women saw the vote as a symbol of an independent status for

women, a status they did not desire. Consisting almost entirely of upper-class women, their opposition reflected their fear that autonomous women would free men to not marry or support wives (Marshall 1986).

Reacting to increasing activism from oppositional forces, an ideological change became apparent when the campaign for women's suffrage moved from an equal justice argument to arguments based on pragmatic considerations of the human good women could achieve with the vote (Kraditor [1965] 1981). For some supporters suffrage was the end and for others it was the means to the end. Attempts at winning women's suffrage had been a long and unrewarding task; suffragists had reached the point where they wanted the vote and they did not care how they got it. In this way, feminists and social feminists alike turned to expediency arguments in order to get what, for quite different reasons, they both wanted.

Prologue to the second wave

The 19th Amendment provides a clear example of the ambiguous quality of social movement success. Winning suffrage gave women the vote, but not the underlying goal of political power, the means by which they meant to raise their status and create a better society. With the victory of suffrage, the unifying issue of the movement was gone. Thus, the various sectors dissipated into separate issues divided by two opposing views: one calling for women's equality and the other for women's protection.

Three years after suffrage was won, Alice Paul wrote the Equal Rights Amendment (ERA) and had it introduced into Congress.[14] Contrasting gender conceptions were openly articulated at this time through support or rejection of the ERA. Woman's Party activists believed a constitutional amendment would symbolically raise women to an equal status with men and do away with the legal barriers to women's advancement in the public realm. Political and economic equality were the focus; changes in patterns of interpersonal relations and family life would follow these achievements.

Other women's groups, including NAWSA (which became the League of Women's Voters after passage of the 19th Amendment), did not support the Equal Rights Amendment. For these groups, women's role in the family was the very condition which must be addressed first. The interest was not just on women but on women and children—the two issues were seen as inseparable. While the NWP saw women as persons in their own right, most women's groups saw women as mothers who needed special treatment to fulfill this role. Thus, they worked not for equality between the sexes, but rather for legislative provisions for maternity and infant health care, restrictions on child labor, and protective labor legislation for women designed to shorten their hours of work and define the conditions under which they could work.

In the end, the movement succumbed to the divisions within. Moreover, women, it turned out, did not vote much differently than men; even more disheartening, to a large extent they simply did not vote. Illinois, the only state in 1920 to tabulate voting by sex, showed 70 percent of eligible males voting with only 40 percent of eligible female voters going to the polls (Papachristou 1976: 197). For women activists, the achievement of suffrage meant both the loss of their rallying symbol and the accompanying recognition that perhaps "their most fundamental feminist assumptions about the spiritual superiority of women" were a fallacy (Showalter 1978: 11).

The following perusal of legislative action during the 1920s shows a marked change in government social programs from the beginning of that decade, when the effects of women's votes were unknown, until the end of the decade when there was no longer any fear of women's voting powers. Immediately after women got the vote, in 1921, the Sheppard-Towner bill for maternity and infancy care was passed. In 1924 reformers celebrated congressional approval of a child labor amendment; however the necessary state ratification failed. Subsequently the Supreme Court struck down child labor legislation as well as minimum wage laws for women. The final rejection came when the Sheppard-Towner Act was renewed in 1927 with the provision that it be automatically repealed two years later (Becker 1981; Chafe 1972; Lemons 1973). With the threat of a female voting bloc gone, additional reform legislation would have to wait until economic collapse forced government involvement in the New Deal policies of the 1930s.

After 1920, subtle emancipatory changes in gender attitude (brought about in part because of the recent suffrage activism) became apparent in social perceptions of the general population. Even dress reform finally came into its own. Ironically though, during the 1920s, the women's movement found itself the victim of "preemptive movement success," a process where the groups' constituency gains a new advantage without the group gaining acceptance (Gamson 1975). With victory in hand, in a relatively short period of time feminism was out of style. Instead, there was the "emancipated woman," who could be seen in flapper dress, short hair, and "loose living"—new mores which were, in fact, disturbing to many suffragists.

Within the movement itself, major personality figures left the American scene as leaders from both sectors spent much of the 1920s in Europe concentrating their efforts on organizing in other countries. Jane Addams dedicated herself to the organization she helped found in 1915, the Women's International League for Peace and Freedom; Crystal Eastman moved back to England, spending most of the decade abroad; Alice Paul worked with international feminist groups and lived in England for much of the 1920s and 1930s; Alma Belmont became president of the National Woman's Party, holding that office until her death in 1933 even though she moved to France ten years earlier and made only occasional trips back to the United States (Becker 1981); Harriot Stanton Blatch went to Europe immediately after the suffrage victory to research and write a book on the outcome of the war, later working on peace issues (Blatch and Lutz 1940); Carrie Chapman Catt traveled extensively in Europe and Latin America, serving as head of the International Woman Suffrage Alliance, the Pan American Association for the Advancement of Women, and the committee on the Cause and Cure of War (Peck 1944).

Important as international work was, feminists leaders left a country still not supportive of women's equality. By 1925 the generalized progressive mood of the country was gone and there was an increasing level of red-baiting of reform groups. After the stock market crash of 1929, the Depression wiped away any audience, political or public, for receiving feminist views on upgrading women's status. During the 1930s, public opinion polls found over 80 percent of Americans disapproved of wives working if their husbands had a job. The federal government itself released 1600 married women from its workforce, and a National Education Association survey showed that 77 percent of school systems would not hire married women and 63 percent dismissed women teachers if they married (Ware 1981, 1982).

With America's entry into World War II, women were catapulted into the workforce through government encouragement, then thrown out at the war's end in order to provide jobs for returning veterans (Hartmann 1982). From the mid-1940s until the 1960s, traditional gender role divisions prevailed as the mythical ideal for American family life, an anomaly in the demographic and family trends that had been occurring in the United States since the turn of the century. The age of marriage dipped, the birth rate soared, and compulsory family togetherness took hold. Simultaneously, changes in the economic structure were gearing up to draw women into an employment role which did not fit the edict of the times. In spite of the cultural promotion of the ideal traditional family, women were increasing their labor force participation throughout these years.

The challenge to women's gender role behavior was spreading, if not the image of their place in society. Dissonance between thought and behavior—the ideological and material contradictions developing in women's lives—as well as the actual constraints of the homemaker role, were to play an important part in women's response to the re-emerged movement of the late 1960s. Yet such undercurrents were deeply buried as thoughts of political power, economic equity, or autonomy had no place in the 1950s' American housewife and mother image. Most people never even knew there had been a women's movement.

Nevertheless, there was an ongoing women's movement during these years. Various women's groups worked for improvement in women's position, some favoring the Equal Rights Amendment and some bitterly opposed. Deadlocked for nearly 50 years over the ERA, women's groups often undermined each others' efforts. Politically, most women activists were not that far apart. There were, of course, personal antagonisms, although few would admit that this was the cause of their lack of cooperation. Rather, they saw themselves as ideologically opposed and defended their positions on that ground.

Ideology, what it means and the ways that meaning changes over time, provides important clues to understanding intra-movement feminist relations during the suffrage campaign and the post-suffrage years.

THE ROLE OF IDEOLOGY IN THE EARLY WOMAN'S MOVEMENT

Although the suffrage movement benefited from the introduction of diverse tactics, it suffered from its failure to develop a multi-faceted view of women or a deeply engrained feminist ideology to hold activists together. In terms of mobilization, one agreed upon goal worked to greatly increase the number of supporters for the movement. However, for the most part (after the 1890s) the movement was not committed to feminism; it was committed to suffrage, and the vote was desired for divergent reasons, sometimes including contradictory ones. The different segments making up the movement submerged ideological conflict by working together for the same goal while ignoring their underlying differences in outlook.

There was no clear direction after the suffrage victory, as it was not just different legislation, but opposing legislation, which separated the segments of the movement. On an underlying level, the primary concern was betterment for women: social reform groups wanted to improve women's lives where they were; activists in the NWP wanted to move them to where they felt they should be. Both valued women, one as independent persons, the other for their "higher" special qualities.

The NWP's isolation was not broken until 1937 when the Business and Professional Women (BPW) endorsed ERA after the Fair Labor Standards Act allowed minimum wage and maximum hour laws for both women and men. Thereafter, other women's groups came out in favor of the amendment's passage, but opposition remained among the League of Women Voters, unions, and the Women's Bureau of the Department of Labor. Those groups in favor of protective labor accused the National Woman's Party of being insensitive to working women's needs; but the NWP argued instead that protective labor legislation hurt women workers by protecting them out of higher-paying jobs.

The continued rejection of ERA by the League of Women Voters was particularly notable given its roots in NAWSA and the joint efforts of NAWSA and the NWP to achieve suffrage. Yet, as discussed earlier, ideological submersion and the conflict/competition between these two groups in the suffrage campaign mitigated against their working together in the later stage.

Various women's organizations were interested in improving the status and position of women in the social structure, but, in spite of the same broad-based goal, some of the leaders barely spoke to each other. Indeed, part of their resistance to supporting ERA in the 1940s and 1950s came from personal and organizational antagonism toward Alice Paul and the NWP.[15] It is interesting to note, however, that individual activists often held overlapping membership in organizations such as Business and Professional Women (BPW), the American Association of University Women (AAUW), the Women's Bureau of the Department of Labor, the League of Women Voters, and the National Woman's Party (Rupp and Taylor 1987).

Single-mindedly working for the Equal Rights Amendment, the National Woman's Party was the only organization during the 1920–60 period that explicitly identified itself as feminist. Carrying the torch for women's equality during a period of extreme anti-feminism, NWP was a lonely group which persisted in lobbying for ERA in spite of denigrating attitudes that they were fanatical old women clinging to their suffragist past (Rupp and Taylor 1987).

This stage in the women's movement was one of basic survival, and the fact that NWP was able to keep the issue of women's equality alive is a credit to their persistence in the face of massive resistance. And, as later developments reveal, the continuity in the women's rights movement was important for the inclusion of sex in the Equal Pay Act and Civil Rights Legislation of the 1960s, and for the resurgence of feminism in the latter part of that decade.

Chapter 3

RESURGENCE OF FEMINISM:
THE CONTEMPORARY
WOMEN'S MOVEMENT

Gradually, without seeing it clearly for quite a while, I came to realize that something is very wrong with the way American women are trying to live their lives today. I sensed it first as a question mark in my own life, as a wife and mother of three small children, half-guiltily, and therefore half-heartedly, almost in spite of myself. . . .There was a strange discrepancy between the reality of our lives as women and the image to which we were trying to conform, the image that I came to call the feminine mystique. I wondered if other women faced this schizophrenic split and what it meant.

(Betty Friedan, *The Feminine Mystique,* 1963)

That was the period when I still could fake a convincing orgasm, still wouldn't be caught dead confronting an issue like pornography (for fear, this time, of being a "bad vibes, uptight, un-hip chick"). . . .I learned to pretend contempt for monogamy as both my husband and I careened (secretly grieving for each other) through the fake "sexual revolution" of the sixties. Meanwhile, correctly Maoist rice and vegetables filled our menus - and I *still* put in hours priming myself to reflect acceptable beauty standards, this time those of a tough-broad street fighter: uniform jeans, combat boots, long hair, and sunglasses worn even at night.

(Robin Morgan, *Going Too Far,* 1977)

Give us this day our daily breath
Deliver us from our daily death
Amen

(Barbara Deming,
*We Cannot Live Without
Our Lives,* 1974)

After an extended period of dormancy, a new activist women's movement erupted throughout American society. The contemporary movement has articulated goals aimed at the transformation of society on the social, political, economic, spiritual, personal, interactional, and cultural levels. And in this era, feminism, with its various emphases and applications, overtly expressed itself in a number of "types" of feminist thought.[1]

When feminist organizing re-emerged in the late 1960s, multiple groups created two distinct sectors of the movement. With the notable exception of Jo Freeman (1975), most work on the organizing stage has centered on identifying and labeling the various groups, rather than examining the relationship of feminist groups to each other and to the overall formation of the movement. This body of literature classified the sectors as "reform" and "revolutionary," or the "moderate women's rights" branch and the "radical women's liberation" branch. The two sectors have often been presented as polarized, sometimes even as opposed to each other (Andersen 1983; Banks 1981; Carden 1974; Firestone 1970; Hole and Levine 1971; Jaggar and Struhl 1978). The National Organization for Women (NOW), in particular, has been singled out as a reform organization with limited goals. For instance, Leah Fritz described NOW as wanting only "equal rights for women *within the present society*. . . . [S]tructural change of the society as a whole is not included" (1979: 42; emphasis in original). Joan Cassell claimed that "NOW members do not seek to transform themselves or their world" (1977: 95).

Another characteristic of the literature has been the tendency to connect the emergence of the contemporary movement to the social movements of the 1960s in a way that often defines the civil rights movement, the anti-war movement, or the New Left as the major (or only) precipitating factors leading to women organizing their own movement (see, for instance, Evans 1980). This view of the origins of the contemporary movement misses the roots of women's discontent leading to the formation of women's groups not connected to other social movements, and fails to recognize the groundwork done by pre-1960 feminist activists. The fact is the new groups making up the contemporary women's movement came into being after important legislation was passed. Already existing women's rights groups and women in government positions lobbied for the inclusion of women in the legislative acts of the 1960s; yet, efforts to create change in the political-legal arena have frequently been ignored or discounted as conservative forms of activism.

Dividing the movement into reform and radical categories is inaccurate, since all of the emerging feminist groups were radical departures from the then prevailing view of women. In addition, feminist groups do not fit into traditional categories of progressive and conservative politics. Freeman stated this when she argued:

It is a common mistake to try to place the various feminist organizations on the traditional left/right spectrum, and concomitantly, to describe the two branches as "women's rights" and "women's liberation.". . . Some groups often called "reformist" have a platform that would so completely change our society it would be unrecognizable. (1975: 50–1)

Rather than ideology, Freeman found the differences between the two branches to be primarily structural and stylistic, and, secondarily, strategic and methodological.

The greatest fear of radicals in the late sixties was that they would be coopted by the system into helping improve it through reform rather than destroying it through revolution. The idea that they could instead coopt institutional resources to their own aims was totally alien. (1979: 180)

Freeman called the two segments of the newly emerging movement the "younger" and "older" branches, because one came into being a year before the other and each initially organized within different age groups. However, her descriptive terms, meant to neutralize the reform-radical designation, fail because radicalism is considered a trait of youth and conservatism of age, despite Steinem's contention that "women grow more radical with age" (1983: 3). More neutral terms to define these two sectors would be *mass movement* and *small group*.

Structure and style tell us much about the way the two sectors organized, but the vehemence with which feminists voiced their disparate views about each other is not explained. For, even if feminist ideology did not play an important role in these early divisions, the fact is that many participants perceived themselves as philosophically opposed and acted on those assumptions as if they were true. Whether they were actually ideologically opposed or not, ideology was used to distinguish activists from each other. Thus, why feminist women chose to focus on differences in feminist orientation, rather than their similar feminist foundation, remains unexplained. To answer this question, it is necessary to examine the groups and the issues they raised during the organizing period of 1966 to the early 1970s.

RE-EMERGENCE OF THE WOMEN'S MOVEMENT

The rebirth of feminism can be traced to the family-centered years of the 1950s. This was an era which re-established women's place in the home after their move into paid employment during World War II. Although women's labor force participation continued to rise in the post-war period, cultural ideology defined the wife/mother role as both women's special duty and path to fulfillment. This meant that work outside the home was done only with much maternal guilt, spousal shame, and "child deprivation."

In questioning the lack of options women had in their lives, Betty Friedan planted a seed for ideological change with the publication of *The Feminine Mystique* (1963). Friedan was protesting the limits of a family-centered role for women; however, there were other groups in American society who had not even had the *opportunity* to attempt this idealized version of family life. In stark contrast to the TV image of "Father Knows Best," disadvantaged groups, African Americans in particular, did not find themselves in an ever-expectant personal fulfillment cycle. White middle-class women were constricted by social expectations, but for black women (and men) even broader constrictions were enforced by law.

The forerunner to the 1960's social movements was black activism in the South. The precipitating event to organizing mass protest occurred in 1955 when Rosa Parks, a member of the National Association for the Advancement of Colored People (NAACP) in Montgomery, Alabama, refused to give up her seat and move to "the back of the bus." This action went beyond the concept of integrated educational facilities[2] and inspired Southern civil rights activists to protest segregation of public facilities in general. Martin Luther King worked on the resulting mass transit boycott and the organizing of the Southern Christian Leadership Conference (SCLC). College-age students in SCLC formed the Student Nonviolent Coordinating Committee (SNCC) in 1961 and began promoting summer "Freedom Rides" in the deep South. Another campus movement of importance founded in the early 1960s, calling itself the New Left, was Students for a Democratic Society (SDS).[3]

With burgeoning activism and a civil rights March on Washington planned for August 1963, crucial policy changes began taking place at the federal level. The first of these were the Equal Pay Act of 1963 and Title VII of the Civil Rights Act of 1964. Although the inclusion of sex in these Acts came about without pressure from a strong women's movement, they were not as haphazard an inclusion as most researchers conclude. The successful achievement of early legislative gains for women have been only superficially acknowledged; however, a review of the events leading to the emergence of a new women's movement shows the importance of these early political gains.

The role of women in government

When John F. Kennedy took office, he appointed Esther Peterson director of the Women's Bureau and relied on her as his adviser for women's affairs. Peterson, who came out of labor union activism, placed her loyalties with working women. Rather than continue the tradition of stressing high-level governmental appointments for women, she persuaded Kennedy to form the President's Commission on the Status of Women (PCSW). Peterson was personally opposed to the Equal Rights Amendment because of her desire to retain protective labor legislation; however, this inclination was not reflective of most women in government positions. Her hope was that a commission could deflect interest in ERA into support for an equal pay law (Zelman 1982).

In October 1963 the Commission presented a report, *American Women,* showing discrimination against women in every facet of American life. Of notable mention was wage discrimination, where women earned up to 40 percent less than men on the same job (Lear 1971: 164). Even though the Commission report came out shortly after the Equal Pay Act, the idea of equal employment opportunities for women had previously been broached by the PCSW. For instance, they had effected reform in the Civil Service Commission by securing Attorney-General Robert Kennedy's cooperation in issuing orders to federal agencies to disregard sex qualifications in hiring practices.

Although the official PCSW stance did not support or reject the ERA, the Commission took the position that equality of rights under the law for all persons must be a part of the Constitution. This approach was taken in order to apply pressure to the courts to reinterpret the 5th and 14th Amendments to include women. As a safeguard in case that failed, the Commission report stated "a constitutional amendment need not *now* be sought in order to establish this principle" (Zelman 1982:34).[4] Thus, they left an opening for support of ERA in the future, while allowing the concept of equal pay and equal job opportunity to take hold in government policy circles. With this action, the dividing issue of protective labor legislation and ERA was partially subsumed under a new conciliatory position which maintained both factions' legitimacy.

In spite of the creation of the Commission and the inclusion of sex in the Equal Pay Act, Kennedy had a poor rating among political women because of his failure to include them in his government appointments. This "woman problem" became a means for gaining a constituency for Lyndon Johnson when he unexpectedly took over the presidency. Early in his term Johnson signed a bill outlawing sex discrimination by private employers and began a Women in Government campaign (Zelman 1982).

These policies coincided with the congressional debate on Title VII, the employment provision of the Civil Rights Bill. Including women in Title VII was seen as a fluke by most observers, since sex was tagged onto this legislation as a way of destroying it. But, the point is, it passed. Credit for this can be attributed, at least in part, to the persistent efforts of women activists, such as the work of the PCSW which gave legitimacy to the question of equal job opportunity, pressure in the House from Representative Martha Griffith (a non-active member of the National Woman's Party), and the intensified lobbying and letter writing by the NWP.

The Equal Employment Opportunity Commission (EEOC) was charged with overseeing Title VII. Nonetheless, the EEOC took no action to insure implementation of the sex provision. In June 1966, at the Third National Conference of Commissions on the Status of Women, a group of delegates met in Betty Friedan's hotel room and wrote a resolution calling for the EEOC to follow its mandate to end sex discrimination. When the resolution was not allowed to be brought to the floor for discussion, they convened to begin plans for the formation of an organization specifically designed to work for social change on gender issues. Out of this meeting the National Organization for Women (NOW) was born.

DEFINING THE ISSUES IN N.O.W.

In the initial organizing stage, a number of schisms in NOW led some members to claim the organization was too radical and others that it was too conservative. At the first national meeting following its founding, NOW members adopted a Bill of Rights which included support for the Equal Rights Amendment and the right of women to control their reproductive lives.[5] Members of the United Auto Workers Women's Commission left NOW because of their opposition to ERA. Other women, disagreeing with NOW's support for abortion rights, left to form the Women's Equity Action League (WEAL).

On the other side of the spectrum, Ti-Grace Atkinson, claiming "irreconcilable ideological conflicts," resigned from the presidency of New York NOW over disagreements related to leadership structure (Atkinson 1974: 9), and Rita Mae Brown left the same chapter because of a lack of support for defining lesbianism as a feminist issue. Later, of course, the UAW backed the ERA, WEAL agreed with the right to choose, and NOW supported lesbian rights.

These splits led to change in other groups or the development of new groups interested in working on specific issues. For instance, UAW women applied pressure on their union to reassess its position on ERA, and WEAL began work on legal issues in employment and educational opportunities for women. When Ti-Grace Atkinson left NOW she organized a radical feminist group eventually known as The Feminists.[6] Rita Mae Brown went on to co-found Radicalesbians, where the idea of lesbianism as a feminist lifestyle was discussed (Abbott and Love 1972).[7]

After Brown raised the lesbian issue in NOW, there was a general purging of lesbians and lesbian sympathizers within the New York NOW chapter. The issue was mainly being addressed internally; the purgings were an attempt to keep it quiet. Many heterosexual feminists feared that a connection with lesbianism would taint the movement and, possibly, themselves.

Nevertheless, once news of the purgings spread, lesbianism became an issue for discussion in NOW chapters across the country. Most heterosexual women had only their culturally defined homophobic assumptions to refer to; hence, they had never given serious thought to the connection between sexual orientation and civil rights. For instance, Betty Friedan described how this issue initially aroused "the creeping horrors" in her. She explained her reaction by relating it to her middle American (Peoria, Illinois) upbringing (Friedan 1976: 159).

By bringing the subject into the open, Sidney Abbott and Barbara Love observe that one of the major considerations guiding NOW members' discussions was the discovery that women they knew and respected were lesbians.

> What happens when respected and valued people become identified with negatively valued ideas? During 1970, N.O.W. members had learned that an important movement theorist (Ms. Millett) and a few national, regional, and local N.O.W. officers were lesbians. Such a tense situation potentially is a powerful one, tending to produce change. (1978: 132)

Over the next year the question of how lesbianism fit into feminism created intense and heated dialogue in NOW. Yet, the dissension this issue created was illuminating and, eventually, diminished when the organization took a position at their 1971 conference which supported the right of each person to define and express their own sexuality. Moreover, a resolution was passed declaring the oppression of lesbians a legitimate concern of feminism. In this way NOW defused an explosive issue by incorporating it into an officially recognized organizational concern; thereafter, the lesbian/straight split created less of a strain within NOW than it did in many of the smaller radical feminist groups.

Organizational disputes are important movement events because they force participants to confront meaningful issues. Rather than maintaining unity by denying the existence of controversial subjects, participants are led to consider the issues and organizations are forced to articulate a position. For instance, ERA, abortion rights, and lesbianism were initially interpreted by some NOW members as representing a radical agenda. Electing to take on these issues, even at the cost of losing supporters, meant the membership as a whole was prepared to be labelled "radical." The outcome of these early confrontations established the idea that NOW would be involved in a range of issues and that, as an organization, principle would override mobilization concerns. But not always, as the issue of structure revealed. Although agreeing with the feminist critique of hierarchy, most NOW members had long been engaged in professional careers and, for them, pragmatic considerations governed questions of organizational structure.

In terms of mobilization, these splits resulted in the formation of new groups and new ideas. In addition, they showed that the women's movement could consist of different types of groups where particular issues would be highlighted. Interested observers were given more options for joining the women's movement and more opportunities for developing leadership skills were created. Thus, early schisms in NOW were able to mobilize a variety of material and non-material resources for the women's movement.

THE SPREAD OF THE SMALL GROUP SECTOR

As some activists were breaking away from NOW, women involved in a variety of other 1960s' movements were questioning why women had not been included in the ideals of social justice that these movements espoused. Highlighting this omission was the contradiction between a liberatory ideology and the helper role women played in these groups. Women's secondary status within social movement circles was nothing new, but their awareness and articulation of dissatisfaction was.[8]

As early as 1964 women in the Student Nonviolent Coordinating Committee (SNCC) wrote a position paper protesting their status within that organization. Hoping to stimulate debate on the issue, they drew, instead, Stokely Carmichael's infamous retort: "the only position for women in SNCC is prone" (Evans 1979: 87). Despite ridicule by male activists, women continued to meet and discuss their situation. In August 1967, at the National Conference on New Politics in Chicago, an attempt was made to get a women's rights resolution onto the floor. When this effort failed, five women surrounded the podium to protest, only to have the Chair reach down, pat one woman on the head, and say "Cool down, little girl, we have more important things to talk about than women's liberation" (Freeman 1975: 60).

One of these women was Jo Freeman, who later was involved in a number of feminist groups and author/scholar of the women's movement, including editor of the first newsletter for radical activists: *Voice of the Women's Liberation Movement*. Ironically, the woman who was patted on the head was Shulamith Firestone. By the end of the year, she joined with Pam Allen to form New York Radical Women (NYRW), the group which organized the first media protest—the 1968 Miss America pageant—which launched the movement into the public eye.[9] Later she was a founding member of The Redstockings and in 1970 the author of a book on radical feminism.[10]

In a series of events not unlike the experience of women delegates to the 1840 London World Anti-Slavery Convention and the 1966 Conference on the Status of Women, once again an all-too-familiar precipitating event led directly to women organizing for themselves. Women's liberation groups were formed to explore women's common gender experiences. In sifting through their theoretical beliefs and experiential realities, the organizing focus of these groups became consciousness raising (CR).[11] According to Ann Snitow, a member of NYRW, consciousness raising groups spread like "wildfire":

> We called ourselves brigades and we founded a whole bunch of other brigades: we cloned ourselves. These groups were a glorious but brief moment, and I say glorious, partly because of the excitement, but also it really was true that we listened to each other and didn't judge the material. In other words, people said the truth.[12]

Snitow adds that, even though there was an honest dedication to an examination of women's lives, there were hidden messages of what was open for discussion. Saying that you loved men or enjoyed penetration was generally taboo. Nor was there any talk about lesbianism or class. Even with these unspoken limitations, a wide array of themes and subjects were raised over the next few years.

Consciousness raising created a sense of unity and strength; however, after engaging in it for some time, many women felt a need to "do something" (Pane 1973). Most of the small groups were not structured to move participants into activism after reaching a point of analytic saturation. Eventually, many CR groups simply folded. Even though they were short lived, it was out of these groups, particularly those organized in New York City, that the major ideas and writings on radical feminism developed.

With NOW, there was no formal structure for the incorporation of CR groups. In fact there was early resistance to using this process; for example, Betty Friedan often described CR as a form of naval gazing. Nevertheless, by the end of the 1960s, NOW members began setting up CR groups within local chapters. The introduction of CR by one sector of the movement and the spread of it to another sector provides an example of a diffusion effect in social movement interaction. Eventually CR became a common practice throughout the women's movement, including within NOW; although in NOW, because of its action orientation, consciousness raising was an occasional activity serving more as a prelude to political activism than a *raison d'être*.

Radical feminism vs. socialist feminism

Throughout 1968 and 1969, small women's liberation groups began forming in major cities in the country. Many members brought with them both revolutionary ideas and antagonism toward working with leftist men. Out of this dual orientation came an interest in developing a feminist analysis of social relations that would subsume the economic analysis of leftist groups. Even though a strong basis for their organizing was to present a critique of the left, many of the leaders of these groups were so thoroughly left-wing that for them feminism included socialism.[13] Therefore, in spite of their common desire to disassociate from their

previous experiences, an early dividing issue centered on the question of working with the left. Moreover, even though there was agreement on their rejection
of capitalism, there was tension built into these groups around the use of Marxist
ideology and open support for socialism.

Political strategists and theorists wrestled with this question (Sargent 1981).
One way this problem was addressed by those activists critical of the left but
still desirous of maintaining a left identity was to form autonomous women's
liberation groups with a specific leftist orientation. The first of these was the
Chicago Women's Liberation Union (CWLU), organized in the fall of 1969.[14] In
a proposed statement of political principles, the Union called itself radical
women who were committed to the right of women to control all aspects of their
lives. Initially, the CWLU did not define itself as socialist feminist, but the principle of the Union was that women's liberation is a revolutionary struggle that
cannot be achieved without all people being free; likewise, women's liberation
is essential to the liberation of all oppressed people.[15] The conceptual framework
of Marxism, that the elimination of capitalism would lead to women's liberation,
was replaced with the need to eliminate both capitalism and patriarchy.

Early papers differentiated CWLU from other women's groups, including
Marxist women, whom the writers called politicos (i.e. women working in male-
dominated groups where the struggle against male supremacy is neglected). For
example, a perspective paper on organizing leftist women into autonomous
women's liberation groups accused consciousness raising groups of exaggerating
the importance of oppression by sex. In a revealing comment, the exclusive
focus on women's struggles was termed a "silly idea." Referring to NOW, the
paper warned of the "dangers and pitfalls of an organization for women's liberation whose constituency and membership is based overwhelmingly in the
middle class" (Radinsky and Gadlin 1969: 2–4). This critique is curious since
socialist feminist groups also consisted of mainly middle-class women, and a
review of CWLU activities shows they were similar to those of NOW (e.g. setting
up speakers' bureaus and women's centers to work on abortion, rape, and equal
employment). Their attitude toward NOW acknowledged that it included quite
militant women but, at the same time, they claimed that for "many (not all) of
these people, 'women's lib' means little more than tenure(d) professors, more
women in certain high-level positions, etc."[16]

In effect, CWLU called for the establishment of an independent, humanistic,
socialistic, women's organization because no left organization seemed likely to
give adequate consideration to questions related to women's liberation. By the
early 1970s, CWLU members were explicitly defining themselves as socialist
feminists. New unions formed, many beginning on college campuses as study
groups. Some defined themselves as Marxist-Leninists while others eschewed
such labels; often unions were involved in the initial stage of the development
of Women's Studies within the academic community. A major area of discussion

in the unions was centered on whether one considered themself to be a leftist first or a feminist first.[17]

Shulamith Firestone elected to be a feminist first. In *The Dialectic of Sex* (1970) she argued that women's subordination was based on the biological facts of procreation. Firestone defined Marxism as an analysis centered on production, while radical feminism presented an analysis centered on reproduction. Thus, the underclass in society, rather than being an economic class (the proletariat), consisted of a sex class (women). Proposing a feminist revolution premised on "not just the elimination of male *privilege* but of the sex *distinction* itself" (1970: 11; emphasis in original), Firestone took the radical feminist analysis of a sex class system to its extreme and called for the removal of sex/gender differentiation by eliminating the family and replacing it with institutionalized child rearing, artificial reproduction, and bisexual sex relations.

The lesbian/feminist debate

The year before Firestone's book came out the lesbian/feminist debate had emerged in the women's movement. Throughout the first wave of feminist activism, the one issue that had not been broached was that of lesbian relationships. In the contemporary movement, lesbian feminists have had an influential impact on legitimating conceptions of sexual politics, the right to control one's own body, and a lesbian-separatist lifestyle. How lesbianism became a feminist issue is examined by historian Liz Craven, who begins with the impact feminism had on lesbians.[18]

Craven traces the history of lesbian organizing, beginning in 1955 with the formation of a secret organization, the Daughters of Bilitis (DOB). The newspaper of this group, *The Ladder,* published research and personal stories focused on assimilating lesbians into society. Because homosexuality was a legal felony, members of DOB were attempting to rid themselves of a deviant status; thus they shared success stories of how they managed to hide their lesbian identity.

In the early 1960s, DOB members allied with homosexual males; however, the male organizations of that time, ONE, Inc. and Mattachine, basically wanted DOB to be an auxiliary organization. Ironically, Craven pinpoints the publication of *The Feminine Mystique* (1963) as a motivating force for a changed perspective on lesbianism. The awareness gained from this book was that gender definitions and gender roles are part of the social structure. If gender-appropriate behavior is a social construction, then perhaps, as lesbians, they were not individually psychologically flawed.

In the late 1960s, lesbians were confronted with the question of aligning with gay men or with women's liberationists. What they found was chauvinism in the male groups and silence in the women's movement. The silence, however, was being broken with the manifestos and organizational philosophies coming out of radical feminist groups. For instance, The Feminists openly defined a radical feminist as a woman who rejected the institution of marriage "both in theory and in practice" (The Feminists 1970: 116). Ti-Grace Atkinson coined the term political lesbian, which came to have a number of meanings: (1) women who adopt a separatist lifestyle; (2) women who live their lives in total commitment to women even though they do not engage in sexual relations with women; and (3) lesbians who become politicized to the nature of sexism through feminism.

This developing lesbian feminist consciousness coincided with the 1969 police raid on Stonewall Inn (a gay bar in New York City), which led to the rise of the Gay Liberation Front (Humphreys 1972: 6). The gay liberation movement provided support to lesbians to concentrate on the issue of sexual orientation and to expect it to be acknowledged within the movement.

In order to bring the issue into the open, lesbian feminists began confronting heterosexual feminists' omission of their concerns and, indeed, of their very existence. One of the early instances of the use of this tactic was the 1970 Women's Strike for Equality in New York City. Scores of women who had not previously been involved in the movement participated in a march carrying signs calling for legalized abortion, government-sponsored child care, and equal educational and employment opportunities for women. The march was a success; however, a second strike held later that year ended in acrimonious debate when armbands and leaflets were distributed stating "we're all wearing lavender arm bands today to show that we stand together *as women,* regardless of sexual preference" (Friedan 1976: 158).

Lesbianism became a divisive issue in part because heterosexual women, fearing that feminism would take on a lesbian identity, hoped to keep the issue quiet; and in part because political lesbians reacted to homophobic bias by proclaiming the only true feminist to be a "woman-identified woman" (Radicalesbians 1971).

For some activists, lesbianism took on a status in which feminist ideals and a lesbian lifestyle were synonymous:

> It is now clear that the lives of Lesbians provide an example of Feminist theory in action . . . The startling fact is that Lesbians already meet the criteria that Women's Liberation has set up to describe the liberated woman . . . For Lesbians live what Feminists theorize about; they embody Feminism. (Abbott and Love 1978: 134).

For lesbians, feminism was an important tool for building a positive self-image; for heterosexual feminists, however, problems arose when identifying politically with women took on the additional moral imperative to also be identified as a political lesbian. As the political lesbian view spread, heterosexual women in radical groups found it difficult to defend their own lifestyle as feminist. It was common to be told that a discussion of women's relations with men was not appropriate for a women's community. Married feminists were often made to feel that the problems they had in their marriages were of their own choosing since they elected to stay in those relationships. Reflecting back on this time, one woman explains heterosexual women's passivity to this assault as guilt: accepting blame as women are taught to do, they bent under the pressure and did not push back saying "this is absurd" (cited in Hansen 1986).

The separatist solution

During this period two books were published which turned the lesbian debate in a new direction. Elizabeth Gould Davis published *The First Sex* (1971), in which she revived matriarchal theory. Jill Johnston called for a woman-committed state based on peer grouping, noting that "women and men are not peers" (1973: 278).

Subsequently, The Feminists' adopted organizational rules which stipulated that only one-third of their members could be married or living with a man because commitment to a man prevents a woman "from uniting with other women and seeing herself as a member of the class of women" (The Feminists 1973: 117). Unlike the separatist tactic of Black Nationalism to offer a sense of unity among African Americans (Essien-Udom 1962), this exclusionary policy created divisions because it defined "the class of women" by separation from men, a definition which divided heterosexual women from lesbian women— and, as it has been argued in the 1980s, women of color from their racial/ethnic community.[19] Later, The Feminists excluded all married women from membership, and moved further into a female countercultural view when members began espousing matriarchal values and female mysticism. In her analysis of the early years of the contemporary movement, Alice Echols argues that these essentialist conceptions and separatist practices were early indicators of the cultural feminism that was to follow the demise of radical feminism in the 1970s (1989: 182).

The years between 1966 and the early 1970s were a time of dynamic growth in feminist consciousness and organizing. It was an exciting period still caught up in the 1960s' decade of social protest; moreover, extensive media coverage gave legitimacy to the importance of women's activism around sex/gender issues. But it was also a time of foreboding, when signs of a changing social climate were emerging and other social movements, some without knowing it yet, were on the wane. Still, pressure from outside forces was minimal compared with what was about to occur in the mid-1970s and 1980s. Indeed, in the early 1970s internal dissension and the exacerbating instability of the radical feminist groups were related as much, or more, to divisions within their own ranks as to the threat of an anti-feminist backlash.

Chapter 4

IDEOLOGICAL PURITY: DIVISIONS, SPLITS, AND TRASHING

> People who have many common features often do one another worse or "wronger" wrong than complete strangers do. . . .[T]hey do this because there is only little that is different between them: hence even the slightest antagonism has a relative significance. . . . [T]he divergence over a very insignificant point makes itself felt in its sharp contrast as something utterly unbearable.
>
> (Simmel [1908] 1971:91)

Georg Simmel argues that similar qualities and common membership in groups often create intense in-group antagonism. But what of those people who purposely join together to bring about social change? Given their similar goals and common enemies, the various groups comprising a social movement should overlook minor within-group differences. William Gamson (1975), in his study of social movements, found instead that factionalism nearly always contributes one of the major blocks to the success of social movements. Although this may be true of social movements in general, what of the feminist movement? In the United States, the feminist movement is premised on egalitarian values, the elimination of hierarchical power relations, and the ideal of sisterhood. Yet, within the movement, antagonistic relations created serious rifts and mitigated against concerted social action.

In this chapter the disputes over ideological purity that evolved in the early years of the contemporary women's movement are examined in further detail in order to analyze the meaning of the schisms that developed. The analytical model of resource mobilization provides a framework for studying the mobilization effects of emotions, symbols, and ideology, three characteristics of social movement organizing often ignored in mobilization studies (Ferree and Miller 1985; Zurcher and Snow 1981). Emotions, symbols, and ideology contribute to the development of interactive group relations, a process within the women's movement closely related to how the various groups defined themselves in relationship to each other. Of particular importance is feminist ideology—how it was used by leaders and activists as a mobilizing resource during the organizing stage and why, at the same time, the feminist groups making up the movement experienced antagonistic relations based on ideological conflict.

THE BURSTING OF THE BUBBLE

Feminist activists from diverse backgrounds initially organized around their own life experiences. The varieties of appearances, styles, interactional patterns, and group structures were reflections of the women leaders, who organized in ways with which they were most familiar. For instance, the founders of NOW were, for the most part, highly educated women who found their career paths limited by their sex category. Because of the resources NOW members had access to, their organizing efforts began by challenging the policy arena of the male-dominated power structure. Other feminist leaders sometimes took these goals to mean that NOW was not critical of the system, although many NOW leaders had backgrounds that included activism in the civil rights movement and other causes.[1]

Although there was dissension in both sectors of the movement, the small group sector experienced the greatest division and therefore warrants the greater attention when exploring the transformation of the movement in these early years. The contribution the small group sector made to the infancy stage of the contemporary women's movement was considerable. However, very quickly many of the women in these groups went from introducing new forms of feminist thinking to a narrowed view of feminist legitimacy.

By the early 1970s, the rapid spread of the small group sector had begun to break down as factions spent larger and larger portions of their energy attacking each other. Radical feminists considered NOW members to be the wrong kind of women (establishment) pursuing the wrong kind of goals (reform). Yet, it turned out that activists in NOW were less of a problem than other radical women, as splits occurred in the small group sector over working with the left, organizational structure, intra-group process, lesbianism and separatism.

Within a short period of time there were three distinct feminist orientations that came out of the small group sector. Activists in this sector, regardless of how else they identified themselves, considered themselves radicals. While NOW had its own internal friction, one of the few areas of agreement among broadly defined radical groups was their efforts to distance themselves from NOW. Nevertheless, sharp divisions arose over the question of what a radical feminist was or, if a woman was a radical, was she radical enough?

Even though all three orientations in the small group sector called themselves radical, they each used the term in a different way:[2]

1. *Radical feminists,* sometimes referred to as CR feminists, developed the original meaning of radical feminism. The term radical is taken to its base meaning: origin or original source; and for radical feminists, that source—the root of women's oppression—was men. This definition identifies the social system as a patriarchal structure premised on competition, power over others, and male superiority. Based on a social constructionist view of gender differentiation, they called for a social transformation of the existing unequal power relations between women and men. Their intent was personal and political action; they were anticapitalist, but divorced from the left.

2. *Politicos,* also called Marxist and socialist feminists, were interested in achieving women's liberation without losing their ties to the left. Radical was interpreted as support for a fundamental restructuring of the social structure in order to achieve political and economic change leading to equality for all groups in society. Marxist feminists particularly focused on the elimination of capitalism, while socialist feminists called for the dual and simultaneous elimination of capitalism and patriarchy.

3. *Cultural feminists* call themselves radical feminists, but also are sometimes known as political lesbians or separatist feminists. Cultural feminism is an offshoot and transformation of the early radical feminist groups (Echols 1989). Taking an essentialist view, cultural feminists celebrate and valorize femaleness. Radical cultural feminists consider patriarchy and masculine values to be the cause, not only of women's oppression, but also of capitalism, war, racism, and the destruction of the environment. Cultural feminism calls for the creation of a wholly redefined world, including change in linguistic, artistic, sexual, and symbolic conceptions of women. Also opposed to capitalism, they nonetheless find the left irrelevant. For separatists, creating a world apart from men is the logical course of action.

Within the radical feminist sector, volatile divisions developed around these orientations: separatist feminists accused heterosexual feminists of being male-defined; Marxist feminists charged that all women's groups were bourgeois; socialist feminists considered radical, lesbian, and separatist feminists to be man-haters; and radical feminists dismissed women who continued to be associated with the organized (male controlled) left. Even as antagonism grew among these variations of radical feminism, antipathy to the "liberal sector" continued unabated, particularly as the National Organization for Women expanded in size.

The contrast between the mass movement and small group sectors is most apparent when growth and decline are compared. By the early 1970s NOW had increased its membership and witnessed the spread of grassroots chapters around the country; but within the small group sector, many of the radical feminist groups were in disarray or had ceased to exist. Part of this demise occurred because the groups had served their purpose. Yet, women who had their consciousness raised, for the most part, did not go into action-oriented groups; they simply dropped out of the movement.

Societal events, such as the end of a radical activist climate and the beginning of an economic recession, contributed to the dissolution process in the small group sector. Structural conditions also played a part in small group dissolution, particularly with deliberate attempts by other radical groups to influence and co-opt feminist activists. For example, members of the Socialist Workers' Party infiltrated various women's groups in order to recruit radical women, in some cases taking them over (Hole and Levine 1971: 163–6).

SWP members were able to disrupt many of the small groups, but were unsuccessful in their attempts to gain control of NOW. The small groups, to varying degrees, tried to function on a leaderless basis with consensus rule. This format, patterned after the participant democracy of the New Left, was believed to allow for the greatest amount of participation with the least amount of hierarchy. Undesirably, it also meant the group could be controlled by a small minority vetoing issues (Freeman 1979). In comparison, the structure of NOW (both nationally and at the grassroots level), with formal bylaws, elected officers, and democratic rule, worked as an effective barrier to such takeover attempts.

The early 1970s saw both growth in the overall women's movement and the beginning of an organized backlash against feminist gains. Throughout the 1970s, there was increasing activism in both the feminist and anti-feminist movements (Chafetz and Dworkin 1986). On the feminist side, new segments of the movement formed: self-help groups, coffee houses, academic women's studies programs, rape crisis centers, battered women's shelters, and national single-issue organizations. Yet the decline in radical feminist groups was occurring at the same time that new feminist activity was emerging. Thus, it appears that much of the loss of the original small groups can be attributed to internal feminist dissension.

Indeed, activists of this period consider the impact of antagonistic group relations to be a major cause of many women leaving the movement. Laurel Richardson describes how, within groups and between groups, charges of elitism, racism, homophobia, and classism were rampant.

Everybody was trashed. Different groups for different reasons at different times. Too radical, too conservative, too liberal, straight, lived with men, had boy children, etc.[3]

As groups began to fall apart, members blamed other feminist groups for their own debacle. Carol Hanisch, an early member of New York Radical Women (NYRW) and Redstockings, blamed the break-up of the latter group on women who "spent much of their time attacking Redstockings both in the group and publicly for its lack of 'democracy' " (1978: 165). According to Pat Mainardi, another member of NYRW and Redstockings, as new people came in they began organizing on the basis of their special qualities rather than on the basis of what women had in common, as the early consciousness raising sessions had done.

The left and lesbian forces infiltrated and seized virtually every independent women's movement center and publication in the years 1969–1973, in many cases establishing the now familiar left-lesbian alliance against feminism. . . . [T]he original ideas of the radical women's movement have been suppressed. (1978: 122)

In describing her experiences in a leftist women's group, a radical feminist speaks of how these meetings were alienating interactions between "them and me."

What it actually was was them speaking New Leftese and me stumbling along in tattered bits—sometimes trying to use their terms, but every time being accused of using them incorrectly, and plain English was no good since they would translate it into New Leftese. . . . My overwhelming feeling was stupidity. I just didn't know what was going on verbally and couldn't respond to it although I knew very well what was actually going on but they wouldn't allow me to speak to that. (Anonymous 1970: 63)[4]

Blame for the decline of the original radical feminist groups has also been placed on the growth of the liberal sector:

It has been only six years since the women's liberation movement mushroomed, and already the radical women who initiated the movement's theory, organizing ideas, and slogans, have been buried from public consciousness and the liberals have taken over. (Sarachild 1978: 13)

In response to these charges, women who joined NOW and other mass movement groups argued that radical women were too young and, as mostly white middle-class students, too sheltered from the real world to understand what women's liberation was really all about. As Beverly Jones described it:

For at least two reasons radical females do not understand the desperate condition of women in general. In the first place, as students they occupy some sexy, sexless, limbo area where they are treated by males in general with less discrimination than they will ever face again. And, in the second place, few of them are married or if married have children. (Jones and Brown 1970: 364)

Radical feminists, in turn, felt they had experienced firsthand the frustration of oppression by male peers. They were supposed to be making a revolution together, but the radical men relegated "their" women to making coffee and running the mimeograph machine. So if they decided not to marry or have children (including, perhaps, reaching out to other women for love and sex), it was, in their eyes, for solid feminist political reasons. Marxist feminists, of course, saw radical and liberal feminist groups as bourgeois cultural nationalists. Each group of activists, in short, saw the others as naive and politically ineffective.

RETROSPECTIVE ANALYSIS

A decade later, radical feminists have reappraised this early period and questioned some of the principles their groups employed. For instance, many now consider their leaderless-structureless style and their practices of dividing tasks by a lot system, setting up rules for limiting speaking at meetings, and refusing to name spokespersons or authors of papers to have stymied individual members' talents and initiative. Moreover, there is acknowledgement that participants who could not expend the time required of consensus decision making were excluded; unchosen and unacknowledged leaders took over; and there was a lack of accountability for actions or for what took place in intra-group relations (Joreen 1973; Morgan 1977).[5]

According to many of the long-term activists interviewed for this research, feminists involved in the various groups actually shared a similar vision. In retrospective reflection on the intense confrontations and deep divisions that arose, activists consider definitions of self to have played a more prominent role in these divisions than was recognized at the time.

For instance, Robin Morgan considers the immaturity of the movement and the arrogance of newly converted activists to have been contributing factors to the demise of some groups.[6] As an example, she recalls the 1969 Bridal Fair action she took part in when she was a member of WITCH.[7] Members of this group protested the fair by attending in black veils and singing "Here come the slaves/Off to their graves" while releasing white mice throughout the display at Madison Square Garden in New York City. Later, she wrote about this action as a "self-indulgent insult to the very women we claimed we wanted to reach" (Morgan 1977: 74). Yet, such actions helped to define the participants as separate from and radical compared with the women attending the bridal fair. Thus the action was meaningful in establishing group identity.

Socialist feminist unions organized with the understanding that their eventual goal was a merger between feminism and socialism (Schmid and Starkweather 1969). While it was clear that they had separated (temporarily at least) from socialist groups, they did not want to be seen simply as feminists. In attempting to carve out a niche for themselves, socialist feminists experienced their own identity crisis.

> We always had this attitude, which I am now so critical of, which is that socialist-feminism is so much better than everything in regular feminism. So any time we came up with something ordinary it didn't sound good enough. It didn't have a socialist component to it. How is that different from what the liberals are doing? And so we didn't do it. (Cited in Hansen 1986: 75)

Separatism became divisive because it contained different meanings among feminist groups. Originally, separatism from men was an essential strategy for the radical groups; the expectation was that there would eventually be "integration with equality" (Leon 1978: 153). But a separatist organizing principle became problematic when the outer limits of this philosophy were stretched to include the adoption of a lesbian separatist lifestyle.

NOW specifically avoided a separatist strategy in the organizing stage, making it clear that the organization was called the National Organization *for* Women rather than *of* women. Anyone interested in working for the improvement of women's lives was invited to join. Nevertheless, the small number of male members represented mostly paper members or men involved through their attachments to women activists;[8] it was common knowledge within NOW that it was essential for women to define and lead their own movement. Indeed, since the founding year, the possibility of men holding national leadership positions has been virtually zero.

Although the idea of women-only groups has been associated since the early 1970s with lesbian separatism, the practice has historical roots,[9] and most feminist groups do practice a form of separatism in their political work. For instance, when the National Women's Political Caucus organized in 1971, some chapters allowed men to be members, and some voted to exclude men.[10] The League of Women Voters originally formed in 1920 as a single sex organization; indeed at its 1972 national convention, league members rejected a proposal to lift the ban against male members. As one member explained, "The League is about the only moderate organization that has power for women. And I don't want to give up that power." Supporting this position, Gloria Steinem adds: "We cannot integrate with men on an equal basis until we are equal. If you admit men, let them do the typing, run the child care centers and donate money."[11]

One feminist who agrees with a separatist strategy considers the perceptions of people involved to be the real defining characteristic of what is or is not separatist organizing. Philosophically, since feminism focuses on women, the entire movement could be defined as separatist.[12] But this way of looking at the issue of separatism was not a part of the consciousness of feminist leaders in the early 1970s; it was, instead, a time when the word separatism was seen only as a representative symbol of fundamentally opposed feminist views.

Given the reality of a movement attempting to organize on behalf of all women, and given the pragmatic considerations of the need for cooperative feminist organizing, why were the battles over ideological definitions and the emphasis on ideological purity so intense? To answer this question, we must turn once again to the importance of ideology in social movements.

THEORY AS IDEOLOGY: A DEMOBILIZING EFFECT

Ideology provides the rationale for how people lead their lives; it is a belief system for how things should be. Disagreement with prevailing ideology leads to the formation of an alternative ideology, a crucial component for social movement development (Ferree and Miller 1985; Gusfield 1970b; Turner and Killian 1957; Zurcher and Snow 1981). An alternative ideology provides a justification for social change and thus can motivate people to action. A second function of ideology is the establishment of a framework for individuals to connect with others through common experiences. The development of a challenging ideology, then, provides an alternative worldview uniting diverse individuals into a group with a common interest in changing the status quo.

Theory is an explanation of why things are the way they are, how they got that way, and what needs to be done to change them. Theories are based on unproven assumptions; hence, there can be more than one theory to explain the same occurrence. The purpose of theory is to contribute to the legitimacy of ideology; thus, even when there are several theories, they can each feed into the ideology because different people may relate to one theory more readily than to another without severing the connection the ideology provides. Ideology should subsume theory and integrate the various assertions and aims of an established sociopolitical system or challenging system.

When theoretical explanations are seen as definitive, they take on the appearance of separate ideologies which create dissension when they are promoted by loyal constituents. For social movements, competing theories become demobilizing factors as disputes over ideological purity override common political concerns. In other words, theory becomes divisive when it is used as an ideological label for self-identification in order to differentiate competing activist groups.

Almost inherently, this way of using theory carries with it an evaluation of who holds the superior (more correct) position. Within the women's movement, disputes over theory turned into disputes over who was most feminist or who was the right kind of feminist.

Part of the ambience of social movements is to argue about strongly held feelings and convictions. This is expected of social activists; what is problematic is the way differences are resolved. Although the various feminist groups reflected different women's realities, and shared exploration could have deepened feminist analysis, activists moved very quickly from introducing new ways of seeing to a narrowed view of feminist legitimacy. Thus, the movement found itself with competitive models of "right thinking." Self-defined radical groups argued over who was really radical, and, in a dismissive manner, they labeled the mass movement sector as liberal feminist. In radical circles, liberal feminism was considered conservative since its goals included reform in the current legal, social, and cultural structures.

This differentiation, however, was not the way most activists in the mass movement sector saw what they were doing. For example, Betty Friedan, a founder and first President of NOW, always called herself a radical feminist (1976), and many NOW members had far-reaching visions of political and cultural change.[13] Radical feminists' ignorance of and disregard for "liberal feminism" failed to appreciate the potential for a revolutionary model this sector of the movement contained (Eisenstein 1981), or the potential for women who joined this sector to become radicalized on issues of sexism, class, racism, and lesbianism.

The adoption of an ideology that found only certain actions, lifestyles, and relationships acceptable is closely related to social movement histories characterized by values of dominance and control. None of the feminist groups in the women's movement was desirous of dictatorial authority, yet the emphasis on ideological purity lent itself to sometimes oppressive mind-sets.

Most movements experience factionalism, many collapsing under the weight of excessive infighting. Within the civil rights movement, at the peak of activism in the 1960s, intense intra-movement conflict and competition emerged among the major organizations vying for money and publicity (McAdam 1983). Lesbians parted with the Gay Liberation Movement in large numbers during the early 1970s, leaving the men in the movement to continue their acrimonious struggles among the various camps alone (Jernigan 1988: 37–41). A pattern of sectarian attack can also be found in the long history of leftist organizing (Gitlin 1987; Oberschall 1978; Sale 1973; Weinstein 1967). Radical feminist women reacted against the male chauvinism they found in leftist groups of the 1960s era; nevertheless, they borrowed heavily from them, including the practice of promoting dogmatic positions on correct thinking.

Women of many persuasions were joining movement groups in the 1960s and

1970s, including anti-feminist groups. The right wing, far from the vision of a monolithic group of like-thinking proponents, also contains schisms and dissension related to dominance and control. Recent scholarship on a neglected part of that movement, right-wing women, shows there are deep divisions in ideology and interest among the women involved (Klatch 1987). But an important distinction between right-wing women and women involved in feminist organizing is that, overall, right-wing groups have maintained a male-dominated leadership structure. Feminist groups, as we have seen, were formed to be led by women for women. It is ironic, then, that in reifying theory and focusing on activist differences rather than on areas of agreement, these groups, in their early years, fell into a pattern of factionalism reminiscent of male-dominated social movement groups.

Because feminism is a movement that exhibits an important departure from other social movements, that is, it is led by women, there is an expectation that it should not be hierarchical, elitist, or controlling of adherents. Indeed, feminism is meant to value, support, and unite women. It was the expectation of "a haven from the ravages of a sexist society; a place where one would be understood" that led to despair when, for some participants, just the opposite occurred (Joreen 1976: 51): In repeated incidents of what became known as trashing, the sense of joy in women discovering themselves was dissipated.

Trashing was destructive because it was couched in terms of philosophical difference, when in actuality it was a form of character assassination. In describing her personal experience, Jo Freeman found that what was attacked was not "one's actions or ideas, but one's self" (Joreen 1976: 50). Freeman blames her own need for feminism and the seduction of its appeal for making her vulnerable to the depths of despair she and other women experienced after being trashed. Indeed, trashing was the ultimate betrayal of the belief in sisterhood; or, as proclaimed by Ti-Grace Atkinson, after being asked to leave the group she had started, "sisterhood is powerful: it kills sisters" (quoted in Joreen 1976: 91).

Trashing could be personal or group oriented, each group finding a derogatory term to apply to the others. It was found in all sectors of the movement, but more so in the small group sector where being radical meant being right. The early years brought feminist ideas that were new and exciting; however, as each position developed, it was seen in polemic terms of "either/or." The high-riding spirit brought with it a high level of insecurity as groups took unbending positions, defending their own particular strategy or ideology as *the* correct line. The end result was particular brands of feminism which bred contempt for those feminists who did not think or organize in the same way.

The focus on destructive distinctions, begun in a generally progressive political environment, continued to play itself out in a more hostile environment characterized by a general economic decline. At that point, when feminists could have focused their efforts on issues of concern to poor and working-class women, they were fragmented and fighting over labels.

Defining the self in definitions of feminism

In the formation period of the contemporary movement, the spread of feminist ideology by different groups was mobilizing. It created an immediate and rapid dissemination of feminist ideas within different sectors of society. From the beginning, however, the creation of a radical identity was an overriding concern for many feminist activists. Being radical carried with it a commitment to separate from the establishment, and that meant the necessity also to define oneself as different from women considered to be connected to the establishment. Because so many of the early small group feminists came out of social movement activism of the 1960s decade (Deckard 1983; Evans 1979; Freeman 1975; Hole and Levine 1971; Thorne 1975), their radical identification preceded their involvement with feminism. Being radical was not just part of their definition of themselves as feminists; it was a fundamental aspect of their self-identity. For instance, radical was part of the names of their groups—New York Radical Women, Radicalesbians, Westchester Radical Feminists—and was used to describe their personal orientation, as in "Notes of a Radical Lesbian" (Shelley 1970). The act of naming their brand of feminism "radical" helped activists to define themselves as substantially different from "reformist" women.

Seeing themselves as opponents of the status quo, as agents of social change, radical feminist leaders tended to oppose any idea or person considered to be part of the current system. If capitalism was to blame for women's oppression, then attempts to gain entry for women into high-level positions were indicators of implicit support for an oppressive system. If male domination was the cause of women's oppression, then aligning with a man meant helping them to oppress women. If "compulsory heterosexuality" underlay patriarchal control (Rich 1980: 647), then choosing heterosexual relations made a woman part of the problem. The various conflicts, although labeled ideological, went beyond ideology as they posited how women should live their lives.

On close inspection, the various views of feminist acceptability represented lifestyles most suited to those who advocated them. What was overlooked was the differences among women. Thus, instead of unifying feminist activists, feminist ideology and theory became a means to separate movement women from each other.

The common goal of suffrage produced effective mobilization in the first wave of feminism, but the woman's movement experienced intra-movement hostility and decline after the vote was achieved. Although there were personal antagonisms and strong disagreements over tactics during the suffrage campaign, activists contained factionalism by focusing on the attainment of the vote while ignoring their differing underlying views of womanhood. Many factors contributed to the demise of a concerted women's movement in the 1920s: the Red Scare, associating social reform with communism; the home economics movement, with its emphasis on housewifery as a valued occupation; an economic recession following industrial demobilization after the war; a focus on class and race with the rise in labor unrest and lynchings of blacks in the South; the view that women were emancipated after winning the vote; the gains in entry to white-color occupations; and the diffusion of women's activism into numerous civic, social, and peace organizations.[14] Nevertheless, the failure to achieve a sustained movement for feminist advance, and the dissipation of scores of suffrage activists,[15] can also be partly attributed to the lack of a shared ideological foundation among women's rights proponents.

Unlike the earlier movement, the contemporary U.S. women's movement did not fail to debate and promote an ideological base for feminist activism. Moreover, it created a number of well-developed theories to account for women's secondary status. The problem in the organizing years of the contemporary movement was that competing theories were used as competing ideologies. Rather than producing creative dialogue, theory and ideology became a means of establishing a particular feminist identity. The effect this had on the movement as a whole was to draw lines among feminist women. Moreover, the acting out of radical identities left an impression on the general public that the women's movement was not for ordinary women, since the goal of some of the tactics was to distance radical feminists from other women rather than to induce them into the movement.

Ten years after it began, contemporary feminism had created a new awareness of the relations between women and men and made important advances on a number of levels. Early victories can be attributed to participants in all sectors of the movement, who organized and publicized women's demands for change. But, within the movement itself, factional disputes contributed to painful personal attacks and a climate of competition among feminist groups. Staking out a position and defending it contributed to the proliferation of feminist idealogues rather than social change agents. Ideology, an important resource for garnering social movement support, became a negative factor in sustaining commitment, particularly in self-defined radical feminist groups. During this phase of the movement, the ideal of sisterhood was strong, but the practice was still struggling to emerge.

Chapter 5

SOCIAL MOVEMENT TRANSFORMATION: THE WOMEN'S MOVEMENT FROM 1975 TO 1982

We have a large family, seven children, and I used to be in business for myself and it seemed like I never had time for politics and political issues. Then I went to a statewide women's conference to put together issues and a slate of people to go to Houston for the International Women's Year Conference. This was the first time I ever saw democracy fail.

There were 240 of us who had gone for the whole weekend. We started Friday night and went all day Saturday and until noon on Sunday. We went through all the issues—older women, rural women, reproductive rights, sexual preference, the ERA, just a million issues—and when we came out of our last workshop and walked up the hill to vote, there were 500 anti-choice people who had been bused in just to vote. We stood five abreast for five hours waiting our turn. It was incredible.

And, of course, it turned out that an anti-feminist slate represented the state of Missouri. I called my sister who is a good feminist in Nebraska and she said the same thing happened there. They couldn't stop it either. We got on the phone to Kansas to all the people we knew there and we didn't catch them in time. So we— me and my three sisters and my mother who is a strong feminist—went to Houston to watch from the gallery. The only issue Missouri voted yes for was women and credit, which made us think that they wanted to keep their credit cards. They were not concerned at all with any other aspect of women's lives.

So that was the beginning of my getting involved with the women's movement.
(Ann Boyce, president, Freedom of Choice Council)[1]

The re-emerged women's movement is now a quarter of a century old. Many of the original groups are no longer in existence and other groups active in later years were unformed in the organizing years. Some issues have been won, new ones have emerged, and old ones have taken on new identities. In other words, the women's movement and the social environment have changed since the late 1960s. Yet, until recently, the contemporary women's movement has been studied almost exclusively in terms of the formation and early years of movement activism.[2] Without ongoing research and analysis, earlier definitions of the movement continue as if there had been no change in direction or consolidation of feminist meaning. Polarized conceptions of feminist groups are frozen in time; and often, as shown in the following quote, reveal themselves as subjective views containing inaccurate information:

> The National Organization of [sic] Women . . . Founded in 1966 under the auspices of Betty Friedan and like minded women, N.O.W. was initially wholly dominated by their types' concerns . . . [in which] a power struggle in the early '70s between the dominant bourgeois reformers and a socially and politically more radical faction within N.O.W., the Red Stockings, [sic] resulted in the defeat of the latter and a temporary resistance to broader progressive goals within the organization (Lewis 1985: 32)

There is little recognition of a growing feminist consciousness or of movement transformation when writers concentrate on where women came from rather than where they are aiming to go. The fact is that by the early 1970s most feminist groups considered themselves part of a movement going beyond limited conceptions of women's rights. For instance, in an editorial from the NOW president, 1970 was declared "the year of Dogged Determination—determination to implement our program for full liberation" (Hernandez 1971: 176).

The literature on the women's movement is a mixed assortment of maintaining old assessments and objecting to the continuation of earlier categorizations. Until the latter part of the 1980s much of the literature continued to categorize movement groups by a reform/revolutionary designation (Andersen 1983; Banks, 1981; Fritz, 1979; Richardson 1981). However, since Freeman's observations (1975, 1979) other voices have joined her in questioning the continued appropriateness of these labels. Indeed, Maren Lockwood Carden (1974), a proponent of the early categorization scheme, changed her position when she did an update on the movement and found "the old distinction between 'Women's Liberation' and 'Women's Rights' (also called the 'younger' and 'older' branches of the movement) is no longer valid" (1977: 5–6). Other researchers have called for the end of purist thinking (Chafe 1977), and the need to recognize a core ideology underlying all feminist groups (Whitehurst 1977). The early classification scheme did not fit in Verta Taylor's analysis of the post-70s movement (1986); and Ferree and Hess (1985) found diverse feminist groups in the 1980s interacting in a complementary rather than a competitive way. Chafetz and Dworkin agree that there has been convergence, but contend that, in spite of internecine attack, this conversion actually took place much earlier. Indeed, they argue that by the "early 1970s the two branches were coalescing into one movement, characterized by substantial ideological, tactical, and organizational diversity," with "a set of common themes, concepts, and goals" (1986: 164–5).

This new literature provides us with a view of a transformed women's movement; however, for the most part, it fails to tell us how this change came about. As Jo Freeman points out in her review of *Controversy and Coalition: The New Feminist Movement* (Ferree and Hess 1985), this work provides us with only partial information by reviewing the various social movement organizations' achievements and failures. What is missing is the internal dynamics and alliances of these groups (Freeman 1986: 64–5).

To understand how this change came about, we must go back to events occurring in the early 1970s and analyze the effects of environmental and movement-related developments on the direction feminism would take in this decade.

A FORGETTABLE AND NOT-SO FORGETTABLE DECADE

By 1973, as the original radical feminist groups were dissolving, new segments of the women's movement were forming. Centers and service groups were established by women from the various sectors of the movement, some from NOW, some from CR groups, some with separatist orientations, and some from within socialist feminist unions. In addition, national single-issue organizations were being formed or becoming more prominent, for example, the National Abortion Rights Action League (NARAL)[3] and the National Women's Political Caucus (NWPC).[4] Older women's groups such as the League of Women Voters began to take up feminist issues, finally coming out in favor of the Equal Rights Amendment after it passed Congress. Women's caucuses were formed within a wide variety of established groups and separate women's professional organizations mushroomed throughout the country.

A self-conscious feminist culture spread with the formation of self-help groups, coffee houses and women's centers. Women's music emerged, some, such as Maxine Feldman's recording of Angry Atthis/Bar One, containing an explicit lesbian sentiment, and in 1974 the first National Women's Music Festival was held at the University of Illinois (Ladyslipper 1983). It was within this growing women's culture that the view of women as victims began to be replaced with a view of women as possessors of higher values.

NOW began to strengthen its base of operation by incorporating a Legal Defense and Education Fund (LDEF) for the purpose of initiating and funding precedent-setting legal cases based on sex discrimination. The President of NOW

LDEF, lawyer Sylvia Robert, won the case of *Weeks v. Southern Bell Telephone Company,* which established the principle that an employer must open all jobs to women who wish to apply. Protests and legal action centered around sex-segregated want ads were held in major cities around the country, eventually resulting in restrictions on this practice. Other legal actions followed, mostly centered on regulations affecting women's accessibility to get hired or promoted. In 1970 alone, NOW filed sex discrimination complaints against 1,300 corporations. By 1974 NOW LDEF had participated in over 50 major legal cases covering a wide spectrum of issues including family law, property rights, civil rights, and employment discrimination (National Organization for Women 1974; Webb and Bacon 1985).

After almost 50 years of lobbying, the Equal Rights Amendment passed Congress in 1972, with 22 states rushing to ratify in the first year. In 1973, with the Supreme Court ruling on *Roe v. Wade,* abortion became a legal option for women faced with an unwanted pregnancy. Later that year, AT&T, the nation's largest private employer and largest employer of women, lost a wage discrimination suit filed by the Equal Employment Opportunity Commission (EEOC). Over $30 million in back pay and future salary adjustments were awarded to women and minorities (Epstein 1975; Spokeswoman 1974a).

Feminism was no longer a joke. On the contrary, it was taken seriously enough for a strong backlash to organize against it.[5] In the early 1970s small groups supporting traditional gender roles sprang up; for example, HOTDOG, an acronym for Humanitarians Opposed to Degrading our Girls, and HOW, standing for Happiness of Womanhood (O'Reilly 1983). Books based on the philosophy of feminine virtues as female power became best sellers.[6] The organized conservative response began in earnest in 1973, after the ERA passed Congress. STOP ERA[7] was founded by Phyllis Schlafly in October of that year; likewise, the National Right to Life movement organized within a few months of the Supreme Court abortion decision. After the settlement with AT&T, women's equality was seen as an expensive and threatening reality to corporate interests. Thus, in 1974 Paul Weyrich founded the Heritage Foundation, a right-wing think tank.[8] In contrast to the organizing years of the contemporary movement, when a major problem was to be taken seriously, "women's lib" had become big business.

Conservative opposition was assisted by the shock of the 1973 oil embargo, and the resulting recession created barriers to further advance for progressive social movements. In the women's movement, activists were reflecting as early as 1974 on the negative effects of the economic downturn for women and minorities. Activists decried the plight of women workers and watched with dismay as economic strains created instability in their own organizations. One activist optimistically hoped that people would ultimately see beyond their immediate problems and address "what the current economic situation says about overall power relations in this society" (Spokeswoman 1974b). How many people reached that conclusion when faced with their own monetary fears is unknown, but what is clear is that by the mid-1970s the women's movement had entered a new phase, one of defensive rather than offensive action.

1975: A WATERSHED YEAR

When the ERA passed Congress in 1972, the vote in the House of Representatives was 354 to 23 and in the Senate 84 to 8. In that same year 22 states ratified, with eight more doing so in 1973 (Pleck 1983). What had at first looked like a rapid ratification process, however, began to slip away as the opposition organized and individual states began to stall. Clearly the tide had turned as New Jersey and New York, two liberal states which had earlier ratified the national amendment, turned down a similar proposal for their own residents. The defeats heralded the new anti-feminist/New Right coalition: Phyllis Schlafly's STOP ERA, the Mormon Church, fundamentalist churches, the John Birch Society, political conservatives in general, corporate leaders, anti abortion groups, and the hierarchy of the Catholic Church. A second Schlafly group, The Eagle Forum, coalescing numerous discontents, was formed in 1975. Calling itself anti-ERA, anti-abortion, and pro-family, this group chose the eagle as its symbol because it stood for traditional American values and because the eagle was one of the few creatures in society to have one mate for life (Fishman and Fuller 1981).

The end of the original radical feminist groups

The realization that feminism was in trouble came at the exact time the women's movement was facing one of its most difficult fragmentation points. In the early 1970s, consciousness raising as a major movement activity had peaked and by 1975 the original radical feminist sector had all but disappeared. With the demise of the small groups, also disappearing were the zap actions, witch hexes, and guerrilla theatre demonstrations. These innovative social movement tactics were replaced by the less public women's culture and the service projects which became the new form of small group activism.

A final ending to the intense emotional confrontation within the radical feminist sector was the publication of *Feminist Revolution,* self-published in 1975 by the reorganized Redstockings. Articles in this book indicted liberals, lesbians, and leftists for the breakdown of a radical feminist agenda within the women's movement. The most controversial piece, "Agents, Opportunists and Fools," connected the CIA to *Ms.* magazine and the Women's Action Alliance, both founded by Gloria Steinem. In 1977 when Random House agreed to publish the book nationwide, this article was deleted. A story questioning this deletion in the *Village Voice* (see Borman 1979) drew scores of letters one week later. One letter, signed by eight well-known feminists, defended the deletion by objecting to "self-styled Redstockings, very far from the original group," who have taken it upon themselves to "claim sole title to feminism." The letter closed by stating: "all of us happen to believe that the worldwide women's movement is not the property of any person, group, or central-committee mentality." [9]

Even a reply accusing the letter writers of their personal self-interest through their connections to *Ms.* (two were editors, some of the others were contributors) could not dull the importance of their message: intolerance and dogmatism within the movement had played itself out.

Fragmentation on the left

Socialist feminism was faring no better. A national conference in Yellow Springs, Ohio, was planned in 1975 by the women's commission of the New American Movement (NAM). [10] The organizers assumed the conference would draw 500–600 people, but over 2,000 registered or attempted to attend. What looked like the beginning of a major swell in the growth of socialist feminism, however, turned out to be the height of this organizing orientation in the U.S. women's movement. Instead of a gathering signifying strength among leftist women, activists involved in various Marxist-Leninist and anti-imperialist organizations accused socialist feminists of being bourgeois; lesbians were defined as women involving themselves in a bourgeois decadent practice. The conflict and emotion aroused at the conference left many women feeling they had just been through a "horrendous experience." [11]

Rather than finding unity, the conference became a forum for expounding ideological positions. Interestingly, as one participant later remarked, this conference on socialist feminism, the first ever to be held, did not come across with a strong socialist feminist theoretical position.

> Because the conference was supposedly a socialist-feminist conference, the irony and disrespect of calling a "socialist-feminist caucus" prevented what was probably the majority political position from being presented in a coherent manner in opposition to other caucus views. The anti-imperialist caucus, the Marxist-Leninist caucus, the third-world women's caucus, the lesbian caucus, the older women's caucus, etc. presented statements that were not always consistent with socialist-feminism and were sometimes openly contradictory. [12]

As Karen Hansen describes it in her history of the women's liberation unions, the "Yellow Springs conference confirmed that theoretical unity did not exist and in turn called the strength of the movement into question" (1986: 91).

After the conference, continuing debates over the issue of feminism and petty bourgeois opportunism dissipated vast amounts of energy. Sectarian disputes resulted in the end of the local unions, including one of the last to survive, the Chicago Women's Liberation Union, which disbanded in 1977. In the early 1970s CWLU had been a dynamic union, larger than Chicago NOW, with over 400 members. In trying to understand how such a group could dissolve, Chris Riddeough, a member of CWLU, explains that it was partly their own philosophical vulnerability which contributed to their collapse.

> One of the things the Marxist women did was to appeal to the socialist ideas that people had, and it was at a point in time when I think getting called "petty bourgeois" sparked a reaction in people that you wanted to prove wasn't true. So there was this sense of needing to justify oneself politically. [13]

After the break-up of the unions, socialist feminists joined either other feminist groups or newly formed socialist groups. [14] However, "women who were feminist and worked in socialist organizations found themselves working specifically on feminist issues within that group. For instance, within NAM the Feminist Commission was formed to work on feminist issues." [15] Thus, in joining a mixed-sex socialist group, socialist feminists lost their autonomy and in, some sense, became a movement within a movement.

Internal challenge in NOW

The service groups and growing women's culture remained basically outside the public activist realm. Thus, the political arena was left to the mass movement feminist organizations, most particularly to the National Organization for Women. NOW also experienced a crisis in 1975, which nearly split the organization in two. A challenging group from within, calling itself the Majority Caucus, won a bitterly fought national election with the slogan, "Out of the Mainstream, Into the Revolution" (Majority Caucus 1975).

While there have always been divisions in NOW, serious infighting began at the 7th National Conference held in Houston in May 1974. As the scene of the first contested national election, this conference witnessed considerable personal attack. Intense confrontation arose over the office of president, where Karen DeCrow, a feminist lawyer from New York, won by a narrow margin over Mary Jean Collins-Robson, a long-time NOW activist from Chicago. As the new president, DeCrow found herself in a minority position on a board consisting of a large number of Collins-Robson supporters. In addition, living in New York left her isolated from much of the day-to-day decision making at the Chicago-based national office.

Over the ensuing months, friction developed between DeCrow and the executive director of the national office. By the end of the year, 12 board members joined with DeCrow in forming a "Majority Caucus" to work for structural change within the organization (Belmont 1975). Protesting national board actions, they filed a lawsuit for bylaws infraction and placed their dues in escrow. Eventually "intrust" chapters and states represented a large proportion of NOW members, estimated at around half the membership (California Majority Caucus 1975).

The dispute between the two factions was framed in rhetorical terms of radical and conservative orientations, but little difference actually existed on fundamental questions of goals and organizing strategy. On the question of organizational structure, neither faction ever considered eliminating structure or a national presence.

> To begin with, there is no question as to the need for a national organization for women. Effectiveness requires it. Each of us understands that in approaching local or state industries and agencies we are treated with greater attention and respect if it is understood that behind us there is a national structure with national resources. The question at issue is what structure this national organization should have. (Jones 1975: 7).

Even in terms of tactics, the two groups were not that far apart.

> The first national march, the one held in Springfield in 1976, had originally been proposed by the Chicago faction of the national board, and the only member of the Majority Caucus who thought it was a good idea was Ellie Smeal. Now, as you may recall, the rallying cry of the Caucus was "Out of the Mainstream, Into the Revolution" and that was meant to imply they were going to hit the streets and raise hell. But, ironically, it was the Chicago faction that proposed the march which was in effect hitting the streets and it was the other faction who originally opposed it. So nobody was very consistent in what they were saying.[16]

Nevertheless, the 1975 national conference was full of conflict and high tension. The division was so bitter that accusations of CIA intervention were bandied about (Pombeiro 1975). An outside organization, the American Arbitration Association, was contracted for $10,000 to administer the election. Delays and confrontations over voter credentialing resulted in overtime expenses for space, equipment, and personnel. The largest conference in NOW's history, instead of making money, cost the organization $20,000 (National Organization for Women 1976: 25–6).

The Majority Caucus brought a slate of candidates, a position booklet, and a well-organized campaign team. At the election's end they held 16 of the 25 board seats and all but one of the national executive positions. The insurgents had made a sweep, but many of the elections had been close. For instance,

DeCrow retained the presidency by only 98 votes in which over 2,000 votes were cast (Shanahan 1975; Gordon 1975; National Organization for Women 1976: 27).

Eleanor (Ellie) Smeal, a major organizer behind the Majority Caucus, was elected Chair One. The following year, she was instrumental in leading the membership to accept bylaw changes for delegated conventions, paid officer positions, a reduction in the number of officers, and a residency requirement for national officers in the national office city.[17] At the first election after the new bylaws went into effect, Smeal ran for president and won. The organization under the leadership of Smeal and other leaders from the Majority Caucus moved into a political direction assisted by one of the first changes enacted, the relocation of the national office to Washington, D.C., the heart of the country's political activity.[18]

THE ERA CAMPAIGN

By 1977 the Equal Rights Amendment was the mobilizing issue for feminist activism. NOW was in the forefront of this campaign, and Eleanor Smeal became the uncontested leader behind NOW's growing influence. Smeal, whose educational background was in political science, led NOW into a political direction with the intent of building a mass movement large enough for politicians to take seriously. Using the ERA to mobilize large numbers of women from around the country, NOW grew from 35,000 members in the mid-1970s to 250,000 members by 1982 (National Organization for Women 1982). In 1975 NOW was working with a budget of $500,000; in 1982 the combined organizational and Political Action Committee (PAC) budget was $13 million, and by the end of the ERA campaign NOW was raising $1 million a month (Mann 1982; National Organization for Women). The ERA became more than a mobilizing issue; it also served as a unifying issue for feminist activists. Because NOW had moved into a leadership role in this campaign, it was able to pick up women from different segments of the movement who were unaffiliated by the late 1970s. The ongoing merging of new activists contributed to an energized and more diverse organization.

In 1976, NOW began organizing national marches and demonstrations, starting with an ERA march in Springfield, Illinois, which drew 10,000 participants. Marches and other public demonstrations serve a two-fold purpose for social movements. First, they bring issues to public attention; and second, they mobilize commitment from supporters.[19] For instance, the first march NOW was involved with, the 1970 Strike for Women's Equality, expanded membership in some chapters by 50–70 percent (Freeman 1975; Ferree and Hess 1985).

Demonstrations were staged connecting the contemporary movement to the suffrage movement by wearing white and carrying replicas of the purple, white, and gold banners used in that campaign. Symbols increasingly became a part of the mobilization process. Colors were used to create a sense of belonging to the movement. Green was taken to symbolize "go," in opposition to the anti-ERA forces who carried red "STOP ERA" signs. With the approach of the seven-year deadline for passage of the Equal Rights Amendment, NOW organized an extension march in Washington, D.C. which drew over 100,000 participants. The extension drive, believed by many to be an unattainable goal, resulted in congressional approval for a new deadline of June 30, 1982.

The extension march was held on July 9, 1978, exactly one year after Alice Paul had died. The awareness of her death, before passage of the amendment she had authored, provided an inspirational impetus to many supporters. The use of symbols and pageantry was combined with music, chants, and name-catching speakers. All of these methods drew press attention, increased aware-ness of women's historic activism, and created an emotional response which con-tributed to an effective mobilization process. For instance, in 1980 NOW organized a Mother's Day march in Chicago and once again drew 100,000 participants.

Other organizations were active and other issues were addressed, but for the seven-year period between 1975 and 1982 NOW and the ERA were in the forefront of activism in the political arena. A good portion of this development can be attributed to the force of Ellie Smeal's leadership and appeal. Smeal was char-ismatic to many NOW members, as she projected a sense of power—a taboo characteristic in earlier feminist circles. The importance of a charismatic leader in social movements has long been noted, first by Max Weber, and subsequently by others (Zald and Ash 1966; Friedland 1969) but the contemporary women's movement had discouraged this role because of feminist (and New Left) values of egalitarianism. NOW took a more lenient position, having always been orga-nized with a leadership structure; yet there was distrust of too much focus on one person. None of the previous NOW officers had evoked the emotion Smeal was able to do. Her rise to prominence was partly due to the nature of her personality and partly because the timing was right. As one NOW activist ex-plains, "What she took over, we needed someone to counter Phyllis Schlafly. We needed someone to say, this is what we're going to do."[20]

The noticeable increase in feminist activism paralleled the growth of the New Right as the ERA became the focal political activity for both feminist and anti-feminist forces. With the increased publicity from both social movements, this issue became a rallying cry for progressives and conservatives alike. The ERA could have faded away; instead, feminist activism thrived in a growing conserv-ative climate. Thus, part of the increased commitment by feminists stemmed from the growing strength of the organized backlash.

Moreover, there was the sense that an opportunity might be lost if this issue was not won at this time. When Smeal was elected NOW president there were two years left for the ratification process. She took the position that this was an historical moment which demanded the priority of ERA. She pushed for a concentrated public campaign, and, even when the three and a half year extension was granted, the "historic moment" persuasion was still compelling. The membership responded with a conference mandate for a National ERA Strike Force to plan overall strategy for unratified states. For five years the ERA was a burning passion for scores of activists. In the process of building the campaign, emotions deepened, ERA became a mobilizing issue, and Ellie Smeal became a mobilizing agent. An example of the increased wide-spread support brought about by the ERA campaign was the boycott of unratified states. Started by NOW, the boycott eventually enlisted hundreds of supporting organizations.[21]

The Equal Rights Amendment, which had been one issue among many, became the symbol of women's equality. The failure of an amendment prohibiting discrimination on the basis of sex became representative of women's generalized secondary status. Thus, the Equal Rights Amendment, like suffrage before it, became a highly valued resource as it became more symbolic than tangible. As Zurcher and Snow (1981) suggest, "it might be argued that the resource most important to a movement's mobilization efforts is a symbol that unifies and empowers" (1981: 471). Ironically, this was true for both the pro- and anti-ERA forces, thereby lending support to both factions' mobilizing efforts.

A feminist victory which seeded anti-feminist aftershocks was the International Women's Year Conference (IWY) held in Houston in 1977. Over 1,500 elected delegates attended the conference, along with 20,000 observers (National Commission on the Observance of International Women's Year 1978). On this occasion there was an unusual gathering, one that included both feminists and anti-feminists. Moral Majority forces dubbed it the "Immoral Women's Year," and major confrontations arose over ERA, reproductive freedom, and lesbian rights. Only about 20 percent of the delegates came from the pro-family sector and the resolutions passed at the IWY Conference were all passed with a feminist intent.[22] However, this conference did contribute to the development of the "pro-family" movement, some leaders even calling it their "boot camp" training (Klatch 1987).

In spite of some significant gains, the political climate was actually growing more unfriendly to feminist interests. No state had passed the amendment since the extension; only one had passed since 1975 and several states had voted to rescind their earlier vote. Even as polls showed increasing support for passage, the Republican Party removed ERA from their platform.[23] Indeed, the 1980 elections of Ronald Reagan and a Republican Senate were strong indicators of a more hostile environment for future feminist advance.

THE INTRODUCTION OF CIVIL DISOBEDIENCE

The political process was not working, but, having put so much effort into one issue and strategy, NOW and other politically focused groups held firm to their strategies. Within this environment, smaller unaffiliated groups began to emerge. These groups introduced a new tactic: non-violent civil disobedience. The major force behind this direction was another charismatic leader, Sonia Johnson, a soft-spoken but emotionally powerful speaker. A fifth-generation Mormon, Johnson had been excommunicated from the Mormon Church at the end of 1979 for forming Mormons for ERA. In the early 1980s she organized women, many of whom were religious or coming out of a religious background, into a "spiritual mission" in which civil disobedience became their mode of action. Joining a newly organized Congressional Union,[24] an early action she was involved with was a chaining-in at the White House gates.[25] Twenty women were arrested that day, charged with obstructing traffic and fined $50 each[26] (Fithian 1981: 2; Congressional Union 1981: 1)

The June 30, 1982 deadline for ERA passage was approaching with three states short of the two-thirds requirement. Springfield, Illinois, became a center of activity, hosting intense confrontations between pro- and anti-ERA supporters for the last stage of this 10 year campaign. A Northern industrialized state, one of the first to pass the suffrage amendment and one of 16 states with a state ERA, Illinois was logically seen as a state where ERA was passable.[27] National NOW concentrated activist efforts by targeting states, and in the Spring of 1982 they organized mass lobbying and a march in Illinois. A silent vigil, reminiscent of earlier suffrage vigils, had been conducted in the Rotunda of the Illinois capitol by a downstate NOW chapter since the end of the 1970s. Every day the legislators were in session, at least two women dressed in white, stood silently in the Rotunda with purple, white, and gold banners. Added to this was a NOW lobbying table placed in one corner of the Rotunda with green and white colors. Across from the NOW table was a red and white STOP ERA table with signs, buttons, and printed hand-outs.

At midnight on May 17, seven women, including Sonia Johnson, began a 37-day fast in the Rotunda of the capitol. Declaring the fast a solemn witness to women's "deep hunger for justice," the fasters sought "to touch the hearts of the nation's lawmakers that they might be moved to fulfill the nation's 200 year old promise of equal justice under the law."[28] In solidarity with the fasters, the Religious Committee for the ERA (RCERA) declared every Wednesday through June 30 a national day of fasting, prayer, and renewed work for passage. Supporters were asked to wear a white ribbon as a sign of fasting.[29] A week after the fast began, Eleanor Smeal, wearing a white ribbon, visited the fasters and arranged for NOW to provide hotel accommodations for the women, who had been sleeping on the floor of a church.

On June 3, a group calling themselves "A Grassroots Group of Second Class Citizens" chained themselves inside the Capitol. Springfield officials decided to let them stay. The militants found themselves sitting around an empty capitol building for the weekend while the NOW march was taking place outside.[30] After four days and nights, in a pre-dawn eviction, they were forcibly removed. They repeatedly returned over the next few weeks, holding sit-ins at the Governor's office and once on the floor of the House. Arrests followed and 12 members were sentenced for contempt of court. Ten of the 12 arrested spent four days in jail for statements they made during their hearing in court. At a later date, eight members of the group were charged with a felony and fined a total of $3,600 for a blood-writing demonstration.[31] The result of these efforts was dismal; no new Yes votes were gained—in fact, one legislator changed his vote to No, claiming he did so because of the fasters.

After the ERA defeat, new assessments began in feminist organizations. The issue which had united and inspired thousands of women was no longer able to do so. Passage now required that the entire process be started anew; and the political climate was not open for this effort. Many groups which had organized specifically around ERA disbanded, centers closed, and membership in the remaining groups dropped. Even though many of the fading supporters were only paper members, they had represented financial support and potential recruits to action. The main arena of involvement for nationally organized groups became electoral politics. Most felt the need to change legislators before attempting the ERA, or any other legislative goal again.

Going in another direction, Sonia Johnson organized a "Women's Gathering" for activists "searching for feminist alternatives to the present direction of the women's movement."[32] The first Gathering drew nearly 200 women from across the country, many—perhaps half of them—NOW members. In an opening address, Johnson spoke to the despair she saw in the women's movement. She warned of the seductiveness of joining the system in order to make changes, when in reality it just "sucks women up." The work women had been doing was described as bolstering the patriarchy rather than recognizing and building the power within themselves. The essence of her message was that women cannot solve problems of the system by working in it.

The victory of suffrage is often blamed for the demise of the women's movement of that era. In the 1980s the defeat of the ERA acted as a brake on the energetic commitment of many feminist activists. It was a significant defeat, even if it was expected. In truth, either victory or defeat of a major goal can lead to movement decline. The failure to pass ERA was more than the loss of an important goal. It was also the end of a symbol of feminist unity; and it was an indicator of larger social changes that had taken place over the previous ten years—now firmly in place.

Chapter 6

CHANGING ORIENTATIONS IN IDEOLOGY AND ACTIVISM

I'm not as idealistic as I used to be. My experience as an organizer is that we don't know how to make things change. I think that most of the people who debate in elaborate theories on how to create change are not at all involved in trying to make those theories work. I believe very strongly that the best theory and the best strategies emerge out of trying things out, actually trying to make them happen, and then being reflective on that to figure out what you've learned.

Charlotte Bunch (1983)[1]

By 1980 the Equal Rights Amendment had become a goal for activists across the feminist spectrum. Although there were feminists who believed it was more symbolic than substantive, the force of the opposition, and the fact that legislators kept saying NO to legal sex equality, spurred even those who felt it was a waste of time to give their support. As one member of a civil disobedience group explained it:

I thought it would pass without me having to do anything. I was kind of peripherally involved, you know I'd go to a rally if it was convenient. But I kept noticing that the ERA wasn't passing—and it just seemed like this real simple thing. I guess I finally realized what we were up against. And then I knew that it was going to take my efforts and all of our efforts to get it passed.[2]

In the last stage of the ERA drive those activists who had left the battle to NOW and other ERA-focused groups began to see that those groups were not achieving this one "very small" goal. Deciding at this point to get involved meant either joining an already established group or forming a new one. Joining NOW was the most logical course of action but, among women who formed alternative action groups like the Grassroots Group of Second Class Citizens, another type of activism was felt to be needed—a type of activism that would awaken people out of passivity.

> Something disruptive action does that other kinds of actions don't do is it calls attention to the fact that you're doing something you're not suppose to do. So it gets in the newspapers and catches the attention of people.[3]

For some direct action activists, NOW held little appeal because they remembered negative interactions they had experienced at an earlier time.

> I was a member of Chicago NOW in 69 and 70. In 69 we were just trying to get our chapter started. There was no real interest in ERA then. I remember talking to an attorney in our chapter about the ERA and she didn't think it was necessary. I still wanted to have discussions about it, but there was no freedom of speech in the Chicago NOW chapter in the early 70s. The president passed out the chairperson-ships according to how people voted—if they voted with her, then they would get to chair a committee.[4]

Or, they simply had no interest in doing the type of activism ERA-focused groups were engaged in:

> I wanted to do something other than waste gas money driving back and forth to Springfield talking to those clowns that don't even care. . . . You know, there's a lot of drudgery involved in the movement, letter writing, all the time it takes to make a contact, follow up, and that kind of thing.

Lobbying legislators was a particularly offensive activity for some direct action activists:

> I wrote a few letters and then I went with the Religious Committee for ERA to Springfield and talked with the legislators. I worked a little bit with the ERA coali-tion here in town too. I got bored with it. But there was another thing. See, I couldn't vote, so they didn't have to please me. Some of those legislators, they talked to me like I was a stupid kid and I didn't know what I was saying. You know, "what did I care anyhow, I wasn't through college, why would I worry about it?"[5]

Civil disobedience was seen as working outside the system, a more interesting and emotional involvement. For those activists who had been involved with other social movements in the past, it was also a continuation of the type of action they were used to, and, for those who knew the history of the suffrage movement, it was seen as a replication of those militant efforts:

> Some of us had been active in the civil rights or peace movement. So we were familiar with a lot of direct action tactics. Also a number of us had background in the history of the suffrage movement—for instance two of us are historians—and we were using the original Congressional Union as precedence.[6]

Sonia Johnson and the D.C. chapter of the contemporary Congressional Union tried, at the 1981 NOW conference, to get NOW members to endorse and participate in a civil disobedience (CD) action. During the conference, notices were posted announcing a CD workshop to plan an action for the next day. Over 200 NOW members showed up for the workshop, leading some NOW leaders to accuse Johnson of "attempting to take over the conference."[7] Through negotiation it was decided to bring the issue to the floor for a discussion and vote.

Plans had previously been made for a pageantry style demonstration at the Lincoln monument; NOW leaders urged members to retain the original plan. As chair of the 1981 conference, Eleanor Smeal was accused of opposing CD and holding down members who wanted to use direct action tactics. Smeal's reply to this accusation was that members were free to vote for any action they wanted the national organization to implement. Further, they could get together with women during the conference and plan direct action strategies for local actions.[8] Many, in fact, did get together during the meeting and discuss such plans. Smeal maintains that NOW considers its options open, limited only by what the membership as a whole decides to be the most effective method at the time. "NOW is not opposed to civil disobedience, but the timing has to be right."[9]

After heated discussion from both sides, the CD action was voted down. Although there were NOW members who were interested in doing civil disobedience actions, there was also the hope that the present strategy would still work. The organization, as a whole, elected to stay the course, although individual members were free to involve themselves in any kind of alternative action they desired.

Resistance to throwing away their previous efforts was also connected to the unstated assumption that their energies had been wrongly placed. Some NOW members reacted to this assumption (whether real or not) by questioning the motives of civil disobedience activists.

> It's not that I'm opposed to civil disobedience, but when they talk about wanting to do something meaningful, and that something meaningful is to lay down in the street to stop traffic—and maybe get on TV and be arrested—and then go home with your war story to be told and retold for years to come, I wonder who this

action is meaningful to. Here we are, doing grunt work for years and years, and they do one action and tell us they're doing something meaningful.[10]

In a sense this assessment was true. The meaningful part of CD, as Sonia Johnson explains it, is not that you think this action is going to win a goal; it is to give women a feeling of empowerment. "You have to see CD as something besides changing the system—you do it to get women happy."[11]

In actuality, cooperation between the mass movement sector and newly-emerging direct action groups was hampered more by assumptions each held about the other than by the strategies they each employed. One that particularly rankled NOW members was the lingering notion that NOW consisted of white middle-class women who were interested only in white middle-class women's advancement. As one NOW activist recounts:

> I was once told something to the effect that "you middle-class NOW women, with your Lord and Taylor jackets, are just doing your club work to keep yourselves busy." I looked at my friend standing next to me—we were both from the same steel mill town—and asked her if we were the only working-class members of NOW. We knew that wasn't true, our whole chapter was. Then I looked at my jacket. It was from Sears and it was the only one I had.[12]

In spite of the fact that NOW members repeatedly speak of the need for broad-based fundamental change, some direct action activists define NOW as a reform-ist organization not concerned with restructuring the system. New activists are often eager to point out how they differ from NOW in their desire to change the economic structure. But, as the following quote demonstrates, they are not sure how to do that:

> I'm not a member of NOW but my impression of NOW is that they are mainstream, a feminism that just reforms. We can't reform this system, we have to restructure the system, dismantle the structure—find other alternatives, explore other options. Although I don't have a formula.[13]

Or, they may find NOW unappealing because they feel it is not radical enough in general:

> Well, I've never belonged to NOW but I see a conservative element there that just reforms rather than dismantles the system. And I would say the same thing for *Ms.* magazine. One issue of *Ms.* had a headline "how to get power"—with neon lights—and it told you how to do it, that is how to get into the system. Both NOW and *Ms.* are hesitant, they draw the line at certain issues and say the analysis doesn't go beyond this point, like questioning things that represent what is natural or normal such as heterosexuality.[14]

In the above quote, NOW is being charged with not being receptive to lesbianism, even though during these years over half of the NOW leadership was fairly openly lesbian, and some activists in direct action groups spoke of the acceptance they found, as lesbians, when they were involved with NOW. Indeed, one member of the Grassroots Group declared that her earlier involvement in NOW "allowed me to come out as a lesbian, really gave me that freedom." [15]

Long-term activists interviewed for this research did not describe NOW in such negative terms. But the image of NOW as a conservative organization remains among newer converts more familiar with the early literature than NOW activists themselves. For instance, the following view expressed by Sonia Johnson is considered radical in that she speaks of a war against women:

> The truth of the matter is that there is a war going on against women. People always say to me "Why do you hate men? Why are you fighting men?" I have to point out to them that, in fact, the war is against women. We are the enemy in a patriarchy. What are we doing to men? Look what's happening to us. Four rapes a minute are reported, the wife battering, incest. Who is fighting who? . . . If we would stop the war against women which is what the women's movement is asking, we would stop the war against the rest of the planet. [16]

Yet, Eleanor Smeal sets a similar tone when she expresses her "suspicion of any approach to change if it is devised by men."

> When people talk about great schemes like socialism, they're talking about grand schemes that men have invented already which still have females as the dependent class. That's why we don't think in terms of left or right, we're thinking in terms of, OK, how is this system designed so that one class of people, named females always end up on the bottom. [17]

And when Smeal addresses the issue of women and power, she does not apologize; indeed, she adopts a maximalist position by seeing it as a feminist imperative:

> It took us a long time to decide that we counted, that we were going to raise money, that we were going to gather power, and that we were going to change the world for us, for our children, for our society, and for the world. [18]

DEFINING FEMINISM IN THE EARLY 1980'S

Even though differences remained, some real and some perceived, working on the same issue did bring a sense of unity to feminists involved in the ERA drive.

The year after the amendment's defeat, when the bulk of the interviews for this research were done, long-term activists defined the meaning of feminism in ways that show a convergence that was absent in the pre-1975 period. The convergence is found in a number of areas but, as shown in the following quotes, one of the most notable is the encompassing and broad-based definition of feminism that activists from diverse groups reveal. According to Charlotte Bunch:

> Feminism is a movement for the liberation of women which, because women's oppression is deeply embedded in everything, must necessarily, then, be a movement for the transformation of the whole society.[19]

National NOW officer Barbara Timmer simultaneously advocates women's equality in the social system and protests the way that system is structured.

> It means both legal equality and changing the world. If you look at NOW's statement of purpose about bringing women into the mainstream and then you analyze the mainstream you may not want to be there. Being in the present mainstream, then, is not your ultimate goal.[20]

A civil disobedience activist calls for change on both the interactive and the structural level.

> Feminism to me involves an analysis and a commitment to change that are quite general in human relationships and structures of society, not just a matter of in some sense equalizing women's role in the existing society, which is totally impossible. It is impossible to equalize the position of women in any part of the present social system because the system rests on the inequality of women. But to equalize women is to destabilize and eventually eradicate the system.[21]

A dual understanding of two aspects of feminism, as both individual and social, is expressed by Ann Snitow, who began her activism in early radical feminist groups:

> One is the aspect which you really identify with women, our situation, our struggle, and our strengths, given the practices that we've lived through. At the same time, you have to understand that we're an oppressed group like any other oppressed group.[22]

In these statements, a rejection of the current system is tied to its multistratified structure. Women's equality is seen as revolutionary not just for women but also for the effect it would have on creating a new social order. Naomi Ross, a NOW activist, develops this perspective when she speaks of how the concept of equal opportunity is meaningless unless the social structure promotes equality between groups.

> Feminism represents the best of what it means to be human. Anybody can be a feminist, except you have to work at it. Basically, to me, it is the belief that everybody should have the opportunity to be the best that they can be and we ought to have a world that encourages that.[23]

In a like manner, a member of a civil disobedience group describes how feminism would create an enriched environment for women which would also result in a better environment for men.

> My definition of feminism is women being associated with other women and working for women to create a better world over all, but especially a better space for women. I'm not real concerned with making it a better place for men per se because I think that will happen anyway with feminism, that more egalitarian relationships will develop and that it will help men too to break out of stereotypical roles.[24]

Instead of narrowly defined categories, these descriptions of feminism are inclusive rather than exclusive. Sonia Johnson suggests a philosophical rationale for the necessity of using a broad-based definition:

> I used to have a definition of feminism down pat and then it began to slip away because it wasn't inclusive enough. You begin to wonder who feminism belongs to; I mean, who has the right to define it.[25]

In adopting an encompassing definition of feminist activism, people who are not involved in a social movement, but who hold generalized feminist values, could also be included. For instance, Carole King, a NOW officer, suggests that, even if a woman's actions are only the sort that improves her own life, it can be considered a feminist act:

> My personal definition of a feminist is someone who is participating in the women's movement by refuting sexism either in a personal or a public way. I think of feminism as active. A feminist, though, to me is anybody who will not tolerate being thought of as inferior to anybody else merely because of their body difference.[26]

Joyce Trebilcot, an academic feminist, makes a similar point by including in her definition "changing your life in some way."

> A feminist is a person committed to making the lives of women better. That's a very broad definition in that it accommodates men, for example, whom some

would want to exclude from the definition. It's narrow in the sense that I take
commitment to imply actually doing something. You can't be a feminist simply by
saying that you approve of or support certain feminist positions. You have to be
committed to doing something about women's lives which means changing your
life in some way in those directions. It's having the commitment and acting in
accordance with it.[27]

For others, such as Chris Riddeough, a participant in a wide variety of feminist groups, some kind of activism beyond personal empowerment is an essential
part of being labeled a feminist.

I think being a feminist means being for women and that really means working for
equality and liberation in social, political, and economic arenas—all aspects of
life.[28]

Social activism is fundamental to most social movement activists, but adopting a broadly defined concept of "who is a feminist" is a purposeful decision
meant to encourage more women to relate to feminism in their lives.

How one acts to improve the lives of women varies widely. I suppose one could
push me, push this definition in the direction of saying that a woman out to improve
only her own life, then, is a feminist. And I think I'd have to say yes. I want it to
be very broad, and that's a political decision to want a definition that would bring
in very large numbers of people, rather than a more exclusive definition.[29]

No longer intent upon attacking each other or declaring one position right and
others wrong, these responses indicate a recognition of women working in a
variety of ways to create a better world. Even those feminists who consider
themselves radical in their vision and activist methods explain the necessity for
all types of involvements:

I think the women's movement is an even broader term than feminism because the
women's movement to me is that whole spectrum of women who are trying to
change the condition of women in society. And I would include groups like the
American Association of University Women, groups like that, that I don't think
are particularly feminist but I do think they are part of the women's movement in
the sense that they are doing activities to try and improve the situation for women.
So to me the women's movement is very diverse with all kinds of groups. And
feminism is the ideology that is at the core of that movement to improve the lot of
women.[30]

Activists' definitions of feminism in the early to mid-1980s reveal a focus on
attempts to create change rather than a focus on holding the correct political line:

> I both take seriously women as a category politically and socially and historically; and at the same time, I'm a gender skeptic. I'm very leery of feminist organizing that romanticizes the category of women since I think it's a role also of oppression. But I don't want to even say that, because I'm in sympathy with all feminists and all forms of organizing efforts.[31]

Indeed, long-term activists in this study were resistant to using any type of classification scheme of where they fit within a feminist typology. Most simply refused to do it. The general feeling was that these classifications create false dichotomies, are divisive, and do not reflect the true nature of who they are or what they are about. They spoke instead of the importance of relating to the similarities between themselves and other feminists. Often, activists who used to identify themselves as socialist, radical, or separatist identified themselves simply as feminists.

Similarities are what stood out in the interview material. For instance, activists from both the mass movement and small group sector emphasize the devaluation of women within a male-defined system as "the problem" they are working to change. Socialist feminism in the United States is weak in name, although part of the philosophic underpinning of the American women's movement is connected to socialist thought. A number of women interviewed for this research identify themselves as socialists; however, they place feminism as their primary commitment. For most long-term activists in the United States, feminism includes some form of an economic transformation. All of the activists interviewed for this research find fault with the exploitation of women (and other groups) under capitalism; nevertheless, they do not feel socialism per se is the answer. Feminism is seen as broader and more inclusive than socialism.

For instance, Sonia Johnson argues that, if you understand what feminism is about, you know it is inherently radical beyond any other liberating philosophy people espouse:

> I see all isms, socialism and all the others that I know about, as part of the patriarchy. I say to women that what we ought to do is build a new structure; we have to do things we've never seen or heard about. There isn't anything proposed on this earth that takes patriarchy into account, that "sees" feminism. Any structure that is hierarchical says that some people are better than others and deserve to have more rewards. Both capitalism and socialism have hierarchical structures.[32]

In a similar manner, Eleanor Smeal describes why modifying terms for feminism are superfluous when describing the goals she finds in NOW:

> I wouldn't describe NOW as liberal feminist, nor as socialist feminist. We are feminist. We are trying to create a world where women have a greater stake in the decision making and resources, in everything. We are working toward change. The

word "radical" in my definition is working for fundamental change and the type of things that NOW is advocating go to fundamental change.[33]

During the interviews many activists talked about how they themselves and the movement had matured. The various types of feminist groups all see themselves as seeking fundamental social change and the end of male dominance. As more than one activist put it,"radical feminism is a redundant term."[34]

Not only did feminist visions become more alike, but the definition of radical activism also changed. Lobbying is traditionally seen as a conservative strategy, but in the early 1980s it was frequently described as difficult and committed work. Some women who had done lobbying report they would rather "go to jail" than continue to ask for their equal rights from "those small town used car salesmen." One activist described how lobbying state legislators had given her a new understanding of the concept of states rights—that is, a structural arrangement which allows local legislators, mostly male, the ability to maintain power.[35] The point is, radical activism was being defined not just as the unusual, daring, or attention-getting action; but also as the hard, boring, long-term commitment of efforts to effect change.

CONTRIBUTING FACTORS TO CHANGING VIEWS

The formation years, 1966–73, contained a high level of energy and excitement. As one activist described it, "things were just bubbling."[36] Anything could happen and the expectation was that it would happen tomorrow—or soon afterward. In contrast, during the ERA drive and in the period immediately after its defeat, feminists extended the time range necessary to achieve their goals. At this point, long-term activists no longer expected to see the changes they hoped for in their lifetime. The issues were seen as more complex, more deeply rooted, and more difficult to achieve than they had seemed in the earlier period.

Moreover, activists found it increasingly more difficult to define success. This ambiguity is related to the fact that feminists are working on short and long-range goals. Although the contemporary movement was put on the defensive after 1975, it grew in numbers, created a unity among diverse feminist groups, and spread awareness of feminist issues throughout society. A Harris Opinion Survey done in 1982 showed an 18 percent swing in support of ERA between 1979 and 1982. When ERA failed in the legislative halls, 63 percent of the population favored passage (The Harris Survey 1982). Thus, the understanding of what constitutes success became blurred.

Issues themselves changed in meaning over time. Even as ERA became a focus of the movement, it was symbolic of a range of issues surrounding women's lives. In actuality, issues broadened and deepened. In the 1960s a major issue was equal pay; in the 1970s it was affirmative action, and in the 1980s feminists were challenging the low value associated with "women's work" by calling for equal pay for work of equal value (also known as pay equity). Throughout the 1970s and 1980s, poverty, racism, and sexual orientation increasingly became routinely included in the feminist agenda. In addition, a connection was made between violence against women, destruction of the environment and the military mentality of the nuclear arms race.

A noticeable change can be seen in the phrase "The Personal is Political." This concept came out of the consciousness raising groups and meant that what was happening to individual women was happening to women everywhere; thus these were political not personal problems. However, the CR groups basically consisted of women who were friends or came from the same social circle; hence, they were seeing their problems as universal, while missing problems of women who lived very different lives. Women of color and third world women challenged the movement to broaden its scope and include problems particular to them. The "personal is political" came to be seen as too limiting—an insight to be used as a first step, but then one had to go beyond that recognition to examine what it is like for other women in order to truly make this a movement for all women.

By the early 1980s, multiple factors had contributed to changing views of feminist group relations and ideological beliefs, which led activists involved in this research to generally agree that: (1) there are more similarities than differences in philosophy among feminists today; (2) this overlap or blending in ideology has occurred because of the maturation of the movement; however, the ideologies have never been as distinct as they were perceived or written about; and (3) there is a new way of understanding feminism. For instance, long-term activists describe feminism as a process, not a thing or category.

In summary, by the early 1980s activists from diverse segments of the women's movement showed significant convergence in their definitions of feminism. Ideological agreement consisted of a desire for the equality of women, a breakdown of all artificial barriers premised on gender/sex characteristics, fundamental change in the social, political, and economic structure, the empowerment of women and a raised valuation of female values.

Distinctiveness in ideological thought constitutes a smaller proportion than similarities. Distinctiveness is represented in cultural feminism by a separatist tendency; in socialist feminism by a strong anti-capitalist or Marxist perspective; and in liberal feminism by the inclusion of women's groups which do not necessarily define themselves as feminist, but which have increasingly supported feminist issues.

Ideological overlap reveals a core feminist belief system with variance between levels of support in particular applications of thought and practice. For instance, socialist feminism and radical cultural feminism share an orientation for communal living with no hierarchy; socialist and liberal feminists share the activist practice of working in the political arena; and, liberal and radical feminists would overlap to a much greater extent than socialist feminists on a perception of women's higher values.

Thus, within the various feminist orientations of the early 1980s there developed a blending of ideology and an appreciation of different types of activism. In this environment of changed attitudes and changed group relations, the movement itself was reconstructed and the terminology redefined.

CONSIDERATIONS OF FEMINIST PRACTICE

The fact that activists in the early 1980s generally expressed similar beliefs and supported the same issues, does not mean that there were no differences between them. The various groups did contain distinctive characteristics, and the most noticeable was how they employed feminist practice. Feminism has been defined as consisting of different types of belief systems which lead to particular kinds of practice. But another way of seeing this dynamic of ideology and activism is that adherence to a similar ideology can lead to different types of practice dependent upon characteristics of group members other than belief systems.

Previous research has shown distinct types of feminist practice, but the difference in the early 1980s was that ideology did not automatically define the type of activism or social movement practice feminists were engaged in. Freeman's (1975, 1979) analysis of organizational and style differences in determining feminist sectors is similar to this comparison of feminist practice; however, an important change in the early 1980s was that feminists displayed a self-conscious awareness of commonality among themselves. Conflict related to self-identity issues no longer played such a divisive role, as evidenced by activists' own reports of similarity in feminist ideology. In other words, activists were confirming what Freeman pointed out before: their differences more strongly represented personal preferences than ideological division. It is this changed perception that is important for understanding the internal process of social movement transformation within a changing external context.

In the same way that activists reveal a convergence in feminist ideology, they also show respect for variation in type of activism, a marked contrast to the pre-1975 period.

When we talk about the women's movement we tend to forget those women who don't even define themselves as feminists who have fought the battles outside of any organizations at all, like the stewardesses who did the first big case under the Civil Rights Act. This is an important part of a social movement, people outside of the organized aspects of the movement who pick up the issues of the movement and move in to implement them in their own lives, or through the courts or whatever. I think whenever you have a group of women get together to work on an issue or to do consciousness raising that you are witnessing an important locus for social change.[37]

The above quote was expressed by a civil disobedience activist who is broadening the definition of activism, even though she is incorrect in the detail of the example she uses (the stewardesses' action was not fully outside of organized feminism—some of the stewardesses who led this fight were NOW members and the organization gave extensive support to their efforts).

Failure to win a major issue by the 1980s brought back more diverse methods and, as a member of the Grassroots Group expresses it, there was a generalized perception that all methods are needed.

When we first started organizing we talked about the necessity for some kind of disruptive action. I just think that one way to achieve a goal is unrealistic. Other types of action, like writing petitions, are part of the democratic system. Civil disobedience is another type of activism, one that calls attention to the system itself.[38]

Ann Courtney, Illinois NOW president during the last part of the ratification drive, rationalizes why work in all arenas is important and necessary.

Being a feminist is to be outside the parameters of the male experience. I think being a feminist is something that means that a woman can be what she wishes to be and that no artificial barriers are thrown in her way. And that extends to every level of our society from the legislative to the legal, to the educational to the political, to the family to the raising of children, to athletics to whatever area. . . . And because of the fact that you are a feminist and believe this, this also means that you want the same thing for everyone.[39]

POLITICAL ACTIVISM AND DISCURSIVE POLITICS

Service work can be considered feminist activism and/or employment. Rape crisis centers, battered women's shelters, women's studies, feminist bookstores, etc., which start out as unaffiliated volunteer activism, often become over time more professional and formal work structures. Activists in these arenas began this work attempting to create environments with little hierarchy, shared decision making, and emotional relating. Women involved in this work come from a wide variety of feminist orientations, including some today who may not specifically define themselves as feminist. NOW stresses political activism rather than long-term service work; members are advised to organize crisis centers, then get out and leave them to other women to run.[40] Although there is still a strong feminist orientation and many committed feminists are involved in various types of service work, often these organizational settings fall outside of social movement activism. Therefore, the following analysis on change in feminist ideology and activism that occurred between the 1975–82 period is a comparison between political activism and discursive activism among self-identified social movement groups.

Political activist groups consist of national mass movements such as the National Organization for Women, the National Women's Political Caucus, Democratic Socialists of America, National Abortion Rights Action League, Women's Equity Action League, etc. Discursive political groups consist of small, sometimes temporary, feminist groups involved in direct action tactics; and the various components of cultural feminism. Specific examples of these are civil disobedience groups such as A Group of Women, The Grassroots Group of Second Class Citizens, and Women Rising in Resistance; in the women's culture are found women's coffee houses, music festivals, communes, spirituality groups, and the more elusive orientations expressed through cultural/personal change processes.

These two forms of feminist practice are called primary orientations in order to make clear the overlap and connection between them. They are not exclusive types of activism practiced only by those groups identified under each heading. They are merely the most frequent form of activism practiced by these groups. More importantly, participants are frequently members of several groups. It would be a mistake to presume each type of group, orientation, or practice has a distinct population involved in it.

There are many examples of overlap in type of practice. For instance, a dual orientation is shown in the desire of NOW members to be involved in civil disobedience or to take part in Women's Gatherings, music festivals, and women's spirituality events. In the past, NOW has held one-day fasts, picketed, and included street theatre in their actions. In 1978, National NOW officers discussed the probability that, if the extension campaign failed, they would "go for broke," meaning begin militant actions.[41]

Other examples of overlap in practice are Sonia Johnson's presidential campaign on the Citizen's Party ticket. Running for President of the United States did not fit perceptions of not joining the system, and there was much heated discussion among her followers over whether she should run. Johnson also ran for the presidency of NOW. In this case, both she and NOW members demonstrate overlapping orientations for political and discursive activism, as the response she got in this campaign (winning 40 percent of the votes) revealed strong support among NOW members for her militant tactics. Another example of overlapping orientation was Mary Lee Sargeant's bid for the Board of Trustees at the University of Illinois. Having been one of the main organizers of the Grassroots Group and later of Women Rising in Resistance, this was a move to put herself into the political activism side and effect change within the system.

With this understanding of non-exclusive categories, political activism and discursive politics are outlined below in terms of their primary orientations along the following characteristics: motivation, structure, leadership, arena, strategy, and tactics.

Motivation

For political activist practice, the primary motivation is to be effective. Pragmatism is imbedded in much of the thinking and planning. There is a constant balancing between principle and reality; thus, compromises are often made. For the discursive political groups, a primary motivation is to promote feminist principles. Adherents are less willing to compromise as they stress the importance of living their lives according to feminist values.

An example of these motivational differences comes from the 1984 presidential election. NOW and the National Women's Political Caucus were the main groups that were instrumental in getting Geraldine Ferraro the Vice Presidential nomination. They felt this was important, even though the Democrats lost, because of the precedent it set and the role-modeling effect. In contrast, Sonia Johnson argued that the Democratic Party was not much different than the Republican Party; neither would raise important women-centered issues. In running on the Citizen's Party ticket she had a chance to travel the country raising these issues, demonstrate women's possibilities (i.e. presidential status), and symbolically reject the present two-party system. Many, perhaps most, feminists would agree that Johnson's position was more in line with feminist ideals. However, the question for political activists was "How effective would this tactic be?" Johnson did run for President and travel the country speaking, but not many people heard her. In fact, most of the people that did were committed feminists already involved in the movement. In retrospect, both campaigns served an important function. Ferraro had an impact on public awareness of women candidates for high office and Johnson had an emotional impact on activist feminists. Thus, it makes sense that a not uncommon sight during the campaign was feminist activists wearing campaign buttons for both candidates.[42]

Structure

Political activist groups have a national orientation, although some, such as the National Organization for Women, also have a grassroots chapter structure. These groups see themselves as mass movement organizations. Increasing the number of members is an important organizational goal, both for the practical effects of large numbers and for the image of representing the majority of women.

During the 1970s, feminist organizing became more involved with centralized formal structures; nevertheless, small decentralized structures continued to emerge. These groups represent the interactive/expressive orientation of discursive politics. They structure themselves as autonomous groups while maintaining connections with other groups through newsletters, other published sources, and personal correspondence. Seeing themselves as a core group, they do not necessarily feel they represent the majority of women, even though they are advocates of all women. In some sense, many of the involvements within this sector serve as an oasis from the present social/political system.

Leadership

Most feminists have a philosophical leaning toward the type of leadership arrangement found in discursive political groups. This is a practice based on consensus decision making and rotating leadership positions. This preference goes back to the beginning of the contemporary movement and, as was true then, is basically found only within a small group structure. But, even in the small groups, this idealized group process is not always able to be practiced. Operating by consensus and shared leadership requires a heavy time commitment. For women with careers and/or family responsibilities, participation is restricted. In reality, most groups are run by a few members who are able to put in the time. In addition, some people will take on more responsibility than others and, in effect, become leaders even when they are not holding an official title.

In the larger groups, size becomes a determining factor in how these groups are structured. It is not possible to operate under a consensus rule when there are 2,000 members voting on policy decisions. For political activist groups, majority rule sets the agenda for the entire organization. Because of the varying levels of activism, larger groups are structured with elected officer positions. This is done to establish responsibility lines for the implementation of goals. Seeing this type of structure as both fair and effective does not totally ameliorate resistance towards hierarchy. Nevertheless, an acceptance of some hierarchy is congruent with the desire to be successful in achieving goals.

Arena

Political activism takes place in the political and public arenas. Lobbying, letter-writing campaigns, and petitions are undertaken to convince legislators to vote on issues these groups support. Education of the public is an important part of their activism, as is attested to by the marches, workshops, and public speaking in which they engage.

For discursive politics, efforts are more frequently placed in the personal and symbolic realm. Decentralized structures are often, as Jenkins suggests, a product of "deliberate choices by redemptive or personal-change movements attempting to embody ideals in the hope that these will serve as models for emulation" (1983: 541). For instance, the women's culture which provides women with enrichment through music and poetry is primarily meant for the women themselves. However, expressive/interactive groups are not formed solely for the purpose of personal contact and enrichment. Indeed, Women Rising in Resistance, a post-ERA direct action group, organized with the intention of using confrontational tactics against the present system, particularly to raise awareness of violence against women.

Women's Gatherings were expressly structured to provide participants with experiences meant to develop feelings of raised self-esteem and personal power. Described as new tools for social change, participants were introduced to three processes of discovery and personal empowerment: Visioning (What kind of world do we want?), Freeing Ourselves of Internalized Oppression (What in us would have to change to make us feel powerful enough to achieve it?), and Hearing Into Being (How can we make these changes?).[43]

Strategy

Political activists are geared to gain power for women within the system. This method of creating change does not preclude their desire to also change the system in this process. The goal is the empowerment of women through structural change; the vision is to create a more humane system developed through women's input. The type of expressive action found in discursive politics is geared towards achieving power within the person. The goal is the empowerment of women through a changed self-image. These strategies are not mutually exclusive, as political and expressive groups see a need for both kinds of changes. What the two forms of practice express is a different time reference for achieving these goals.

For political activists, the mission of a social movement is to change the social structure so that women, as a group, will be identified with higher valuation. The belief is that when changes are accomplished in laws, institutions, and the work structure, new opportunities and attitudes will benefit women throughout society. With these social changes women will begin to have a higher valuation of themselves. It is from this point that they will begin to be more powerful in their personal relations. As Eleanor Smeal describes it:

> You are working for equality and you do that by trying to change the system, and
> in the process you make sure you are not going to do that at the expense of any

other group, so you make sure you are working to eliminate racism as well. In addition, if you get full equality in pay equity, social security, eliminate insurance discrimination, etc., there's a profound change that affects the lower class, that is the people who make less money, mostly women. We want to improve women economically and lessen their dependency.[44]

For expressive/interactive activists, it is just the opposite. Women must begin on the personal level to rid themselves of internalized oppression. It is after personal change has taken place, when women begin to feel psychologically strong about themselves, that their interactive relations improve. Then they can go out and make the structural changes that are needed. Sonia Johnson explains this position:

Women have to begin to see themselves as people who manifest themselves in this world. What we do is feed into the misperception that we can really only affect little places like the job and the home. This is not enough. Women have got to expand beyond that and they've got to begin to see themselves as a person who can change the world, really begin to have that vision of yourself and your whole vision of what you can do to create change. Once you have that changed self-concept you begin to see opportunities where you can make changes which you didn't see before, when you didn't think you could do anything about it.[45]

In these views, both personal and fundamental social change are desired, only the order and method of how to go about achieving them differ.

Tactics

The tactics each type of practice utilizes differ in accordance with the size of the group and the arena of protest. Political activists use legislative means because they believe they have an opportunity to have an effect on laws that are being passed. In this form of activism, numbers count. Another area where they have advantage over the smaller groups is in the courts. They have enough financial resources to participate in legal cases which may be class-action suits.

Expressive/interactive groups have followed two directions: one, to work in the service and cultural arenas where they have a direct impact on women's lives, and two, to use direct action tactics in their social movement involvements. Zap actions, street theatre, and civil disobedience are seen as ways to gain attention and psychologically empower women which lend themselves well to these groups' size limitations.[46]

REVIEWING INTRA-MOVEMENT GROUP RELATIONS

During the latter part of the 1970s and the early 1980s the U.S. women's movement felt the effects of the anti-feminist backlash and a growing conservative climate. The strength of the campaign against ERA acted as a stimulant for a re-evaluation of intra-movement group relations. The participant observation and interview data for this research show that during this period feminist activists involved in the ERA struggle developed a broadened definition of feminist ideology and activism. Antagonistic relations between groups lessened as it became clear how fragile a divided movement was in the face of powerful opposition forces. In addition, skills were gained in the political arena and the movement grew more sophisticated in its understanding of social movement mobilization processes.

The concerted efforts of diverse groups contributed to a generalized view that the mobilization process of the women's movement was dependent upon the engagement of many "types" of women working in multiple arenas. Greater tolerance of difference and less focus on "correctness" allowed activists to take seriously the notion that the women's movement is for all women. Rejecting women's subordinated position in society, valuing women and egalitarianism, the glue which bound diverse groups of activists together during the ERA drive was the effort to achieve the same goal. Recognizing a common foundation and common effort allowed for divergence on analysis of cause, type of action, arena of protest, and organizational structure. Finally, even if "unity feminism" was a superficial cover for more deeply held divisions and was to last only temporarily, the fact that diverse activists recognized themselves as intersecting strands of the same movement and that many participants actively sought more cooperative feminist relations, demonstrates the desire of activists to see themselves differently than feminists had in the organizing stage.

Chapter 7

AMERICAN WOMEN AND THE WOMEN'S MOVEMENT DURING THE REAGAN/BUSH YEARS

In accordance with affirmative action requirements, the new coal-leasing commission consists of "a Black, a woman, two Jews and a cripple."
(James Watt, Secretary of the Interior—Reagan 1st term appointee)

On pay equity:
"The looniest idea since Looney Tunes."
(Clarence Pendleton, Chair, Commission on Civil Rights—Reagan 1st and 2nd term appointee)

Feminism and the contemporary U.S. women's movement continue the challenge to the established social order begun a quarter of a century ago. But the movement has changed and so have the social/political/economic conditions of the country. This chapter examines the anti-feminist post-ERA period, looking at the effects of this social environment on feminist goals and the status of women in American society.

CONSERVATIVE TIMES: THE SOCIAL AND ECONOMIC IMPACT ON WOMEN

With the 1980 election of Ronald Reagan, what started out as an indication of hard times ahead became a period of continuing loss and discouragement. By the end of the decade the ERA was all but forgotten in the general public's mind, and some activists were projecting it would probably be the next century before it could be passed.

Moreover, two previous victories, the legalization of abortion and affirmative action, were in danger of being significantly reduced if not lost all together. Immediately after the 1988 presidential election of George Bush, the administration requested a review by the Supreme Court of *Webster* v. *Reproductive Health Services,* an abortion case from Missouri which contained a clause declaring that human life begins at conception. By this time Reagan had succeeded in appointing half of the judges on the federal level, including three new Supreme Court Justices, all of whom had passed the anti-abortion litmus test (Glasser 1989).

Affirmative action cases show a Supreme Court which had taken a decided turn to the right as it became clear that Reagan's last appointee, Justice Anthony Kennedy, was not a swing vote in the manner of his predecessor, Justice Lewis F. Powell, but a committed conservative. In a number of rulings before the end of 1989, the newly entrenched conservative majority whittled affirmative action down to the point where it had become considerably more difficult for women and minority men to prove discrimination in employment. Further, the Court made it easier for white males to challenge affirmative action policies when it let stand a lower court decision that "White men who did not take part in a case leading to an affirmative action plan may later attack the plan as reverse discrimination" (Epstein 1989a).

What these cases demonstrate is a new Court that basically does not acknowledge that racism and sexism still exist in society. For instance, William Bradford Reynolds, head of the Justice Department's Civil Rights Division under Reagan, explained these decisions as the effect of the Court "looking at a civil rights landscape that is different from what it was 20 years ago. Twenty years ago we had a Black-White problem . . . this new court majority is making sure that the law works in an even handed way so no group has an advantage" (cited in Epstein 1989b).

Such a race and gender neutral position is criticized by opponents as anything but neutral.

> Failing to notice a person's race or gender is not an example of "not being sexist or racist" . . . A colorblind social policy in a racist society, a gender-neutral social policy in a sexist society, simply guarantee that both racism and sexism will be strengthened and perpetuated instead of eradicated . . . treating everyone "equally" when their circumstances are different perpetuates inequality. (Rothenberg 1989: 18)

Criticism from feminist and civil rights activists fell on deaf ears in the political and economic environment of the 1980s, a decade which can be characterized as the rise of conservatism and increasing poverty. The anti-feminism that was so apparent in the 1980s under Reagan and Bush had its roots in the 1970s and was grounded in a generalized conservative backlash reacting to negative nationalistic feelings generated by the Vietnam War, a loss of faith in government during the Watergate affair, and an economic decline which began in 1973 with the first oil embargo. A return to traditional ethics, values, and lifestyles became the response to disruption and decay. By the end of the 1970s the "Moral Majority" pro-family movement was organized to coalesce a wide range of interests into a policial right-wing agenda for the nation. An indicator of the success of this impetus was the expansion throughout the 1980s of fundamentalist religious groups espousing traditional roles for women and men.

Economic decline in the 1970s and 1980s created anxiety for people in general and real deprivation for the most vulnerable segments of the population. The deindustrialization that took place in the United States throughout this period left working-class and poor families in increasingly marginal positions in society. Structural change resulting from technological advances and the loss of industrial union jobs meant that some segments of the population would be either unemployed or forced to take jobs in the expanding service sector that paid less money and usually provided no benefits (Axinn and Stern 1988). A non-family wage and a high divorce rate resulted in an increase in female single-headed households with concomitant increases in poverty-level families.

As people's real income declined, cuts in aid from the federal government were instituted (Burt and Pittman 1986). In just one year, the first of Reagan's administration, programs for the poor were reduced on average 10 percent; although some, such as school meal programs—where catsup became a vegetable—lost up to 35 percent of their funding. Overall, social services for children, employment, legal services, and day care experienced severe decline, creating extensive hardship for poor families (Kimmich 1985). Funding for housing programs was cut by more than 75 percent, from $32 billion to $7.5 billion since 1981. The National Coalition for the Homeless estimates there are approximately 3 million homeless people, with 40 percent of the increase consisting of families—mainly women and children (*On the Issues* 1988a). Far from the reactionary claims that the increase in poverty can be blamed on the welfare policies established by liberal politicians (see Murray 1984), are the documented assaults on welfare that occurred under the Reagan/Bush administrations.

The contemporary women's movement has existed in a time of accelerating change in American society. From 1960 to 1980 fertility declined, the proportion of women in the workforce dramatically increased, and the divorce rate doubled. The rising rate of divorce plunged large numbers of women into downward mobility, and created an increasing percentage of families that are female headed and poor. With the advent of "no fault" divorce in the early 1970s, divorced men's economic standard rose by 42 percent while women's declined by 73 percent (Weitzman 1985).

In a society where women still make at least one-third less income than men and where the majority of families require a two-person income, the economic hardships caused by divorce have left women and children in a vulnerable position. There has also been a rise in never married mothers. In 1988 three-fourths of black women who gave birth to their first child were unmarried, a marked increase from 1975 when that figure was 54 percent. For white women the figures went from 12 percent in 1975 to 20 percent in 1988 (Boyd 1989). The 1980s phrase "the feminization of poverty" is a reflection of the sharp increases in divorce and single-mother households since the 1970s.

The rise in female-headed households is associated with a decline in wages and employment opportunities for men. Thus, the changing economic structure of the United States can be blamed for much of what has happened to the position of women and to the poor, and for the increasing instability in family life during the last 20 years; for example, on a world economic scale the U.S. went from a production level of 52 percent of the world's goods in the 1950s to 22 percent by 1980 (Bluestone and Harrison 1982). Likewise, the failure of the women's movement to make gains for women in their social/economic position can be explained by the fact that women were attempting to improve their status when the country was responding to an economic downturn. From a Marxist perspective, it is the economic transformation—the final crisis of capitalism—not Ronald Reagan or the right-wing, that has created the underlying problems preventing progress for disadvantaged groups during this time period (Fishman 1987).

A poor economic structure is a contributing cause, but not a sufficient explanation for what happened to women in the 1980s, since it can still be argued that the failure of anti-poverty programs, and the disproportionate representation of women and people of color in the ranks of the poor, have more to do with politics and ideology than with a lack of economic capacity (Danzinger and Weinberg 1986). The 1990s bode even more dreary economic forecasts. It is ironic that, as socialism collapsed in Eastern Europe, American economists eagerly offered their expert advice at the same time the Savings and Loan fiasco and an ever-increasing deficit loomed over the U.S. economy. Yet, even as American capitalism may be in trouble, the feminist position that it is men—white middle- and upper-class men—who are in powerful decision making positions is still true. It was from these lofty political circles that the Equal Rights Amendment was defeated and it was from the same powerful decision making positions that the military budget increased at the same time cuts were made in child care, housing subsidies, job training, financial aid for education, affirmative action, pay equity, abortion funding, and welfare.

OUTCOMES OF GENDERED SOCIAL ROLES: FAMILY AND WORK

In spite of the fact that the rate of women's participation in the workforce rose from 27 percent in 1940 to 44 percent in 1985 (including more than half of all women with a child under the age of 1) there is still no government-sponsored child care or parental leave policy in the United States (Hayge 1986). Even with government predictions that five out of every eight new workers between now and the year 2000 will come from the female population (Broder 1989), social institutions are still operating on a 1950s' middle-class family model. Failure to accommodate to the changing role of women is not found only on a societal level: studies on dual-earner families show that women perform 65–80 percent of family work (Berheide 1984; Geerken and Gove 1983). Thus, the major obstacles to women's emancipation lie in both the lack of government-sponsored social service support and the sex/gender relations of the family (O'Neill 1989).

Juggling both job and family responsibilities is not new to working-class and poor women, but it is the increasing likelihood that this is the norm that has created a sense of crisis for women as a group. Rather than enacting social policy to address the needs of women who have been struggling with dual roles, often in poverty, there has simply been an increase in the numbers of women finding themselves in this position.

Feminist social analysts claim that it is the fear of being left alone with children and a low-paying job or welfare that prompts anti-feminist sentiment among those women who have attempted to prevent further erosion of a traditional family model. The fear they express is real. Barbara Ehrenreich (1983) argues that it was "men's flight from commitment" which women reacted to in their support or rejection of feminism. The anti-feminist reaction took the form of a pro-family movement to bring back the middle-class family model of breadwinning men supporting homemaking wives and children. The feminist reaction to men's lack of commitment was to change the social environment so that women could live independently if they chose to or were forced to do so. In both cases there was a distrust of men. For anti-feminist women, it was an underlying fear that men would leave their wives if there were no legal ties to restrict them, and for feminists it was a recognition that "all women are just one man removed from welfare" (Klatch 1987: 139).

Another fear, not just for the traditional woman but for heterosexual women in general, is the thought of never marrying or being divorced and remaining single for the rest of their life. In spite of the rise of women in the workforce, women are still largely defined by their relationship to a man and such attachments still provide status. Women, as well as men, desire intimacy and connection in an insecure world. Most people hope to marry someday or establish a long-term relationship with someone to share their life. In a social milieu fostering a fear of loneliness, *Newsweek* added a gender-specific alarm with a cover story on the "male shortage" in American society (1986). From a study by social scientists at Yale and Harvard, we learn that education and career for women, particularly as they pass the age of 30, place them at high risk of falling into the demographic category of never married. According to the researchers, there is only a 5 percent chance of marriage for highly educated women over the age of 35 and "forty-year-olds are more likely to be killed by a terrorist" (*Newsweek* 1986: 55).

The *Newsweek* article implicitly, but starkly, blames feminism's "unrealistic" expectations of female self-development and "demanding" criteria of acceptable men for the doom awaiting ambitious women. Following the article's publication, discrediting responses raised questions regarding faulty statistics and distorted conclusions (Pollitt 1986). For instance, researchers pointed out that contrary data showed eight out of ten college women do marry and a "male shortage" exists only for a narrow cohort (Rosenfelt and Stacey 1987). Other objections went further, claiming the real intent of the media in heralding this study was to control women's behavior (Ehrenreich 1986). The original article's message, however, overshadowed follow-up critiques. While it is apparent the study was flawed, what remains is the powerful image of the loneliness "uppity" women can expect as their reward for success.

Anxiety over high rates of divorce, single parenting, and poverty could now be joined with life-long singlehood for those women who do not stay in their place. Of course, not all women could or desire to stay in their place; indeed, some have never had "their place" to stay in.

Dependent upon lifestyle commitments and social location, the idea of women's equality can be interpreted as opportunity or threat (Mueller and Dimieri 1982). The anti-ERA movement consisted of a high proportion of full-time homemakers who defined the amendment as devaluing the homemaker role and taking away protections for women such as alimony and child support. Becoming an employed worker holds little appeal when work opportunities are limited to a segregated occupational structure which offers few intrinsic rewards. Studies have shown that, although women have increased their labor participation, there has been little change in gender economic equality. Moreover, as their employment rate has risen, women today have less leisure time while men have more (Fuchs 1988).

Women who are not in traditional family roles desire equal rights to improve their position in a sex/gender stratification system. They hoped the ERA would improve their opportunities for occupational advance. Employed women are less likely to have the option of staying home full time; improvement in their work and economic condition is a primary concern. Women on both sides of this issue are acting in their own interest to defend their status positions. Thus, full-time homemakers are more likely to be opposed to feminist goals, while those in the workforce are more likely to support the idea of equal rights.

From a feminist perspective, full-time homemaking can be a fulfilling lifestyle and an important social role. But, in a gender-unequal world, it does carry risks. Fundamentally, the traditional family ideal places a wife in the position of depending on the goodwill of her husband. And, while faith and trust in another human being are important values, it is an unfortunate fact that not all men have goodwill. In an economic dependency situation, if "faith and trust are broken, the woman has a great deal more to lose than the man" (Hegger, Ryan, and Weston 1983: 15).

DEFECTORS FROM THE FEMINIST CAUSE

In addition to the onslaught of opposition forces, the 1980s also witnessed the defection, or position reappraisal, by previous feminist supporters. Two examples of this reversal stand out: (1) men, who claim they are feminists, writing anti-woman books; and (2) feminist-identified women attacking the women's movement for neglecting maternal needs.

In the first case, books by Harry Stein (1988) and by Warren Farrell (1988) report on early male converts' confusion today. Both Stein and Farrell decry the lack of gratitude women have given them for their efforts at being sensitive to issues of women's equality, particularly since men are now being neglected as women no longer take care of their needs. In reviewing these books, Sara Frankel notes that in each book the authors complain that women's main source of income is men. In effect, they want women to pay their own way; however, as Frankel points out, "neither Stein nor Farrell pays much attention to the economic and political barriers still impeding the equality they claim they'd like to see between the sexes" (1988: 49).

The second case consists of two examples of non-feminist writing by women who identify themselves as feminists. In *A Lesser Life: The Myth of Women's Liberation in America,* Sylvia Hewlett charges the women's movement with ignoring issues of real importance to women, like child care and maternity leave, because when the movement began "the focus was on individual redemption, not on promoting societal change" (Hewlett 1986: 153). Responding to Hewlett's assertions, Lois Reckitt and Toni Garabillo call her book revisionist history. They point out that a great deal of attention was paid to child care, including a concerted campaign for legislation to set up a federal system of child care, which resulted in a comprehensive bill passed by Congress in 1971, although later this bill was vetoed by President Nixon.[1] (George Bush similarly vetoed parental leave in 1990.)

Indeed, what was happening throughout the 1970s and 1980s was that child care bills promoted by feminist and social activists became increasingly difficult to get out of congressional hearings. In 1988 the Act for Better Child Care Services (ABC) and Parental Leave Act made it to the House floor, but were tabled in order to do what Senator Robert Dole called "business that is important" (cited in Simpson 1988: 82). In opposition to feminist efforts, the United States continues to be the only industrialized country (with the exception of South Africa) with no federal program for maternal leave or a child care system.

In the second example, an article published in the *Harvard Business Review* (Schwartz 1989) claimed mothers are a corporate liability because they cost business money with maternity leave and sick pay; thus, investing in expensive training means an economic loss to companies. The author, Felice Schwartz,[2] argues for a new lower-pressure career track for those women who place their family obligations in high priority. Citing the need to develop employment policies that help mothers balance their obligations, she suggests women would fall into either a career-primary track or a career-and-family track (dubbed the "mommy track" by the popular press). Feminists responded that the article was full of sexist, racist, and classist assumptions, such as the assumption that employment for all mothers is optional. Moreover, they argued that Schwartz was carelessly conflating the biological role of maternity, which is done by women, with the social role of child rearing, which can be done by either sex.

What Schwartz did in her article was to present a sexist solution to a very real problem of women's work/family role conflicts. Rather than address the need for dual parenting responsibilities, non-penalized flexible work schedules and social service provision, she suggests a formula for keeping women in a secondary position in the workforce. Barbara Enrenreich and Deidre English consider the publicity generated by this article to be an indication of a negative reception to women in careers in general.

> It should never have been taken seriously, not by the media and not by the nation's most prestigious academic business publication. The fact that it was suggests that something serious *is* afoot: a backlash against America's high-status, better paid women, and potentially against all women workers. (Ehrenreich and English 1989: 58; emphasis in the original)

ASSESSING THE PAST

After the defeat of the Equal Rights Amendment, books and articles were published to explain what went wrong: too little direct action such as civil disobedience (Carroll 1986); strategical mistakes particularly related to NOW's position on the military draft (Mansbridge 1986); proponents' inability to achieve the necessary consensus to overcome structural barriers associated with passage of constitutional amendments (Berry 1986); better organization on the part of the opposition (*Ms.* 1983); failure to allay the fears of traditional women (Conover and Gray 1983); and ERA proponents themselves—their ideological purity, volunteer troops, and lack of success in making their case (Mansbridge 1986).

Feminist activists tend to take a different view when analyzing why ERA did not pass. What they see is that the world became a different place in the 1980s than it had been in the 1970s and 1960s. From their perspective, the defeat of ERA was simply the most manifest indication of what was occurring and what was yet to come. Activists found themselves caught up in a "political opportunity structure" that was not as favorable to civil rights and feminist goals as had been the case earlier.[3] Despite postmortem accounts of where the movement went wrong, activists consider the strength of the backlash and the increasingly conservative social environment to have operated as an effective barrier to any kind of social movement advance, feminist or otherwise.

From long-term activists' perspective, critics have expended too much analysis blaming the proponents instead of examining the social/political environment. For instance, in response to a charge in Mary Frances Berry's 1986 book that feminists' timing was off, former NOW President Karen DeCrow quipped: "Our timing was fine. Our friends in the Republican and Democratic parties did us in" (1988: 7). In answering a second charge in Berry's book that in 1972 proponents did not allocate major resources for state passage, DeCrow remarked:

> The truth is that in 1972, the supporters of ERA did not have the financial resources. The National Organization for Women, now operating on a multimillion dollar budget, had little money. National officers, now paid a dignified salary, were unpaid. Our expenses were supposed to be reimbursed, but the board never had the funds to do so . . . The opposition, on the other hand, has always been well-financed.(1988: 7)

The aftermath of a failed campaign left an opening for the kinds of analyses that faulted feminist activists for their "mistakes." Many of these critics' comments were insulting to those activists who had put years of their lives into planning, strategizing, and working to gain passage of the amendment. Admonitions of oversight and advice for the future were not well taken when it was felt they came from people who had not been out there on the line. Often such reports were less than accurate, such as the following interpretation of the early image feminists projected in the opening debate on ERA ratification:

> Much of the public perceived the rhetorical and nonverbal images used by segments of the women's movement as essentially strident and negative (radical, loud-mouth, militant, stringy-haired, anti-male, braless "libbers"). (Mayo and Frye 1986: 87)

In actuality, at the outset of the debate the public did not know very much about feminists or the ERA; and it was at the outset that political support was strongest—the ERA passed both houses of Congress and 22 states in the first year. It was later, long after the "stringy hair" and non-existent "bra-burning" were over, that the anti-ERA forces grew and the political climate cooled. Mayo and Fray (1986) further criticize the ERA campaign by claiming that "supporters failed to perfect affirmative rhetoric that fit prevailing cultural concepts of women" (ibid.). In this critique it is not clear if the authors' miss the point of what the women's movement is about or if they are asking feminists to mask their message. Since feminism challenges the prevailing cultural concept of women, it would have been problematic to "perfect" affirmative rhetoric to fit that concept and at the same time be true to feminist goals to create positive opportunities for women outside of traditional norms.

Other critiques of the movement also indicated that feminists should have compromised, given in on some issues, or distorted their real intent if they wanted to be successful. In critiquing the critiquers, Kristin Luker's review of books by Mary Frances Berry (1986) and Jane Mansbridge (1986) wonders if their suggestions for securing the ERA might not be impossible or irrelevant. She questions what the outcome might have been if the policies Berry and Mansbridge suggest were successful. For instance, she considers the policy Mansbridge suggests—a "deferential" model for women in relationship to the draft— to be a policy that might have led to a deferential ERA. An amendment which allowed exceptions "could have proved a fatal flaw" because it would have "left unchallenged the idea that men and women could legitimately have different treatment based on sex alone" (Luker 1986). Of course, the insistence on no differential treatment by sex has its own internal inconsistencies, since there are biological reproductive differences between the sexes, and there are gender differences related to child rearing (the question of whether or not there should be, not withstanding). What equality really means is that all barriers to equal treatment should be removed, including barriers such as the *lack* of policies such as maternal leave and child care provisions.

SUCCESS FROM A FAILED CAMPAIGN

Regardless of the cause, the loss of ERA did strike a blow to the movement. The Equal Rights Amendment had become a unifying mobilization issue for supporters and activists. The failure to achieve ratification left the movement fragmented over future direction, leading to the re-emergence of divisive issues related to class, ethnicity, race, pornography, sexuality, and spirituality.

The aftermath of defeat—a divided movement and the loss of mass activism—should not, however, negate the benefits the ERA campaign provided for the dissemination of feminist ideals. Of the needed 38 states, 35 passed the amendment, representing over 70 percent of the population. Opinion polls showed that, by the time ERA failed, 63 percent of the people supported it; however, that level of support was lower than the 74 percent support found in 1974, a figure that shows the success opponents had in creating a level of unease about the possible negative effects ERA might produce. In spite of a decline in the percentage of the population favoring passage, the majority always supported ERA and, once the "Mom and apple pie" rhetoric died down, a Harris Poll found that by 1988 there was an increase in support, with 78 percent of respondents favoring the amendment (National Organization for Women 1989a). Other polls in the mid-1980s showed that 56 percent of women identify themselves as feminists, with 71 percent of respondents reporting that the women's movement had created some level of improvement in their lives (Gallup 1986). It appears, then, that even though it did not get the necessary votes for ratification "ERA won the popularity contest" (Pleck 1983: 12).

Going beyond popular support for the amendment, the ERA campaign helped women gain other advances.

> The debate over the ERA served as the impetus for changing the course of public policy on the status of women in court decisions, federal and state laws, and bureaucratic procedures. It was accompanied by a virtual revolution in public opinion on the proper role and rights of women in society. Furthermore, the conflict mobilized women on both sides of the issue; it brought them together in coalitions and into politics. The political role of women changed. (Boles 1986:61)

Within a resource mobilization framework, the ERA was highly successful. The campaign not only increased public awareness, but was also instrumental in drawing in large numbers of activists for the movement. Small groups emerged to participate in diverse ways during various phases of the ERA drive, and the mass movement sector experienced a steady increase in monetary assistance and membership rolls.

The loss of ERA meant a decline in these resources (Jonasdottir 1988). However, even when people were no longer active, having once been involved their feminist commitment was likely to be maintained. Many women who found it necessary to drop out of activism wound up working in ways where they could continue to support and promote their feminist ideology.

A contradiction emerged in the 1980s between support for feminist goals and declining participation in women's movement activism. A feminist consciousness represents support for feminist issues and an identification with women as a group, whereas a receptivity to feminist ideas may indicate support for feminist goals even though a conscious awareness of women as a sex class may not exist

(Katzenstein 1987). It appears the latter is representative of much of what has occurred. For instance, younger women have voiced their objection to the term feminist, although they have accepted the ideal of women's equality. In interviewing college students and recent graduates after the ERA defeat, Susan Bolotin found that "feminism had become a dirty word" and that young women believe feminists are bitter toward men or that they are lesbians (1982: 30). College women accept that aspect of feminism which gives them the freedom to strive to be successful and independent, but if being a feminist also means alienating men they do not want to be called feminists.

Other research has also concluded that younger women want to "have it all" and they believe they can do this on their own, without a social movement agitating for social reform (Renzetti 1987; Komarovsky 1985). In an early 1980's survey of 10,000 women, Carol Tavris found over half the respondents planned to have a $25,000 a year career; further, they expected no problem with interrupting their career for a two to six year period to stay home and raise children (quoted in Bolotin 1982: 106–7). Expecting to have a career with a flexible schedule and a salary higher than 98 percent of other women workers leaves little desire or awareness of the need for a women's movement.

What stands out in these assumptions is a high level of agreement with feminist goals in combination with a weakening perception that there is still a need for feminist activism. These surveys reveal new gender role expectations; however, personal remedies prevail rather than group action. Placed within the context of the economic decline of the 1980s and a decade uninspired by the 1960s' protest movements, individualistic efforts predominate (Klatch 1987).

Although feminists can lament the frequently expressed individualistic attitude of younger women towards feminism, this attitude does not have the same implications as the rejection of feminism expressed by traditional women. For anti-feminist women, equal rights does not make sense because women and men are seen as fundamentally, innately, different. If each sex has a separate role to play in society, then what feminists are attempting to change is the natural order of separate spheres. This acceptance of biologically defined gender roles, though, represents a small minority of the population today.

Whether one calls themselves a feminist or not, joins or does not join an activist group, or even if one does not believe the women's movement is needed any longer, there clearly has been a diffusion of feminist thought throughout the country. Indeed, one of the defining characteristics of the contemporary women's movement has been a shift in collective consciousness about gender relations (Mueller 1987).

Even before the mid-1970s, survey data showed the general public had become more aware and supportive of feminist beliefs (Poole and Zeigler 1981). Public opinion research shows that since 1977 a pro-feminist trend has been occurring in all socioeconomic groups of the population (Mason and Lu 1988).

Working-class women are as likely to identify themselves as feminists as are professional women. Indeed, 57 percent of women with family incomes below $20,000 per year called themselves feminist as compared with 55 percent of women with family incomes over $40,000 (Gallup 1986).

By 1980 the majority of people in the U.S. believed that the differences in men and women's lives were due to how they were raised rather than to innate abilities. The percentage of people who supported efforts to advance women's rights grew from 44 percent of men and 40 percent of women in 1970 to 69 percent of men and 73 percent of women by 1985. Seventy-five percent of the population believed that women's roles in the future would be different than today and only 10 percent thought they would revert to a more traditional lifestyle (Klein 1987).

The growth of a collective conscience is important and contributes to building for the future. In a similar way that "the operation was successful, but the patient died," the spread of a feminist consciousness occurred even though ERA went down in defeat. Most activists believe that the next generation will support feminist goals and, as they experience discriminatory policies in their attempts to integrate career and family roles, they will become more involved in social change efforts.

Continued efforts to create an environment that recognizes gender inequities is essential for a feminist consciousness to develop and movement goals to succeed. As Cynthia Kinnard found in her research on anti-feminism during the nineteenth century, "ground has been lost whenever feminists let up their guard" (1986: xiv). Because history provides insights into the present, it is also important to note that Kinnard's research shows that the slow pace of change was due not to feminist complacency, "but rather that the foe was so vigorous, protean, and persistent" (ibid.).

Recognizing that social movements follow an uneven cyclical course helps deflect feelings of hopelessness during a regressive period. Moreover, as shown by the low level of change in stereotypical gender attitudes among adolescents since the 1950s, it may well be that life experience is a necessary ingredient for individuals to commit themselves to activism (Lewin and Tragos 1987; Tavris and Baumgartner 1983). If it is the case that personal confrontation with sexist attitudes is needed for social movement involvement, then it is likely that a new generation of activists is waiting in the wings.

None of this is to say that no mistakes were made in attempting to win ERA or even in putting so much focus on one issue. Nonetheless, the Equal Rights Amendment did make feminism a regular part of the daily news and of the general public's conversation. And it was a close race: in some states only a few legislators prevented passage. Rather than blaming feminist activists for failing to win constitutional approval for women's equality, it is possible that capitalist/ economic decline and "the rise of a conservative backlash after an era of war, turmoil and social reform is as much as one has to say to explain the defeat of ERA" (Pleck 1983: 1).

In an optimistic view, the populace is more in favor of women's equality than was the case when the Equal Rights Amendment was first introduced in Congress and long-term social and demographic trends appear to be working on the side of progressive change. The conditions that lead women to accept feminist goals—higher education, employment, fewer children, divorce, discrimination, and poverty—are all continuing factors of modern life. This change means that the future, under a more favorable political climate, should result in passage (Dehart-Mathews and Mathews 1986). Paradoxically, though, some of these same conditions, such as divorce and poor economic conditions, are also factors which led to the growth of the anti-ERA pro-family movement.

Controversial constitutional amendments have a history of extended debate, for they indicate dramatic shifts in cultural life. Given that the ERA is involved in defining women's roles and position in society—indeed, is part of a larger conflict over the meaning of womanhood—it is not surprising that it has not been achieved after more than half a century. It took 72 years to get women's suffrage; the ERA drama is part of a story that has yet to run its course.

The Independent

VOLUME 84   NOVEMBER 1, 1915   NUMBER 3491

MARCHING FOR THE VOTE

TWENTY-FIVE THOUSAND WOMEN AND 2500 MEN PARADED UP FIFTH AVENUE LAST SATURDAY,
TEN DAYS BEFORE ELECTION, TO CONVINCE NEW YORK VOTERS OF THE MAGNITUDE
AND EARNESTNESS OF THE SUFFRAGE CAMPAIGN

1915 suffrage march in New York City. *Photo from the Schlesinger Library, Radcliffe College, Woman's Rights Collection.*

National Woman's Party members picketing outside the White House gate, July 20, 1917. *Photo from the Library of Congress, National Woman's Party Collection.*

Alice Paul as a young woman and suffragist leader. *Photo from the Schlesinger Library, Radcliffe College, Alice Paul Collection.*

(*Above*) 1st National ERA March, Spring-field, Illinois, 1976. 10,000 marchers carrying pre-printed red or blue ERA signs indicate the early stage of this campaign. Within a few years green became the symbolic color for the pro-ERA forces and creative symbols, pagentry, and staged drama were employed. *Photo by Gene Parvin.*

(*Left*) Eleanor Smeal, National NOW president, leading a workshop on organizing for the ERA at the Illinois NOW State Convention, 1977. *Photo by Elizabeth Neeley.*

(*Above*) Kick-off announcement of the ERA Caravan in Illinois by the National Organization for Women, 1978. The Caravan tactic was a replication of the Caravan for Woman's Suffrage organized by the National Woman's Party and a NOW strategy implemented the previous year before Kentucky passed the ERA. *Photo by Elizabeth Neeley.*

(*Below*) ERA extension march organized by NOW in Washington, D.C. with 100,000 participants dressed in white. Held on July 9, 1978, the march was dedicated to Alice Paul who had died on this date the previous year. Photo from the National NOW Action Center.

(*Above*) A Group of Women on day 8 of a 37 day Fast for Justice held in the rotunda of the Illinois capitol in the spring of 1982. Shown from left are Sonia Johnson, Dick Gregory who sat in on the fast for three days, Mary Ann Buell, and an unidentified man opposed to the fast. *Photo from Wide World Photos.*

(*Opposite, top*) Rally after the 1978 Washington, D.C. extension march held on the Capitol lawn. Participants dressed in white and displayed purple and gold banners to indicate the connection between the ERA campaign and the suffrage campaign. *Photo by Gene Parvin.*

(*Opposite, bottom*) View of the 100,000 participants at the rally following the NOW organized Mother's Day March for the ERA in Chicago, Illinois in 1980. *Photo by Gene Parvin.*

(*Above*) Members of 'A Grassroots Group of Second Class Citizens' display the international symbol for woman during a sit-in at the Illinois State House of Representatives, Spring 1982. *Photo from Wide World Photos.*

(*Opposite, top*) Celebration of women in front of the White House on August 26, the anniversary of the passage of woman's suffrage. Later participants invoked a civil disobedience action when they blocked Pennsylvania Avenue by dancing and singing in the street. This action was planned at the first national Women's Gathering organized by Sonia Johnson, Washington, D.C., 1983. Photo by Barbara Ryan.

(*Opposite, center*) Rally after second national Women's Gathering prior to a civil disobedience action. Signs and apparel reveal participant's diversity of goals and connection to the women's culture. St. Louis, Missouri, summer 1984. Photo by Barbara Ryan.

(*Opposite, bottom*) Street theatre held outside Republican Headquarters mocking Ronald Reagan. Participants demonstrated against Reagan's re-election bid and supported Sonia Johnson's symbolic run for the White House. Organized by Women Rising in Resistance during the Second National Women's Gathering, St. Louis, Missouri, 1984. Photo by Barbara Ryan.

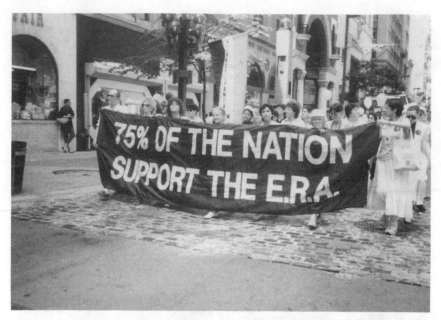

(*Above*) March showing NOW's continuing promotion of the ERA. National NOW Convention, Philadelphia, PA, Summer 1987. *Photo by Barbara Ryan.*

(*Below*) March for 'Women's Equality, Women's Lives' which drew close to half a million participants in the wake of the U.S. Supreme Court's decision to review Webster v. Reproductive Health which allowed states the right to place restrictions on abortion availability. This April 9, 1989 march was organized by the National Organization for Women, Washington, DC. *Photo by Blanche Kauffman.*

CHAPTER 8 ───────────────────────

DIVISIONS REVISITED: PORNOGRAPHY, ESSENTIALISM/ NOMINALISM, CLASS AND RACE

> Feminism is the political theory and practices to free all women: women of color, working-class women, poor women, physically challenged women, Lesbians, old women, as well as white economically privileged heterosexual women. Anything less than that is not feminism, but merely female self-aggrandizement.
>
> (Barbara Smith; quoted in Moraga and Anzaldua 1981: 62)

The conflicting views represented by different perspectives, social roles, and life circumstance are illustrations of the enormous problem the women's movement has in attempting to represent a constituency with multiple views and needs. Because a major source of activism for a prolonged period had been the effort to pass the Equal Rights Amendment, interactions among feminists were affected by the loss of this goal. Once organized labor changed its position on protective labor legislation, the ERA became a symbol of women's worth and equality which created a temporary sense of unity among feminists. Even though activists themselves represented marked differences in orientation, tactics, and lifestyles, working on a common issue promoted an image that there was an underlying commonality among diverse groups of women. Without this shared focus, the challenge to the concept of universal sisterhood re-emerged with new energy.

The loss of a highly publicized mobilizing issue created an environment for other issues, many of which had been partially submerged, to become a focus of movement concern. Divisions over issues and social characteristics increasingly became public and confrontational. Paradoxes that had developed were critically examined as anger and disagreements were openly raised once again. Major divisions focused on: (1) the role of pornography and what constitutes a feminist position on this issue, (2) how to reconcile equality with equity claims, and (3) the problem of gains for some women, mainly white middle-class women, at the same time that there was an increase in poverty of poor women and women of color.

THE FEMINIST PORNOGRAPHY DEBATE

One of the most explosive issues to erupt within the women's movement in the 1980s was pornography. Even though Susan Brownmiller's 1975 book *Against Our Will: Men, Women, and Rape* opened the debate on pornography as a feminist issue (Sellen and Young 1987), there was no mention of pornography in either the recommendations of the National Commission on the Observance of International Women's Year in 1976 or the National Women's Conference held in Houston in 1977 (Ferree and Hess 1985). In 1978 a conference on Feminist Perspectives on Pornography was sponsored by Women Against Violence in Pornography and Media to address violence against women through sexual and violent images. The following year Andrea Dworkin's book *Pornography* (1979) was published and Women Against Pornography (WAP) was formed in New York City. WAP organized a Women Against Pornography conference, began distributing anti-pornography literature, and gave guided tours of the pornographic district in Times Square.

Thus, in the late 1970s pornography became a priority issue for small numbers of feminists. Although generally felt to be offensive, pornography was not an issue most feminists cared to organize their activism around. There was, however, a growing interest in exploring the topic of women's sexuality. The theme "Towards a Politics of Sexuality" was chosen for the Scholar and the Feminist IX Conference held at Barnard College in October 1982. Controversy emerged when some of those in attendance protested the failure of conference organizers to include anti-pornography speakers. Further, in an acrimonious attack, presenters were accused of supporting patriarchal sexuality. It was at this conference that a deep division developed among feminists over how to view, and what to do about, pornography (Turley 1986).

Anti-pornography feminists take the position that pornography is at the root of violence against women; in fact, is the cause of this violence. Symbolizing this position, they have adopted the slogan "pornography is the theory, rape is the practice."[1] While they emphasize pornography that depicts violence towards women, it is not only violent pornography that is opposed. Indeed, Andrea

Dworkin argues that "most pornography is deeply violative of a woman's integrity" because it not only "generates crimes of violence against women," it also "creates bigotry, hostility, and aggression," which lead to "attitudes and behaviors of sex discrimination" (*On the Issues* 1988b: 5).

By identifying pornography as the foundation of women's oppression, anti-pornography feminists thought they had found an issue around which to unite all women. Ironically, it became an issue that provoked bitter debates leading to the kind of name-calling reminiscent of the early years of feminist organizing in the contemporary movement. In essence, anti-pornography feminists were accused of being anti-sex while anti-censorship feminists were charged with not being real feminists.

The first attacks occurred at the Barnard conference when a leaflet was distributed protesting the advocation of "the same kind of patriarchal sexuality that flourishes in our culture's mainstream, that is channeled into crimes against women, and that is institutionalized in pornography" (cited in Ellis 1984: 104). In response, Carole Vance argued that the conference planners were interested in focusing on women's sexual pleasure because "to speak only of sexual violence and oppression ignores women's experience with sexual agency and choice and unwittingly increases the sexual terror and despair in which women live" (1984: 1).

After the Barnard conference, anti-pornography feminists accelerated their campaign of picketing and introduced a new innovative tactic to use the legal system for women's protection rather than the protection of pornographers. Andrea Dworkin and feminist lawyer Catherine MacKinnon wrote a civil rights ordinance which assigned pornography to the realm of sex discrimination. Charging that pornography was damaging to women, the ordinance allowed any woman to bring civil suit against the makers and distributors of pornographic material. Introduced in Minneapolis in 1983, the ordinance was passed by the city council, but vetoed by the mayor. The next year a member of the city council in Indianapolis, a Republican who had opposed ERA and abortion, hired MacKinnon as a consultant. During the Indianapolis hearings, support for the ordinance came from Christian fundamentalists, the Moral Majority, and Eagle Forum activists (Turley 1986).

The anti-pornography movement was now aligned, although not happily or for the same reasons, with the conservative pro-family forces that had been active in anti-feminist causes since the mid-1970s. When an anti-ERA legislator introduced a second ordinance that same year in Suffolk County, New York, feminists opposed to the anti-pornography movement organized the Feminist Anti-Censorship Taskforce (FACT). Although often defined simply as supporting the First Amendment, FACT is opposed to the anti-pornography movement for reasons going beyond the rights of free speech. In terms of tactics, they find that a civil rights ordinance on pornography does not affect sexism found in the mass

media or advertising, and, even more importantly, the ordinance gives censorship power to a patriarchal legal system.

> Although the ordinance was written by radical feminists, the judiciary will inter-
> pret it. Judges are schooled in the preservation of the status quo, a male version of
> reality. They rely on legal precedent and laws designed to protect the interests of a
> White male propertied class in a system structured by men. . . . By offering this
> law, feminists are giving power to the state, not to women, to make more decisions
> about women. (Turley 1986: 90)

And finally, perhaps the most divisive feature of the pornography schism, anti-
censorship feminists believe that it is not male violence towards women that is
being debated, but sexual politics. Because historically women have been sex-
ually restrained, anti-censorship feminists argue for greater tolerance for sexual
openness and the acknowledgement of women as sexual beings. By over-
focusing on the negative aspects of sexuality—male violence and the objectifi-
cation of women—sex is identified with a world of "dirty" images which could
once again lead to the suppression of a wide range of sexual expression. It was
not that long ago that information about birth control and abortion were considered obscene and legally banned in the U.S. The 1980s witnessed the Supreme
Court upholding a sodomy law in Georgia where it is legally permissible to
arrest consenting adults in their own homes for engaging in acts of "deviant"
sex. From this perspective, then, anti-censorship feminists argue that the topic
of sexuality needs to be liberated, not closed down.

> If feminists define pornography, per se, as the enemy, the result will be to make a
> lot of women ashamed of their sexual feelings and afraid to be honest about them.
> And the last thing women need is more sexual shame, guilt, and hypocrisy—this
> time served up as feminism. (Willis 1983: 462)

The schism that developed over pornography led to charges by anti-
pornography activists that members of FACT were "cynical slime . . . insane,
demented feminists . . . a front for the pornography industry and not truly feminist" (See, Turley 1986: 86); that they were traitors: "The Black movement had
Uncle Toms and Oreo cookies. The labor movement has scabs. The women's
movement has FACT" (MacKinnon 1990: 12); and that because pornography represents patriarchal sexual relations based on male power and force, anyone who
does not oppose its existence or, even worse, any woman who finds pleasure in
pornographic images and sadomasochistic sexual relations is male identified.
Further, if women believe they like sexual relations with men, it is because they
have been socialized to believe this through a patriarchal culture, since what we
know about sexuality has been defined and constructed by men for their pleasure. In defending this position, Andrea Dworkin states:

The argument isn't just that I or other feminists are for censorship, it's that we're trying to take these people's sexuality away from them. When they're talking about censorship of speech it's almost a euphemism. What they mean is censorship of their sexuality and their sexuality is based on dominance and submission. (Cited in *On The Issues* 1988: 16).

In countering that position, Ann Snitow argues that the ostensible presumption in the feminist anti-pornography stance is that heterosexual sex relations are oppressive for women and that any woman who rejects this analysis has been brainwashed by patriarchy and is, thus, operating under a false consciousness. An unacknowledged underside to this analysis is that women are helpless and invisible, as it denies women "any agency at all in the long history of heterosexuality" (Snitow 1985: 118). Moreover, Ellen Willis argues that the reduction of pornography to male sexual violence offers no distinction between consensual sex relations and rape. As pornography becomes an analogy for male lust, sex with men becomes pornographic. Attacking pornography while equating it with heterosexual sex implies a condemnation of both those women who enjoy some forms of pornography and those women who enjoy sexual relations with men. And this, she says, is "familiar ground" (Willis 1983: 465).

Resistance to the anti-pornography campaign has tended to come from those feminists associated with early radical feminism, left, and liberal traditions. Socialist feminism does not trust a capitalistic patriarchal state, radical feminism of the late 1960s promoted women's sexual liberation, and liberal ideology values individual choice in people's lives. The anti-pornography faction arose among cultural feminists of the 1970s who identify themselves as radical feminists, a transformation of the earlier radical feminists, according to Alice Echols, through the infusion of lesbian separatist ideology. Echols argues that in this "reincarnation," there is a resurgence of the "female principle" in which the differences between women and men are emphasized, rather than the similarities (Echols 1983). This emphasis has led to a re-awakened interest in the cultural vs. the innate components of gender, an argument known in the past as the nature/nurture debate and today called the essentialist or minimalist perspective.[2]

ESSENTIALIST VS. MINIMALIST VIEWS

Are women and men basically the same or do they have physical and psychological differences which make them distinct types of people? If they are more the same than different, why do we find such divergent attitudes and behavior among them? And, are such differences innate or culturally constructed?

This historic argument underlies the heart of the issue of gender relations.

During the suffrage campaign, competing nature/nurture views often resulted in contradictory rationales taken by social feminists and equal rights feminists. The social feminist position of the late 1800s argued that women, because of their unique reproductive role, needed protection in order to bear and raise children and, also connected to their biological and cultural role, were innately more nurturing than men. Thus, women needed a political voice in order to contribute to a kinder social environment. The equal rights position argued that women and men had essentially the same capabilities and that women had been placed in a secondary position because of their reproductive role. Equal rights feminists wanted to eliminate the penalties that were connected to mothering and give women a chance to succeed in whatever realm they chose.

Another view found during the nineteenth and early twentieth centuries came from anti-feminist forces opposed to suffrage. For them, the physiological differences between women and men led to inherently separate, but complementary, social roles. Relying on biological determinism and religious teachings, this position posited a social world in which women stay within their "natural" place of homemaking and child rearing while men engage in the competitive world of work. Since this is a woman's role, preordained by nature, it is not placing her in a secondary position in the social order. Men are meant to be the head of the household and rulers of the country because they have the greater capacity for it. Women are meant to be helpmates; indeed, Eve was created out of Adam's rib in order to provide him with companionship in his world.

In the modern-day debate, the anti-feminist position has remained within a natural order argument. However, feminist views have taken on nuances that maintain aspects of the similar/difference perspective of the earlier version, but at the same time add a more complex analysis.[3] In what is called the essentialist (or maximalist) position, women and men are believed to constitute two dichotomous groups. Some essentialist proponents believe the cause of this differentiation is biological, others that it is social conditioning, and still others that it is a mixture of the two. In any case, the differences are so deep that the result is two distinct sex/gender-related worldviews and cultural adaptations. In this conceptualization, women are nurturing, loving, gentle, and desireful of connectedness; while men are aggressive, competitive, forceful, and attuned to separateness.

In contrast, the nominalist (or minimalist) position argues that gender differences are social constructions elaborated through myth, religion, law, norms, and ideology for the purpose of creating and maintaining a hierarchical status division. In this view, women and men are social constructs, there is no essential core of identity other than our life experiences, and our life experiences are acted out in a social structure that is patriarchally defined.

While these feminist conceptions differ on attribution of cause, both stress that gender is not really about difference, but is in actuality a system of dominance (MacKinnon 1987), and that gender differences are exaggerated in order

to form one of the foundations (or, in radical feminist conceptions, *the* foundation) of social stratification. In spite of the level of agreement on structural outcome, the contrasting conceptions of origin have profound differences in theoretical prescriptions for remediation. For instance, the essentialist position posits
innate sex differences in which women's biological traits are a positive force and
men's are a threat. This argument represents a shift in radical feminist analysis
from protesting a social structure premised on male supremacy to one which
vilifies men. "By interpreting masculinity as immutable, the cultural feminist
analysis assumes that men are the enemy by virtue of their maleness rather than
the power a patriarchal system lends them" (Echols 1983: 443).

Because so much of the feminist anti-pornography message incorporates an
anti-heterosexuality message, it contains not only an anti-male component but
an anti-heterosexual female component as well. This is a multifarious transformation of the social purity campaigns of the last century which attempted to put
checks on male sexual behavior in a context where birth control was illegal and
common venereal diseases (before AIDS) were fatal (DuBois and Gordon 1984).
Moreover, it is a far cry from the stated intention of joining women into a united
sisterhood. Indeed, disagreements on issues related to sexuality and pornography have led to mutually bitter accusations of betrayal. Coming full circle, some
1980s' radical feminists have reserved the feminist mantle for only those women
who adopt "correct premises," as when Catherine MacKinnon claims that only
radical feminism is truly feminist because it is unmodified—all other types of
feminism are simply modified endeavors to adapt women to men's systems
(1987).

However, feminists may personally feel about pornography, the evidence on
its effects are mixed and the possibility remains that anti-pornography remedies
will not only fail to eliminate pornography but will also create new arenas of
repression. Further, most feminists consider it unrealistic to expect that the end
of pornography would also mean the end of violence against women or the
elimination of poverty and lost opportunities women experience in their attempts
for self-fulfillment and economic independence.

The bitter exchanges accompanying the pornography debate led to a new era
of acrimonious intra-movement attack, and the issues, while not as heated as in
the past, remain unresolved. There was however, a positive outcome to this
debate: a re-consideration of the sameness/difference argument as a serious issue
going beyond pornography or sexuality.

EQUALITY AND EQUITY

Throughout the 1980s the dilemma of how to achieve equality in a social system
structured around male patterns of behavior led to the development of policy

positions which strive to achieve sex/gender *equity*. Child care, maternity/paren-
tal leave, and pay equity are all issues that attempt to equalize sex/gender differences so that women would have an equal opportunity in the social structure.
Equality with men, on male terms and on the basis of male needs, is no longer
seen as sufficient.

One of the problems with the nineteenth-century woman's movement was its
failure to address sex/gender differences and to incorporate those differences into
policies that would achieve sex equal relations. Equal opportunity to compete
with men, when women and men are tied to different biological and social functioning, only leaves women in an unequal competitive arena. However, attempts
to provide protections for women have kept women in a subsidiary position
because protections have also been restrictive of opportunities. The problem is
how to achieve sex equality without ignoring sex/gender differences. It was the
failure to incorporate both equality and equity that prevented a broad-based continuance of the women's movement after suffrage was attained (Cott 1987).

The problematic nature of difference and sameness, which surfaced in the
early part of this century, continues today. Child care is part of this debate because the lack of affordable, quality child care affects women's ability to enter
the work structure to a much greater extent than it affects men's ability. It may
be that a policy in which there is no government-sponsored child care is a sex
equal policy, since neither sex is entitled to it; but it is not gender equity when
women are more likely to be the primary care taker of children, and would
therefore suffer an opportunity loss that would not affect men. The point that
both women and men should be responsible for raising children, although well
taken, is not the reality in most people's lives. Child care, as it is presently
structured, is a woman's issue and a gender equity issue. It is also an issue
related to class and race, since the poor are less likely to be able to afford child
care and are more affected by the lack of government-provided care than the
middle class.

Maternity leave policy is also a women's equity issue. Whereas child care is
a gender role issue—that is, it is a socially defined behavioral expectation—
pregnancy and childbirth are sex role issues because they are biologically controlled behaviors. Only women fulfill this role because only women are physi-
cally capable of it. The lack of maternity leave which allows women release time
without the penalty of losing their jobs, means that women are handicapped in
their career development because of their biology. It may be that you have equality between the sexes because men do not have time off for pregnancy leave
either, but it is not equity since men do not need it. Work-related benefits that
do not provide maternity leave are premised on a male model of need; or, as
Julius Roth cynically defines it in a paraphrase of Anatole France: "The law, in
its majestic equality, forbids men as well as women to benefit from childbearing"
(1988).[4]

Parental leave goes further than maternity leave and includes release time for the *care* of a new born, sick child or aging parent, all of which are gender-related role behaviors. The importance of parental leave, rather than just mater-nal leave, lies in the message it contains: either sex or both can be responsible for family needs. Even though countries such as Sweden, where parental leave is state policy, find that in 90 percent of the cases it is women who use this leave, the notion that family care is a societal issue and not a woman's issue dispels the belief that women's place is in the home and that the work structure need only be organized around a traditional male model.

Equality/equity differences are also found in the implication of policies based on either affirmative action or pay equity. Under affirmative action, the goal is to give women and minority men opportunities to be hired and promoted in occupational fields that have not been receptive to them in the past. This legis-lation has contributed to the integration of job markets that have traditionally been reserved for white males. We now see women police officers, mail carriers, lawyers, doctors, and professors where previously there were none or only a few. While affirmative action has opened up some possibilities for hiring, it has not impacted retention and promotion after the initial hiring process; nor has it had much effect on breaking down the entrenched segregated work structure.

Pay equity (sometimes called comparable pay) acknowledges the reality of a sex-segregated work structure and attempts to create a different rating system. The rationale behind pay equity is that socialization encourages women to desire and prepare for particular types of work that are different from the types of work that men do. While there is nothing intrinsically wrong with men and women "choosing" different occupational goals, the problem is that the economic valu-ing system has rewarded the work men do more highly than the work women do. Because the conception of equal pay for equal work established under the Equal Pay Bill of 1963 addressed only those occupations in which women and men do the same job, and because most women and men do different jobs, pay equity has attempted to change the wage structure itself. It specifically addresses those occupations known as "women's work" which have historically been de-valued and underpaid.

The difference between affirmative action and pay equity is one of class. Af-firmative action is more likely to move middle-class women into traditionally classified men's work and has been most successful in the professions and semi-professions, while pay equity addresses advancement for traditionally defined women's work, which tends to draw employees from the working class.

Men and women have always constituted a segregated work structure with a different valuing scale attached to each sector. The establishment of a differential male/female pay scale was "legitimized" in the 1800s by the idea of men deserv-ing a family wage. With the rise of industrialization, the ideal middle-class fam-ily constellation became the model of a man who works and provides for his homemaking wife and children. The rationale was that men needed more money than women because they had to provide for a family. Thus, men's wages were usually about twice the amount of women's, even when they were doing the same job. This conception was, of course, a class-biased and sexist conception because there were then, as now, many working-class and single women who had families that were dependent upon their wages, and many single men who enjoyed the benefits of a family wage without the responsibilities of a family.

Today, the pay equity argument is that women and men should be paid for their level of training/education, job responsibility, and skill level. This means that we have to question why an electrician makes more than a school teacher, a tree trimmer more than a nurse, or an administrative assistant more than an executive secretary; and, in so doing, we have to question our sex/gender value system all together. One of the things we know is that not all societies value the same type of work in the same way. For instance, medical doctors in the United States (who are primarily male) are highly valued with prestige and economic rewards, whereas in the (former) Soviet Union medical doctors (who are primarily female) receive a low level wage and have little prestige. There are many examples of this occupational status variance around the world, and often what we see in looking at these comparisons is that what is being valued is not the status of the occupation, but the status of the worker.

In his analysis of the work structure, Thorstein Veblen argued that predatory societies value exploitive behaviors such as are found in politics, war, and sports; whereas those behaviors which do not involve prowess come to be seen as unworthy, diligent, and dull. In modern societies, this distinction between exploit and drudgery is enacted through "an invidious distinction between employments" and occupational valuation (Veblen [1899] 1953: 29).

> Those employments which are to be classed as exploit are worthy, honorable, noble; other employments, which do not contain this element of exploit, and especially those which imply subservience or submission, are unworthy, debasing, ignoble. The concept of dignity, worth, or honor, as applied either to persons or conduct, is of first rate consequence in the development of classes and of class distinctions. (Veblen [1899] 1953: 29)

Value and status judgments, Veblen argues, are wielded by those in power specifically to create a "distinction of a personal kind—of superiority and inferiority" (ibid.: 25). Thus, following Veblen's thinking, allowing women into the workforce, while retaining a lowered valuation of them as a social group, perpetuates differential status levels in the work they do and the type of work they are expected to do.

In a similar vein, Barbara Reskin reasons that resistance to the idea of pay equity should not surprise us since the conversion of a sex category into gender difference has never been an historic oversight, but rather is a social process meant to create and maintain a hierarchical reward system that favors men over women. Reskin argues that because dominant groups write the rules which benefit them and the rules they write enable them to continue to write the rules, affirmative action and pay equity are unlikely to offer much benefit to women (Reskin 1988). While Reskin supports the underlying principle of affirmative action and pay equity, her thesis is that "men will respond to women's challenge in the workplace by emphasizing how they differ from men" (Reskin 1988: 68). From evidence already accumulating, she predicts that organizations will change the rules on how to succeed in order to make it more difficult for women; for example, reminders of women's wife/mother roles will be emphasized and men in individual households will continue to resist sharing in housework and child rearing.

The basis for the continuation of inequality in the private and public sphere under Reskin's analysis is a continued focus on differences between the sexes because "differentiation is the sine qua non of dominance systems" (Reskin 1988:64).

> Differentiation—the practice of distinguishing categories based on some attribute—is the fundamental process in hierarchical systems. . . . In a hierarchical context, differentiation assumes, amplifies, and even creates psychological and behavioral differences in order to ensure that the subordinate group differs from the dominant group. (Reskin 1988: 62)

When placed in the framework of what is needed in order to achieve sex/gender equity, the question of whether the differences that exist are innate or socially constructed becomes a moot point. Whether or not biological differences go beyond reproductive functioning, we know that gender valuations and hierarchical systems based on these valuations are socially created. And we know that they can be socially deconstructed. It is not a matter of whether or not it can be done, or even how to do it; rather, it is a problem of resistance.

Aside from policy implications, analysis of gender similarity and difference led to esoteric and divisive debates in Women's Studies. Couched in the language of essentialism/minimalism (along with academic discussions over postmodernism, post-structuralism, and deconstruction), such debates have provided for interesting intellectual exercises. Although the creation of feminist theory is necessary to continue to develop analyses of gender reality, an essentialist/minimalist debate that focuses on the level of determining the validity or primacy of innate characteristics is limited by (1) the inability to definitely determine whether the influences that affect our thinking and behavior come from our genes or our environment since they are experienced together; and (2) the inability of such definitive answers (if they could be determined) to change sex/gender power relations. If we are serious about attaining sex/gender equity, what is needed is a consideration of the conditions needed to create a society that fosters equity in gender relations and committed efforts to achieve those conditions. This means, of course, social change directed at the structure of work, family organization, ideological thought, religious institutions, political systems, interactional relations, and psychic understandings—in short, the culture itself.

ISSUES OF CLASSISM AND RACISM IN THE WOMEN'S MOVEMENT

The essentialism/minimalist debate looks at the similarities/differences between women and men. Likewise, both gender equality and gender equity focus on eliminating inequality between the sexes. What is missing in these views is an understanding of gender relations that also takes into account differences *among* women and men. Indeed, the most damaging attack on the concept of sisterhood has been the charge of classism and racism in the women's movement. A serious challenge to feminist analysis, then, is the task of organizing around a gender category without losing sight of the structural and experiential differences of women's class and race identifications.

From the early days of the contemporary movement there were feminists who raised concerns about race and class differences among women and the difficulties those differences implied in organizing a movement focused on gender inequality. These concerns were generally submerged within the movement by the primacy of sisterhood until the early 1980s when new confrontations over the lack of racial and ethnic diversity arose. An analytical and operational shift occurred in the post-ERA period when activists and academics focused on integrating gender, race, and class in their research and organizing efforts. Still, charges of racism continue to be raised; and the popular press has repeatedly (and often gleefully) pointed out that, although the movement purports to represent all women, it consists almost solely of white middle-class women.

In looking over the past 20 years, there is no doubt that there has been advance for women as a group. Increases in the proportion of women in professions show that today women constitute 1 in 4 graduates in medicine and business compared with 1 in 20 two decades ago (Associated Press 1989). From 1975 to 1985 women's percent of dental degrees went from 3 percent to 21 percent, and law degrees rose from 15 percent to 38 percent (O'Neill 1989: 313). Paradoxically, it has also been women who have increasingly made up the ranks of the poorest segment of society. Poverty is no longer sex neutral; women now make up 60 percent of poor adults (McLanahan, Sorensen, and Watson 1989). The question confronting the movement is how to explain the achievement of gains for some women, such as the increase of women in professions, while at the same time women in general have fallen further into poverty-level classifications.

One in six families today is female headed, up from one in nine in 1970, and figures related to living at or below the poverty level show that more than half of all people who live in poverty are families headed by women. If these figures are broken down by race, we find that 52 percent of black families are female headed, as compared with 16 percent of white families and 25 percent of Spanish origin families (cited in Gimenez 1987: 421).

Although feminist goals such as ERA, abortion, child care, parental leave, and affirmative action are generalizable across populations, those gains that have been made in career and economic advance have benefited white middle-class women to a much greater extent than poor women and women of color. Despite the fact that class/race disparities exist largely because of an established social order, and women are rarely in the kind of policy-making positions that contribute to the placement of women and minorities at the lower rungs of stratified systems, such gaps between women do not constitute success for a movement that considers itself as representing all women. Hence the women's movement, in demanding equity for women within a social structure that differentiates among women on the basis of class and race, is faced with the question of how to address race and class issues.

Feminism and women of color

The popular press has long described the women's movement as a white middle-class movement. In adopting this view, the diverse components of feminist organizing are missed. Defining feminism and the women's movement as white and middle class excludes those organized groups which represent the interest of women of color,[5] feminist groups composed of mainly white women who have seriously concerned themselves with issues of race and class, and the many women of color who have worked in white plurality groups to create a more comprehensive agenda that addresses their concerns.

Moreover, such a narrowed view ignores the feminism that women of color have long been committed to in their personal lives and social change efforts. For instance, African American women have established nurturing relations among women through the black church and women's clubs, and their organizations are almost always "feminist in their values" (Dill 1983: 134). Public opinion polls have consistently shown black women to support feminist issues like ERA to a higher degree than white women (Gallup 1986). It is not the case that women of color are not feminists or do not believe in feminist goals, but they are making decisions about where to put their energy, and that energy tends to be on issues within their own community. As Bonnie Thornton Dill says, "sisterhood is not new to Black women," but the "political identities of Afro-

American women have largely been formed around issues of race" (1983: 134). Thus, the priority for most women of color is working for advancement of racial conditions.

> To me, the greatest obstacle for African-American women is color. It's simply color. I think when we're dealing with our own men that sexism is the factor involved. But when we're with white men and white women, it's race. So Black women cannot be empowered until we also end racial discrimination.[6]

Uniting with white women on issues of gender is often interpreted as dividing black women from their racial group and the problems that need to be addressed there.

> I just don't feel we can afford the luxury of splitting the Black community. Number one, our men are not in control of anything and that accounts for part of their behavioral problems, because they've been emasculated. So we know they have some problems handling that, but I still feel that that's what we have to work with, to unify our agenda. That's where I put my energies, not with some white women.[7]

In speaking of her long commitment to the National Association for the Advancement of Colored People (NAACP), Margaret Bush Wilson argues that "the problems of Black Americans are ones in which men and women are in jeopardy and our efforts must be geared for the good of both groups." Wilson believes so strongly on a united front that, even after executive director Benjamin Hooks reportedly called her "a bitch" during a board meeting, she was reluctant to admit that sexism was sometimes a problem in the NAACP.[8]

Black women have self-consciously and purposely engaged in struggles that empower "women and men to actualize a humanist vision of community" (Collins 1990: 39). This has been the case, even though the "masculinist perspective itself, concerning the manhood of the Black race, has always occupied center stage in the drama of Afro-American literature" (Hernton 1985: 5).

African American women have had to contend with defending themselves against the myth of black matriarchy (Marshall 1990) and the opposition African American men have expressed to black women about joining a movement that they see as working against men.

> [M]en quite effectively used the matriarchy issue to manipulate and coerce Black women into maintaining exclusive commitments to racial interests. . . . Black feminists Pauli Murray and Pauline Terrelonge Stone both agree that the debates over this issue became an ideological ploy to heighten guilt in Black women over their supposed collusion with Whites in the oppression of Black men. Consequently, these intraracial tensions worked against the public articulations of a feminist consciousness by most Black women. (King 1988: 55)

Similarly, Chicana feminists have been accused of creating ethnic division on the grounds that feminist ideology is Anglo inspired and undermining of the unity of the Chicano movement (Garcia 1989). Such accusations put pressure on women of color to resist working with white women and to refrain from confronting men of their race of sexist treatment towards them.

Although many women of color do not feel their racial and ethnic organizations have taken women seriously, they also do not feel that the women's movement has addressed their needs adequately. Welfare, public housing, tenants' rights, inner-city schools, poverty, drugs, racial rates of imprisonment, unemployment and underemployment are the kinds of issues women of color want the women's movement to work on. As Audre Lorde phrases it, "Black feminism is not White feminism in blackface. Black women have particular and legitimate issues which effect our lives as Black women" (1984: 60).

There is resistance by women of color to radical feminism's focus on the patriarchy as the cause of female oppression, because it denies the oppression of black males and it implies that all women suffer the same oppression (Lorde 1984). The insistence on the overriding importance of patriarchy means that the concept of sisterhood "places one's womanhood over and above one's race" (Dill 1983: 136). Women of color find themselves in a position of having to choose gender oppression over racial oppression, when they are oppressed on both levels. They ask what good it does to improve their status when their children's lives are being maimed?

> Some problems we share as women, some we do not. You fear your children will grow up to join the patriarchy and testify against you, we fear our children will be dragged from a car and shot down in the street and you will turn your backs upon the reasons they are dying. (Lorde 1984: 119)

A recognition of similarity exists among women of color which has led to many joining together to remind the women's movement that there are different versions of what feminism means based on differences in social condition (Hull, Scott, and Smith 1982; Moraga and Anzaldua 1983). Because they often feel like outsiders or tokens in white feminist organizations, separate organizations for women of color have been promoted. Self-definition and self-validation have been sought through working with others who have similar experiences to share (P. Collins 1986). In speaking for Asian American women, Ester Chow argues that "social bonding and group allegiance are much more readily established, and common issues are more easily shared on the basis of race and ethnicity" (1987: 293). Self-definition and organizing on one's own behalf are seen as a means to empowerment (Radford-Hill 1986), and being fully autonomous is believed to lead to the ability to deal with other kinds of people because a solid base of strength has been established (Smith 1983).

In conjunction with a desire to maintain separate organizations, women of color have also worked with white feminists to create more racially integrated feminist organizations. In this process white women have been confronted by women of color about racism within the movement. At the 1983 annual meeting of the National Women's Studies Association (NWSA), a plenary session titled "Racism and Anti-Semitism in the Women's Movement" spoke to this problem.

Addressing the cleavage between black and Jewish women over the way that anti-Semitism has been defined and of the role of Israel in the Middle East, Evelyn Torton Beck called for more understanding by admitting that "none of us is entirely free of the prejudices of the dominant cultures and subcultures in which we live. Even less comfortably, let us admit that this is equally true for those of us who are members of one or more oppressed minorities" (1983: 11). Barbara Smith also addressed this issue by asking women to examine systems of oppression throughout the world (not just as they manifest themselves within the women's movement) in order to understand the diversity of women's lives.

> [I]f we begin to deal with each other with some integrity and with some sense of the complexity of all of the horror, all of the pain, all of the violence that we hold within ourselves and that has been visited upon us by the systems of oppression under which we live, then I think there might be the beginning of some hope between us. (Smith 1983: 9)

In spite of these conciliatory words, the angry response from members of the audience at the close of this session revealed a high level of antagonism over issues of race and class. Throughout the 1980s, and into the present time, the charge of racism in the women's movement continues to be an emotionally difficult issue (Endor 1989).

Interactive effects of gender, class and race

White feminists have responded to women of color's anger in various ways. Minnie Bruce Pratt talks about her feelings and fears in addressing this issue.

> I get afraid when I am trying to understand myself in relation to folks different from me, when there are discussions, conflicts about anti-Semitism and racism among women, criticisms, criticisms of *me*; when, for instance, in a group discussion about race and class, I say I feel we have talked too much about race, not enough about class, and a woman of color asks me in anger and pain if I don't think her skin has something to do with class. (Pratt 1984: 73—emphasis in the original)

One response, then, has been a reluctance to speak out for fear of being called a racist. Another has been resistance to what is sometimes seen as conflating race and class issues.

Although there is a strong correlation between race and class position, class also cuts across racial lines. Class, like race, is fundamental to identity and life experience, and this is true even for women who are in a privileged status based on their skin color because opportunities available to people are largely determined by class location. Even though blacks are three times more likely to be living below the poverty line than whites, two-thirds of all poor people in the U.S. are white. Class, then, affects whites as well as people of color. White women who are working class known they are not additionally burdened by racial prejudice, yet they do not tend to think of themselves as privileged women in the same way that they see women of the middle and upper class. Thus, neglecting to look at class issues often leaves poor white women feeling alienated from women of color's demands.

However, class is complicated; it is much more than just how much money you make or what your class background is. Primarily, factors related to race and ethnicity create different levels of deprivation, even within the same class location. For instance, Luana Ross relates how being poor and treated as a "dumb Indian" created a different perspective for her than what is found in "mainstream poverty" in America (1989: 7). Racism and economic deprivation do not occur in a vacuum; the association between the two is connected to how one sees the world and how one is defined in that world. Or, as Rose Brewer describes it, the "political-economic base of race inequality is overlayed with ideological racism which is part of the consciousness of Whites in U.S. society" (1980: 222).

Wage gap figures which show only a slight difference in wages between white, black, and Hispanic women are sometimes interpreted to mean that there are only slight economic differences between women. Research has reported that in 1987, for every dollar white males earned, white women earned $0.63, black women, $0.61, and Hispanic women $0.55 (National Committee on Pay Equity 1988: 1). Figures such as these have been used to imply that black and white women's economic status are nearing parity since black women earn almost as much as white women in white-collar jobs and around 90 percent of what white women earn in blue-collar jobs (see Westcott 1982). But a crucial component of class within a gender and race analysis includes women's relationships with men, since women's economic position is interwoven with the economic status of the males they are connected to in their family of origin and, for heterosexual women, through adult attachments of marriage and cohabitation. As a group, whites are of a higher class level than other groups in society and, as a group, white women benefit economically from their attachments to white males more than women of color do from their attachments to men of their race/ethnic background. Thus, for there to be near equity in income distribution between women, there would need to be near equity in wages for black, Hispanic, Asian, Native American, and white males.

Taking the example of black and Hispanic males, unemployment figures show they have a higher unemployment rate and a lower rate of income than white males. Although the proportion of men who are employed has dropped during the last 20 years, this is even more marked for black men. From an 80 percent employment rate in the 1930s, the proportion of black males employed in 1983 fell to 56 percent (Wilson and Neckerman 1989: 518). In looking at the wages of those men who are employed, for every dollar white males earn black men earn $0.71 and Hispanic men earn $0.65 (National Committee on Pay Equity 1988: 1).

Sociologically we know that the lower the class position the less likely are men able to provide for families; thus, the higher the rate of never-married female-headed families and the greater the risk of divorce among the poor (Wilson and Neckerman 1989). Because people of color historically have been disproportionately located in the lower class and 99 percent of all marriages in the U.S. are within-class unions (R. Collins 1986: 115), women of color are more likely to be single heads of household and to have a greater risk of being among the poorest of the poor in the social stratification system (Mednick 1989). Placing an analysis of class location into a broader framework than wage figures alone demonstrates the interconnectedness between class, race, and gender as well as the unacknowledged economic relationship of the "heterosexual norm." Phyllis Marynick Palmer speculates that this association between class, race, gender relations, and sexual orientations may be one reason there is more interaction between black and white lesbian feminists than between heterosexual feminists (1983: 166). In other words, lesbians' economic position is not affected as much by the status of males, therefore, there is less reliance on men and greater identification with women.

Struggles with diversity

The question of racism within the women's movement continues to be a confrontational and emotional issue. Indeed, by the end of the post-ERA decade, harsh criticisms over the lack of involvement by women of color were still being voiced toward conference organizers attempting to address this issue. (See for instance Endor 1989—report on a Georgetown University conference on "Women in America: Legacies of Race and Ethnicity.")

Whereas the promotion of universal sisterhood in the 1970s downplayed racial and class oppression, the focus on difference in the 1980s heightened the potential for division among feminist women. For instance, "among feminists an accusation of racist-'n'-classist remains a surefire way to dismiss any concept, movement, or individual. It has the added attraction of working whether one gets one's facts straight or not" (Sturgis 1989: 19).

The response of white women has been to feel guilty, until finally some began saying, enough.

I have heard seminars for years and years, and heard programs for years and years, and worked on plans as to what to do about this problem. And I think we have been guilt tripped so much about this issue that I don't feel guilty anymore. I think that white middle class women have been guilt tripped so much their entire life from everybody around them, from the white male establishment, to the minority male establishment, to the religions, to minority women, to everything in the whole wide world, that it is just amazing to me that we are absolutely creeping and crawling on our hands and knees to try and get out from underneath all the guilt. And I think it's time to stop.[9]

Guilt is paralyzing and self-defeating. Rather than guilt, Robin Morgan suggests white women show respect to women of color by getting angry when that is what they are feeling. The expression of mutual anger can produce a working dialogue to resolve conflicting positions. At the same time, Morgan counsels the need to apply an historical perspective to present interactions.

Do we really expect people to be grateful for our finally doing what we should have been doing all along? The rage is enormous, and the rage will continue and will be expressed until it is spent, and until there is a working trust. What, then, does a white woman do if she's feeling very hurt? She feels hurt, and she lives through it, and she continues doing her work and she continues reaching out.[10]

It is instructive to note that it is the women's movement, not the pro-family movement, that has been called racist. Anti-feminist groups such as the now defunct Moral Majority or the Eagle Forum not only are dominated by white adherents, they also promulgate a racist, classist, and homophobic ideology in their opposition to child care, welfare, reproductive rights, sexual autonomy, affirmative action and racial integration. They are calling for a reduction in social programs and a return to the middle-class traditional family which has always been representative of the white majority ideal.

The charges of racism that have been directed at feminist groups are a reflection of the recognition that this is an arena where people will listen. Initially the women's movement did not take racism seriously into account, but criticism of that position has led the movement to reconsider this issue (Paley 1988). Women's caucuses of professional associations now routinely have panels and paper presentations focusing on the connections between race, gender, and class. Many organizations have minority scholarship funds to defray costs for women of color to attend conferences, and different methods have been tried to increase leadership positions for women of color. For example, in the late 1970s NOW instituted an affirmative action plan which resulted in 25 percent of NOW's national board consisting of women of color (National Organization for Women 1988).[11]

Still, white feminists' efforts have frequently been inadequate and, conversely, there has often been little recognition of the efforts that were made to integrate 1980s' feminism into a movement confronting issues of race. Concern with the latter was expressed by Barbara Smith when she criticized bell hooks' book *Ain't I A Woman: Black Women and Feminism* (1981) for failing to acknowledge "that there are parts of the women's movement, especially in the last five years, that define taking responsibility for racism as a top priority" (Smith 1982: 4).

When white feminists ignore racial charges and when women of color dismiss efforts to resolve racial divisiveness, both groups lose. The case of the near destruction of the National Women's Studies Association (NWSA) illustrates this point. In the desire to address race and class concerns "NWSA set up a system that gave members of minority constituencies greater than proportional power" by allowing caucuses extra delegate voting power "based not on the numbers of their members but on whether or not they represented a group that is oppressed in the larger society" (Leidner 1991: 284). This structural component of the organization resulted in increased, and even more emotionally laden, confrontations. Eventually, white heterosexual academic women came to feel that their own needs were not being met and that they were being unfairly attacked because lesbian and women of color caucuses used "their extra power, as well as the moral force of the majority's guilt, to ensure that their wishes override all others" (ibid.: 286). At the 1990 conference a black staff member who had been fired by NWSA took her case to the Women of Color Caucus. Caucus members walked out of the conference after their demand for the firing of NWSA's executive director was refused. The hostility engendered during and after this conference led to the resignation of the entire national office staff and the cancelation of the 1991 conference (off our backs 1991: 6).

The NWSA experience provides a distressing example of the difficulties the women's movement confronts in attempting to overcome group differences by establishing a framework to equalize power for minority members. Although this experiment failed to achieve equal group satisfaction, the women's movement continues to be involved in addressing class and race divisions; and, in spite of the fact that "Black folks have been angry with White folks for nearly 400 years," women of color are still willing to deal with them (Gillespie 1987: 19). The reality is that both white feminists and feminists of color consider the women's movement to hold the promise of creating change on race, class, and gender issues.

BEYOND THE WOMEN'S MOVEMENT

Including the diversity of women into feminist analysis and activist commitments is a fundamental goal of the women's movement today. Indeed, inclusive feminism has become the new feminist catchword. Yet, parallel to that imperative there has been a call for the movement to become less involved with women and more involved with issues such as nuclear proliferation, war, and environmental destruction. Moreover, women in other countries are calling on U.S. feminists to actively oppose oppressive U.S. policies in their countries. For instance, Azizah al-Hibri chides the women's movement for spending time defining Arab women's issues as veils and clitoridectomies, when for women in Lebanon the major issue is survival:

> How much horror should we undergo before you demand that your war machine come to a halt? You are arming both sides in the Middle East with deadly weapons . . . The women's movement in this country has a moral duty to speak out publicly on these issues, to organize and educate . . . I am your sister. My country is under occupation. What are you going to do about it? (al-Hibri 1983: 11)

Confrontations by diverse groups of women have broadened feminist analysis and challenged the movement into a more inclusive strategy of change. These divisions, though, have raised the question of whether feminism can work to eliminate broad-ranging forms of exploitation, such as racism, classism, war, and environmental destruction without losing its gender focus. These are feminist issues—still, as Eleanor Smeal says, "if we don't make women the number one issue, our issue, who will? I'll tell you who, nobody." [12]

Where to put energy and money, what issues to focus on, and how to make this a movement for all women continues to present activists with difficult questions to resolve. Various confrontations over the years have raised the question of whether feminism can understand the differences between women without losing its common political purpose. What has become increasingly clear is that the elimination of discriminatory attitudes and practices within the women's movement, while essential, is not enough. Class and race are structural components of social stratification systems—as is gender. Feminists are faced with the task of eliminating class, race, and gender inequalities by challenging a social system specifically designed to maintain such divisions.

Fears expressed by anti-feminist women—what that indicates about the entrenched position of sex/gender relations—and the continuing divisiveness over differences among women, helps explain why it is so difficult for feminists to unify to achieve change. Ironically, the women's movement faces greater challenges today than it realized existed in the past.

Historically, social thinkers who have envisioned a more just and humane world have spoken of, even if not acted upon, the need for a solution to "the woman question." In the 1800s the French philosopher Fourier argued that "in any given society the degree of woman's emancipation is the natural measure of the general emancipation" (Engels 1935 9:39). Going beyond seeing women as the measure of a society's level of repression, feminism is built upon a belief that there can be no egalitarian society, or peace among people, as long as women are removed from participation in defining the social order. The empowerment of women is fundamental because, as Robin Morgan states, we now know what our opposition probably always knew: that the feminist goal is not only "to change drastically our own powerless status worldwide, but to redefine all existing societal structures and modes of existence" (1984: 3).

Chapter 9

The Search for A New Mobilizing Issue: The Women's Movement after the ERA

> First, old women are devalued and marginalized. "Old" then moves from 60 down to 50, and then women begin to grow uneasy at 40 and 30. . . . Now we are seeing a kind of "child worship," as politicians tell us that what's happening in our lives as adult women now isn't important: what's important is that "the children are our future." When this kind of belief in discarding the old for the new is pushed along the continuum to the ultimate, we have "fetus worship." And when the fetus is more important than the woman who carries it, feminism is in deep trouble.
>
> (Barbara Macdonald, 1990: 58)[1]

The Women's Movement is dead. So trumpeted the media after the ERA fell three states short of ratification and the U.S. House of Representatives failed to pass a new Equal Rights Amendment in 1982 and again in 1983. The movement had become so connected with the ERA that the press and general public saw that defeat as the end of women's activism. Declaring the movement dead is more wishful thinking than reality; however, such declarations have occurred with historical regularity everywhere feminist movements have arisen. For instance, French feminists read of their demise beginning as early as 1974. After a 1981 cover story "Where have the Feminists Gone?" as well as responding to feminists' own concerns about reduced numbers, Simone de Beauvoir wrote that the movement was alive and well, but in constant danger (1984).

In the United States, reports of the demise of the women's movement began after passage of the 19th Amendment giving women the vote. Because the concerted efforts of large numbers of activists ended in 1920, the general consensus has been that the attainment of suffrage marked the end of this movement and that another movement, the contemporary women's movement, arose in the turmoil of the 1960s. However, recent scholarship has provided us with new knowledge of the women's movement which shows it to be one long movement beginning in 1848 and lasting into the present time, with varying levels of activism in different periods (Taylor 1989). Although lacking a mass movement component, the years from 1920 to the mid-1960s, previously characterized as bereft of women's rights activism, were, in fact, years of continuous and diverse efforts for women's advance (Cott 1987; Rupp and Taylor 1987).

Throughout the 1970s feminist activists scoffed at periodical media predictions of their decline. They were, instead, busy witnessing rising levels of activism and support. Nonetheless, there was concern when even sympathetic journalists began to term the 1980s the Post-Feminist Decade (see Bolotin 1982; Ehrenreich 1987; Goodman 1989). These journalists were responding to the fact that in a ten-year period the women's movement had gone from a state of achieving notable success to bitter defeat. But, when you look at the actors in this social drama, it becomes clear that it was not the women's movement that became "post-feminist," it was the social environment that had become openly hostile to further gains for women. As just one indicator of a changed social environment, it is interesting to note that in 1982 the ERA could not pass a Democratically controlled House even though ten years earlier it had passed the House by a vote of 354 to 23 and the Senate by 84 to 8.

If the movement is not dead, then how is it doing? There is no doubt that feminism has had an impact on American society, but there is bittersweet humor in Nicole Hollander's cartoon caption "If you can't read the fine print, you must be a feminist" (Hollander 1989). In a more serious vein, journalists and feminists alike have good reason to question how it can be that "words like sexism, sex object, and exploitation sound vaguely archaic. . . . [when] what's happened to women is not all that clear" (Goodman 1989: A11).

POST-ERA: DIVERGING PATHS
OF MOVEMENT SECTORS

Even as the general public's support of ERA went up after 1982, the amendment's defeat let to a decline in feminist social movement involvement and, as discussed in the last chapter, a rise in intra-movement divisiveness over issues related to pornography, sexuality, class and race. Moreover, the mass movement and direct action groups that had been active in the ERA Campaign were no longer aligned through working on the same issue. Indeed, each sector took a different direction after the amendment's defeat.

The small group sector and life space fulfillment

For those activists from the small group sector who had been involved in direct
action tactics for the ERA, the period after that campaign was a time of redirect-
ing their involvement or dropping out of activism all together. In 1983 a coalition of women involved in direct action protest formed Women Rising in Resistance to continue implementing alternative strategies for change, but after a
few years even this group began to fade. The same organizational and interactional dynamics that undermined the continuance of the small group sector in
the organizing years of the contemporary movement also affected the outcome
of small groups in the 1980s. Once again, an informal decentralized structure,
while encouraging tactical innovation, tended not to foster the necessary conditions for organizational maintenance (Freeman 1975, 1979; Staggenborg 1989).

Eventually many of these activists became involved, or re-involved, in issues
connected to male violence such as battered women's shelters, rape crisis centers, anti-pornography groups, environmental issues, and the peace movement.
A direction that became more pronounced during the 1980s was the quest for
change from within. Having grown tired of trying to win women's rights from
public officials, segments of the small group sector and the women's culture
engaged in a spirituality search.[2]

A growing interest throughout the 1980s in feminist spirituality, non-violence,
a reverence for nature and womanist values led to the involvement of radical
cultural feminists, anarcho-feminists, and ecofeminists in the prevention of violence to the earth and the earth's people. For instance, the Women's Pentagon
Actions in the early 1980s and the Mother's Day Action at the Nevada Test Site
in 1987 are representative direct action strategies around issues of peace and
nuclear disarmament (Epstein 1988; Van Gelder 1989).

After the decline of the small group sector in the mid-1970s, the rise of radical
cultural feminism often took adherents into causes not usually thought to be
specifically feminist. Questions from within the movement were raised about the
ecological movement and the peace movement draining energy from women's
issues. Feminist activities involved with peace and environmental causes counter
that these are feminist issues because "patriarchy, the domination of women by
men, has been associated with the attempt to dominate nature" and "the despo-
liation of the environment, violence, and militarism are rooted in the culture of
domination" (Epstein 1988: 32).

Because destruction of the environment, war, and militarism are seen as directly flowing from masculinist values, the women's spirituality movement sees
itself as a countervailing force since it is committed to womanist values. Premised on the development of pride in one's group as a source of empowerment,
Goddess worship and the symbols that are attached to it represent female connections to creation and the life force (Stein 1987). Women's spirituality practices have had appeal because they provide adherents with a feeling of having

control over their life. Rather than praying to a higher order to take care of them, Wicca, paganism, and Native American Indian practice are opposed to hierarchy, repression, and dogma, and thus, provide a source of strength and motivation by putting women in touch with the "powerful woman within."

Still, questions continue to be raised about the increasing isolationism of women's spirituality, especially in connection to the New Age movement. New Age is a broad label for spirituality practices that may incorporate feminist principles, such as Wicca and paganism, or may simply be the incorporation of egalitarian ideals into traditional religions. It is an alternative spiritual journey which includes beliefs in reincarnation, astrology, tarot cards, magical practices, crystals, channeling, the power of rituals, self-healing, controlling one's fate, and the need to develop good karma.

In a critique of "Prepackaged Spiritualism" Anjela Johnson calls this trend a self-centered escape which drains feminist energy from activism for social change for women as a group (1988). Followers of women's spirituality practices respond that feminists already "have a well-established tradition of pouring our energies into political movements that put women's issues third, tenth, or nowhere on the agenda" and that the drain of energy from the women's movement predates the rise of New Age spirituality (Sturgis 1989: 17). Rather than drain activism from feminism, adherents argue that spiritual empowerment provides them with a stronger base to continue work in the social arena since "we need religions that don't quarrel too bitterly with our lifestyles and our politics. What could be better than a religion that visualizes god as a woman, that focuses on the goddess within" (Yates 1989: 19).

An example of the incorporation of women's spirituality with social change efforts was the Seneca Women's Peace Encampment.[3] Begun in the Summer of 1983, the camp, located in Romules, New York, provided a base for protesting U.S. nuclear policies through non-violent direct actions and civil disobedience. The Peace Encampment provided a home and occasional resting place for many feminist activists, particularly separatists lesbian feminists. The Seneca Camp followed the model of the Greenham Common Women's Peace Camp which arose out of protests against the siting of Cruise missiles at a U.S. airbase located in Greenham Common, England. Greenham women created a women's space formulated around the ideal of an egalitarian collectivity. Symbolizing women's resistance to militarism and masculinist violence, a permanant camp was established in August 1981 (Segal 1988).

Both the Seneca and Greenham peace camps created an environment which utilized women's spirituality beliefs, witchcraft, healers, psychics, and herbalists along with non-violent direct action challenges to government policy. One Seneca woman describes how this experience enriched and empowered her life:

> Through this work I've learned and keep on learning that our greatest power lies within us. Learning to be powerful means unlearning the patriarchy's terms of

strength, peace, loyalty, and love. Watching the process whereby a handful of wimin take on the US government, and seeing the lengths to which the government will go to silence us has done wonders for my self-esteem. (Blue 1989)

Much of the direct action tactics in the women's movement has come from lesbian cultural feminists who see themselves as the radical element of the activist movement. Yet, by the mid-1980s, as feminist direct action declined and the AIDS crises grew, many lesbians became involved in providing services and support within the gay community for AIDS victims. Although these actions were admirable and succeeded in creating a closer alliance between gays and lesbians, Jackie Winnow questions the practice of lesbian activists putting their energy into providing services for men.

Winnow notes that lesbians have always been in the vanguard of the women's movement, and "without us there would be no rape crisis centers, no women's foundations or buildings, no awareness of domestic violence, no women's music festivals or women's radio programming" (1989: 11). She wonders what will happen to the women's community if lesbians stop working for women. As a victim of breast cancer, Winnow additionally wonders why the same kind of support services offered for victims of AIDS do not exist for people like herself who have other life-threatening diseases. She asks lesbians not to forget that they are women, and that women are raised to be care givers and to regard their needs as less important than men's.

No one takes care of women or lesbians except women or lesbians, and we have a hard time taking care of ourselves, of finding ourselves worthy and important enough to pay attention to. (Winnow 1989: 12)

Sonia Johnson also questions lesbian investment in AIDS work and fears that, like abolition, the peace movement, and Central American politics, these forms of activism sidetrack women into fighting men's battles. She argues that, if women do not take themselves seriously, no one else will either, and "the world can no longer survive women's not having a foremost place on it, and in it, and in our hearts" (1989: 189). Johnson further supports her position by citing the fact that, while 24,000 men died from AIDS between 1985 and 1988, in that same time period over 30,000 women were murdered by men and the gay community did not pour their efforts into ending violence inflicted on women (1989: 189–91).

Johnson is concerned about what happens when women put their energy into causes with men and she is suspicious of New Age teaching and practices. She considers the "New Age Movement" to be a "repository of pseudo-female Eastern thought" in which "one look at women's status and experience in the East should instantly warn us not to import indiscriminately the misogynist messages of Eastern philosophies and religions" (Johnson 1989: 199, 116). Johnson cautions against religious and spiritual escapism; yet, at the same time, she is a well-known advocate of "internal revolution" through disengagement from patriarchal life.

Johnson's leadership in organizing civil disobedience and a fast for the Equal Rights Amendment led her to develop a model for other direct action tactics that were implemented during that period.[4] At that time she felt women's involvement in civil disobedience extinguished their fear, fostered their courage, and illuminated their potential for creating social change. Johnson gained many supporters with her unorthodox methods, but she also found segments of the women's movement opposed, and at times hostile, to her efforts. This negative response led her to feel that, until women rid themselves of patriarchal influence in their lives, they would not be in a position to rid the world of patriarchy in the social system (Johnson 1987).

By the latter part of the 1980s, Johnson transformed the call for developing inner strength in order to change the system to a call for women to develop inner strength by disengaging "psychically and emotionally from patriarchy and all its institutions" (1989: i). Premised on the understanding that the means are the ends, she has argued that by changing our perspective we change reality and it is only then that we can change our way of being in the world. In re-evaluating her earlier activism, she now considers feminist protest to have led to greater levels of misogyny. For instance, she argues that marching and lobbying for the right to choose whether or not we will have children acknowledges that "men own us" (Johnson 1989: 23). Thus, "our participation in a corrupt system facilitates it and corrupts and therefore defeats us" (Johnson 1989: i).

In answer to the question, "What shall we do?" Johnson answers that the question should be 'How shall we be?" With the same knowledge that battered women must leave their husbands, Johnson calls for women to acknowledge the need to leave the patriarchal world we live in. In her own life she no longer reads newspapers or listens to the "old" news on television and radio. Nor does she vote, because voting in a patriarchal world is voting for a system "which is based on the hatred of women" (Johnson 1989: 42). In the end, Johnson advocates a separatist strategy of living the revolution through the creation of women's communities where women can lead their lives in self-affirming ways.

The mass movement sector and party politics

Johnson's "utopian" community has been criticized by other feminists as offering a solution available mainly to political lesbians. Further, her uncompromising patriarchal-dominance analysis is seen as a denial of the debasement of men who do not fit into the ideal of white-middle-class-heterosexual masculinity (*off our backs* 1988). Nevertheless, she is a popular speaker because she inspires women to feel pride in themselves.

Appealing as a "disengage" policy is to politically disillusioned feminists, most activists feel internal revolution does nothing to change the world for those who most need the world changed but are the least capable of doing it. In addressing the issue of inequities in the social system, the question becomes "How can we go about creating change on the structural level?" The mass movement sector of the women's movement has defined its role as changing the structural conditions of an unequal system so that change can be effected in individual lives. To this end, laws and public policy issues such as parental leave, child care, child support, affirmative action, and social security were pursued during the 1980s by feminist groups and traditional women's organizations such as the League of Women Voters (LWV), Business and Professional Women (BPW), the American Association of University Women (AAUW), Women's Equity Action League (WEAL), and the National Women's Health Network (Hartmann 1989).

While promoting a broad range of issues in coalition with other women's groups, NOW continued to call for efforts to reintroduce the ERA (Gardner 1988; Schmich 1988). Continued promotion of ERA was not, however, universally supported by NOW members. At the 1985 national convention, a contested election centered on the future direction of the organization, particularly whether or not to reassert ERA as a priority commitment. Those opposed to reviving ERA considered it "futile to run a race, engage in an issues battle or take up a cause to prove a point when you can not necessarily win anything concrete."[5] Judy Goldsmith, running for re-election as president, considered ERA an exercise in futility and campaigned instead for a multi-issue strategy and a multi-tactic program with less emphasis on marches and demonstrations. According to Goldsmith, "the challenge we face is not to speak louder, but to communicate more effectively."[6]

Eleanor Smeal, who had been NOW president for most of the ERA campaign and who had previously supported Goldsmith, also ran for the presidency. She argued for continued pressure for ERA even when there was no chance of passage because of the organizing advantages such a unifying issue provides.

Contrary to what some say, the ERA doesn't *take* strength from the Women's Movement, it *adds* to it. We can use it to continue to build our political clout . . . Throughout the recent fight for ratification, the ERA was a major recruiter and consciousness-raiser. (Smeal 1987: 218)

Smeal considered the move away from ERA to have been instrumental in declining membership numbers and monetary contributions. To counter this trend, she called for an all-out effort on abortion rights, citing Goldsmith's failure to organize a major march that year in celebration of the January 22 Supreme Court decision legalizing abortion. Defending her emphasis on marches she stated: "It's not that I believe marches alone do the job, but once in a while you have to march for what you believe in."[7]

In her campaign speech, Smeal made it clear that she was interested in pur-

suing whatever worked best for mobilizing efforts "to continue building the largest and strongest organization it was possible to build." She argued against keeping ERA on a "back-burner" while waiting for a more opportune moment,
because such a strategy runs the risk of allowing the amendment to leave public
consciousness. This kind of delay only means having "to start educating a whole
new generation of people, because nothing ever waits for you—you have to keep
it alive." In answer to the question of how money would be raised to run a new
campaign, she answered, "action begets money and money begets action. Do
you think those marches are fund losers? They're fund raisers."[8]

Concurring in this analysis, the vice-presidential candidate on Smeal's slate
spoke to the organizational benefits a symbolic and emotional issue contained:

> It is no accident that NOW reached its zenith in membership and money and visi-
> bility between 1978–1982, the height of the ERA campaign. . . . We captured the
> imagination of this nation and we can recapture the momentum of those years.[9]

Smeal won the election by touching activist desires to re-live the excitement
that had been lost after ERA was no longer a galvanizing issue. During Goldsmith's tenure new issues had been attempted, such as gender discriminatory
insurance rates, but they had not caught the imagination of the membership nor
had they been successful in mobilizing new recruits. The ERA, however, was
also not able to revive flagging interest in feminist activism. When those efforts
floundered, NOW went further into political organizing, a strategy rationalized
as the need to elect candidates to office who support their views, rather than
continuing to petition reticent legislators on the importance of feminist issues.
In this process NOW became strongly identified with the Democratic Party.

The merging of feminist activism with Democratic Party politics is analyzed
by Jo Freeman, who sees this process as part of a 20-year transformation in
Republican and Democratic Party alignment.[10] According to Freeman, the political change process differed for the two parties because of distinct political cultures, particularly in relationship to organizational structure and self-perceptions
of members. Structurally, power in the Republican Party operates in a top-down
fashion, while for the Democratic Party power flows upward. This differing
power flow means that the Democratic Party is a more pluralistic party where
special interest groups count. Attitudinally, Republicans view themselves as in-
siders even when they are out of power, whereas Democrats perceive themselves
as outsiders even when they are in power. This means that other "outsider"
groups feel more comfortable in the Democratic Party than in the Republican
Party (Freeman 1987).

Realignment in party constituency began when the civil rights movement attempted political integration. Protests over representation along racial lines, initially through the Mississippi Freedom Party's challenge to delegate selection

practices, eventually led to a quota system, which changed representation in the Democratic Party from a geographically-based coalition to demographic coalitions. Later, in the 1970s, NOW and the National Women's Political Caucus (NWPC) succeeded in getting sex included in the criteria for delegate selection. The percent of delegate representation for women went from 13 percent in 1968 to 40 percent in 1972, and by the early 1980s women were recognized as an important constituency in the Democratic Party. Subsequently, in both 1984 and 1988 NWPC and NOW members were influential voices in formulating the party platform and in getting a woman vice-presidential candidate in the 1984 race. The Republican Party, on the other hand, was never open to such challenges. Party membership is less demographically representative and party leaders have been less constrained in taking anti-feminist positions on women's issues. The gender gap in voting behavior, with women 8 percent more likely than men to vote for Democratic candidates, is a reflection of party differences in relationship to women's issues (Freeman 1987, 1988).

Even though the Democratic Party was more receptive to women's issues than it had been in the past, moving into the political arena to the extent that NOW did left some members feeling disillusioned with feminist activism. At the 1987 NOW conference, a New York faction, Progressive Action Caucus (PAC), ran against a Smeal-picked slate, United Feminist Action Campaign (UFAC).[11] Molly Yard, the political director of NOW and a former labor activist, ran for president on the UFAC slate with the slogan "The Feminization of Power."

Symbolizing the change from earlier references to women's economic powerlessness found in the slogan "feminization of poverty," the call now was for women to take power by running for office. Reminiscent of the 59 cent button worn during the ERA campaign to highlight the gap in earnings between women and men, the new symbol became a 5 percent button representing the percent of legislators in Congress who are women.[12] To bolster the political importance of NOW's involvement in politics, Congresswoman Patricia Schroeder appeared before the conference speaking about her possible U.S. presidential candidacy in the forthcoming election.[13]

In terms of broad issues, both slates were in favor of getting ERA going again, hitting the streets, and doing political work. In spite of PAC's contention that there were clear differences between the two slates, there were no substantial disagreements on specific issues. The difference between the two groups was more related to who should lead rather than to the direction the organization should be going in. The most vocal argument consisted of PAC supporters calling the entrenched administration a "dictatorship run with poor management."[14] Similarities exist to the hostilities of the election of 1975, but, compared with the harsh words used a decade earlier, this contest was relatively mild. And in this case, it was the prevailing leadership, represented by candidates from UFAC, that won all of the national offices.

Focusing on the political arena is a social movement strategy which may (or may not) lead to a desired outcome. But as a resource mobilization tactic, political engagement itself does not automatically lead to greater levels of movement mobilization unless there is an issue which activates large numbers of supporters. For most people, political activism requires a compelling issue. Thus, even as NOW became heavily involved in the Democratic Party, it continued to use other tactics to achieve its goals, including organizing a women of color conference, a lesbian issues conference, coalition work on multiple social equity issues, and co-sponsoring demonstrations such as the 1987 National Gay and Lesbian Rights March in Washington, D.C.[15] Eleanor Smeal founded the Fund for the Feminist Majority and extended the "Feminization of Power" campaign to a speaking tour of college campuses. NOW members picketed outside the South African Embassy and the Vatican Embassy, which resulted in arrests of NOW officers in both incidents (Associated Press 1987). In all of these actions NOW was looking for an issue to replace the ERA, another issue that could draw in scores of new activists and contributions.

THE RISE OF A NEW MOBILIZING ISSUE

In the Spring of 1989 the issue which had the possibility of accomplishing this task burst into the limelight when the U.S. Supreme Court agreed to review abortion legality once again.

Reproductive freedom is not a new issue. Abortion has been under siege for years, particularly after opponents took the lead with their all-out effort to affect the American public through well-publicized direct action tactics. NOW and other mass movement groups consistently supported abortion rights but, with the exception of single-issue abortion rights groups, they had not made it their number one priority in the way they had the ERA.

Abortion opponents, on the other hand, had instituted a single-issue voting strategy and had progressed throughout the 1980s from picketing to bombing to mass civil disobedience actions. By blocking access at clinics they engaged in acts of harassment and intimidation, with hundreds of protesters being arrested weekly. Indeed, their actions made a mockery of the much smaller and less publicized civil disobedience efforts on behalf of ERA. The numbers were astounding, with arrest estimates running as high as 300,000 from the Spring of 1988 to the Summer of 1989 alone (Green 1989); in 1991 a prolonged campaign in Wichita, KS led to over 2,000 arrests (Goodman 1991; Terry 1991). Although NOW, Planned Parenthood, National Abortion Rights Action League (NARAL), Committee for Abortion Rights and Against Sterilization Abuse (CARASA) and other abortion rights groups continued educational efforts, litigation battles, and escorting clients into clinics, they had not been able to influence voters (and thus politicians) with the media attention the anti-abortion activists achieved with the "terrorist tactics" instituted under Operation Rescue.

The realization that the Supreme Court might use a Missouri case, *Webster* v. *Reproductive Health Services,* to amend or even reverse its 1973 *Roe* v. *Wade* decision legalizing abortion sounded an alarm through activist circles and, more importantly, raised concern among abortion rights supporters outside of movement involvement. NOW had planned a march in Washington, D.C. for "Women's Equality, Women's Lives" to support ERA and abortion rights. Organizers began to emphasize abortion over ERA and sparked a huge response.

On April 9, 1989, between 300,000 and 600,000 people participated in one of the largest marches ever held in the nation's capital, and the largest demonstration for women's rights in the history of the women's movement.[16] Those in attendance represented every demographic category, from senior citizen to toddler, "mothers and daughters, self-described aging hippies and politically emerging college students, Hollywood stars and young professionals" (Toner 1989a). Over 60 organizations endorsed the march, including numerous trade unions and such diverse groups as "the Association of Women Psychiatrists to the B'nai B'rith International, the Ithaca Lesbian and Gay Task Force of New York to the Martin Luther King Jr. Center for Nonviolent Social Change in Atlanta" (Toner 1989b).

A New York Times/CBS News poll taken at the time showed 49 percent of respondents backed continued abortion legality, 39 percent wanted some restriction, and only 9 percent were in favor of a total ban. Broken down by age they found younger people more in favor of keeping abortion legal than older people (Dionne 1989). Indeed, a large number of college campuses had served as organizing points for the hundreds of busloads of student marchers. In reacting to the overwhelming response from college campuses, pro-choice activists predicted "a breakthrough in campus organizing on women's issues" and "a new era for solidarity among women" (Simpson 1989).

Reports from participants spoke to the excitement the march produced and the possibilities for the future it indicated.

[A]fter this march, there can be no doubt who's in the mainstream on this issue. . . . It was a tolerant march, welcoming to difference. . . . It was a united march, with no separate agendas for once . . . April 9 demonstrated that the strength of the women's movement is still growing and is largely untapped. (Tax 1989: 632–3)

Within weeks after the march, pro-choice groups engaged in counter-protests at abortion clinics, leading to the arrests of both abortion rights and anti-abortion activists in some instances (Lyman 1989; Valentine 1989). Seventy-eight "friend-of-the-court" briefs, a record number, were filed related to the Missouri litigation. Every day the Supreme Court sat in session there were abortion rights and anti-abortion supporters picketing the building; a new switchboard had to be activated to handle the volume of calls. Reports from administrative officials at the Supreme Court and congressional offices revealed the impending abortion ruling to be engendering more mail than any case of the 1980s (Carelli 1989).

On July 3, 1989 the Supreme Court ruled to uphold sections of Webster, including a bar on the use of public hospitals to perform abortions. The decision did not de-legalize abortion, but it was a setback for reproductive rights because it invited state legislators to restrict abortion availability in their localities, and it indicated a chipping away at reproductive rights which could eventually result in a reversal of *Roe* v. *Wade*.

The Webster decision allowed restricted access to abortion availability, but at the same time it further activated supporters to become involved in this issue. By October NOW announced there were 250,000 members ready to begin a "freedom caravan,"[17] a membership number up from the previous year when NOW's bi-monthly newspaper circulation was listed as 150,000. In June, the National Abortion Rights Action League (NARAL) reported their membership had increased to 300,000 and that they had raised $1 million by May of 1989 compared with $300,000 the year before; by October NARAL was reporting a membership of 350,000.[18] Both organizations expressed expectations that this response was just the beginning of a massive mobilization effort. NOW president Molly Yard told the press the phone was "ringing off the hook" with people who were calling and asking one question: "Tell me how to join" (cited in Yost 1989).

Although abortion rights continued to be a strongly felt feminist issue after the 1973 Roe decision, Kate Michelman, executive director of NARAL, considers the previous lack of mass activism to be related to the difficulty of arousing people "to work on behalf of something you already have" (cited in Purdy 1989: A10). Thus, with the Webster decision, abortion supporters became more active in the women's movement. It is not surprising, then, to note that there are similarities between reproductive rights and the Equal Rights Amendment. For instance, the lawyer for the Missouri case contends that, in general, how one feels about abortion is in line with how one feels about women.

> It's no coincidence that the denominations that are most vocally anti-choice—Catholics, Mormons, fundamentalists, Orthodox Jews—are those in which women have subordinate roles, and it's also no coincidence that Missouri ranks last among states in the number of women appointed to cabinet-level state government posts. (Susman, cited in Cassel 1989: 8).

Another link between ERA and abortion is found in Kristin Luker's 1984 study of pro-choice and pro-life activists, which reveals similar worldviews that had previously been found in pro or anti ERA positions. Luker reasons that the reason abortion raises so much passion is because it is a referendum on the place of motherhood, and thus the meaning of women's lives. For activist women involved in this issue, abortion is a conflict between two different social worlds in which women's reproductive role can be seen as either a resource or a handicap. Compared with pro-choice women, those women who are opposed to abortion have smaller family incomes, are more likely to be full-time homemakers, have less education, more children, and are strongly affiliated with religion. In sum, Luker finds the two groups of activists to hold different definitions of motherhood which rest on beliefs and values "rooted in the concrete circumstances" of their lives (1989: 551). What Luker and others have determined in their research on recent social movement activism is an involvement premised on "lifestyle politics." In this perspective, participation is based on a belief in how things should be, and that belief is associated with the choices one has made in their own life (Leahy, Snow, and Worden 1983; Liebman and Wuthnow 1983; Staggenborg 1987).[19]

Also examining the social meaning of motherhood is Barbara Katz Rothman, who views it through a patriarchal kinship lens. In patriarchal kinship systems she finds "children are reckoned as being born to men, out of women. Women, in this system, bear the children of men" (1989: 90). Under Rothman's analysis, the bearing of children against one's own desires leads to forced pregnancy, and forced pregnancy is required when children are seen as belonging to someone other than the person who is pregnant.

Fathers' rights groups such as the National Congress for Men validate Rothman's analysis with their view that abortion is taking away something that belongs to them. Throughout the 1980s, fathers' rights groups increased their visibility as they became involved in child custody litigation and attempts to prevent abortions of wives and girlfriends. The position fathers' rights groups have taken is that a man's rights "flow from the conception of his child" and men are entitled to a voice in the abortion decision. As one litigant phrased it: "A part of me was thrown away. My wife's rights and my own should have been considered equally" (cited in Weiss 1989: 277).

In 1976 the Supreme Court ruled in *Planned Parenthood* v. *Danforth* that a provision requiring consent of a husband "was unconstitutional on the grounds that the statute essentially gave the husband the ability to exercise an absolute veto in the abortion decision" (Plutzer and Ryan 1987: 183). Since that time cases for spousal notification (rather than consent) have been brought to the courts. In over 90 percent of abortion cases, men are involved in a mutually agreed abortion decision; however, research has shown that disharmony results between couples who do not agree (Shostak and McLouth 1984). In the majority of cases where married women do not tell their husbands, it is because the marriage is already dissolving, the husband is not the co-conceiver, the wife reports her husband would make her continue the pregnancy or she fears for her physical/emotional wellbeing if her husband knew of her decision (Ryan and Plutzer 1989). Requiring a woman to tell her spouse, then, could result in wives being forced to continue a pregnancy they do not want or place them and their marriage at risk when they make a choice their husband does not like.

Spousal and paternal consent demands are based on the belief that genetic connection overrides other social considerations. In this framework, men have the same rights to children as women based on their contribution to the fertilization process. This emphasis on the importance of "seed" is also found in disputes that have arisen over surrogate mothering cases. Rothman (1989) maintains that it is because men cannot bear children, and do not usually raise them, that they need to control women and reproduction in order to maintain male dominance. Thus, from a feminist perspective, underlying opposition to birth control and abortion is the control of women's sexuality and reproductive functioning, which corresponds to the control of women in other countries through practices of purdah, clitorondectomy, infibulation and polygyny.

The future of abortion as a mobilizing issue

Whether reproductive freedom will fan feminist activism as long or as powerfully as ERA remains to be seen. Unprecedented numbers of participants have taken part in marches and demonstrations in favor of abortion rights around the country (Scanlan 1989). It does appear, as Faye Wattleton of Planned Parenthood declares, that the "Supreme Court has created such an enormous backlash of anger and resentment, real rage, that people who have never come out on this issue are now coming out" (cited in Gillespie 1989: 55). Since Webster the political landscape has already been altered as state-level candidates are being forced to face-off on their position on abortion. Signs of change can be seen by the 1989 U.S. House of Representatives vote to allow federally funded abortions for victims of rape and incest, a reversal of its position the year before (Phillips 1989).[20]

Voting results and exit polls in the November 1989 election show abortion rights was an important political issue in candidate victories. Candidates' position on abortion particularly stood out in two gubernatorial races (New Jersey and Virginia) and the New York City mayoral race. In each case a Democrat who openly supported a pro-choice position won the election. The victory by Jim Florio in New Jersey showed a reversal from a Republican to a Democratic sweep when he won 18 out of 21 counties, the same number of counties won by George Bush the year before (Paolantonio 1989). The day after the election President Bush claimed that abortion was not an overriding issue for voters (Warren 1989), but newspapers began reporting Republican politicians requesting both Bush and the Republican National Committee to ease the party's abortion stance (LeDuc 1989).

As the press touted the advantage a pro-choice position gave candidates, the Democratic Party began to claim this position as its own. Republican political consultant Roger Ailes cynically observed that "The Democrats, after 20 years of not having an issue, came up with one that works" (quoted in Eichel 1989). The 1989 election indicates a turning point in the political battle over reproductive rights, since in the past Democrats and Republicans have divided in "roughly the same proportions on questions regarding abortion" (Boldt 1989). Indeed, the division among Democrats over the issue of abortion was a primary reason the National Organization for Women called for the formation of a third party, a woman's party, at its convention the summer before the November election.

In less than a year the political fate of both politicians and feminist organizing changed. Initial indicators pointed to advance for the pro-choice side of the abortion debate as legislators worried about voters' reaction. Yet, as ERA revealed, opinion poll results are not always indicative of legislative outcome. Thus, in the post-Webster era, the territory of Guam and legislators in the state of Idaho passed restrictive abortion legislation. Louisiana lawmakers passed an anti-abortion bill which made abortion available only to save the life of the woman and which punished doctors with imprisonment for performing the procedure under other circumstances. This anti-abortion bill died when the governor vetoed it as well as a second bill passed immediately after that veto which allowed limited access in cases of rape or incest. However, in a continuing saga, in June 1991, another legislative bill outlawing abortion overrode the governors's veto.

Other states passed varying levels of impediments, particularly parental consent and waiting period requirements. An example of a restrictive anti-abortion bill is the Abortion Control Act passed in the state of Pennsylvania in 1990. A look at Pennsylvania's particular regional conditions reveals a demographic composition and elective history most likely to result in this kind of legislative outcome. Pennsylvania has the third highest elderly population in the nation, the largest rural population of all the states, a constituency with 51 percent of the people identifying themselves as either Catholic or Fundamentalist, an entrenched anti-choice leadership and a legislative make-up in which only 6.7 percent of representatives are female, a figure which ranks this state 46th in the proportion of women legislators in office (Zausner 1989).

Similarly, Louisiana's attempt to outlaw abortion came from a state legislature made up of only three women out of 144 legislators, including an all-male Senate (Barrientos 1990); indeed, Louisiana ranks last in percentage of women legislators of any state. The number of women lawmakers is correlated with legislative outcome on abortion because women legislators support legalized abortion at a higher rate than men; for example, nationally 26 percent of women legislators believe abortion should be banned compared with 38 percent of male legislators (Zausner 1989). A corollary is found in these figures when comparing sex ratio voting on earlier ERA bills, which showed 75 percent of women legislators voted for passage, compared with only 50 percent of male legislators.

At the present time, in terms of resource mobilization, abortion legality is the new mobilizing issue. The Supreme Court decision to allow states to restrict abortion has provided the spur abortion supporters needed to become active. It is an issue that cuts across feminist ideological identification, political affiliation, class position, and race category. Abortion, as was true for ERA, has both a material and symbolic component; and thus, a dual emotional draw. It is likely that feminists in the small group sector will become active on this issue, as they did late in the ERA campaign, because radical feminists have a long history of committed activism for reproductive freedom and the right to privacy with regard to sexuality and the control of one's body. The unity potential of reproductive rights for diverse strands of the women's movement can be seen by looking at "Jane" activists before the legalization of abortion. In the early 1970s feminists in the Chicago Women's Liberation Union began an underground operation known as "The Service" or "Jane," performing abortions out of their own apartments. "Jane" activists represented an assortment of feminist orientations—from NOW members to socialists to separatists (Rew 1989).

A complicating factor in the conflict over reproductive choice is the French abortifacient pill RU486. Although not approved for distribution in the United States, it is likely that this pill will become available some time in the future. If abortion should become illegal, the availability of RU486 in underground circles would probably not curtail activism because as long as this abortifacient is illegal it will be available to only some of the population, and, symbolically, the legality of abortion would still be an issue to arouse activist commitment. Indeed, the tactics that have been employed to restrict abortion—the Hyde Amendment which allowed states to refuse funding for women on welfare, barriers such as parental consent and spousal notification, 24-hour waiting periods, and harassment leading to clinic closures, particularly in remote areas—have already limited which women will have access. Even if *Roe v. Wade* is sustained, poor women, young women, rural women, and married women are all at risk of not being able to obtain abortions if present restrictions are allowed to continue and new ones applied.

With the summer 1990 resignation of Supreme Court Justice William Brennan, a liberal abortion rights supporter, the Court was left with an even split on abortion legality decisions. The written record of President Bush's appointee, State Supreme Court Justice David H. Souter, provided little information regarding rights to privacy vis-à-vis reproductive choice, except that in the late 1970s as New Hampshire's attorney-general he opposed unlimited abortion and earlier in 1976 he argued against Medicaid funding of abortions for poor women (Ford 1990; Ullmann 1990). In a special mailing, NOW president, Molly Yard, notified NOW members that every opinion rendered by Judge Souter was being dissected, but, whatever that research turned up, "we must all remember that he was appointed to his state Supreme Court post by Governor John Sununu, now George Bush's chief of staff. That Sununu supports him tells us he is probably a 'strict constructionist' which does not bode well for women's rights, civil rights or individual freedoms."[21] Confirming this prediction, Justice Souter, in his first Supreme Court abortion case, cast the deciding vote to uphold federal regulations that bar employees of federally financed family planning clinics from discussing abortion as a reproductive choice for patients (Greenhouse 1991).

The challenge to Souter's appointment was unsuccessful, although throughout the proceedings the questioning on abortion and "privacy rights" revealed the prominence this issue held for pro and anti-abortion senators. The attempt by feminist, civil rights and lesbian and gay rights groups to prevent Souter's confirmation recalls a similar protest against Reagan's nomination of Robert Bork to the Supreme Court. In that incident, Bork was denied the position by the Senate, but was soon succeeded by Anthony Kennedy, who promptly set about voting for restrictions to abortion. Given President Bush's stated anti-abortion position and the fact that by the end of the 1980s more than half of all federal judges in the U.S. were appointed by Ronald Reagan,[22] it could hardly be expected that an abortion rights supporter would be appointed to the Supreme Court.

Indeed, with the resignation of Justice Thurgood Marshall (former lawyer for the NAACP and the only African American to serve on the Supreme Court) and President Bush's selection of Clarence Thomas to succeed him (also an African American but ideologically a conservative Republican and a supporter of "natural law" philosophy), the Supreme Court is firmly entrenched with a conservative anti-choice majority (Tribe 1991). The confirmation of Judge Thomas, after the spectacle of an all male Senate Judiciary Committee grilling Professor Anita Hill (also an African American conservative Republican) about her "fantasies, perjury, and unrequited sexual longings" in response to her charge of sexual harassment by Thomas, supports the fear that using the Supreme Court (and perhaps even Congress) as an avenue for creating gender equity is, in all likelihood, a doomed social movement strategy for the rest of this century.

In the November 1990 election, abortion took a backseat to concerns about the economy and taxes as people went to the polls and voted their pocket-books. Overall the election showed a split in electing abortion rights and abortion opponent candidates; however, in ballot initiatives, abortion legality was supported. In Oregon a referendum that would have banned most abortions and one that required parental notification were turned down; and in Nevada voters retained an existing law that makes abortion legal through the 24th week of pregnancy (Rubin 1990).

Given the level of activity to date since the Webster decision, we can expect to see continuing legislative action related to abortion.[23] With the future of abortion legality hanging in the balance, state legislative bodies become the place where abortion restrictions and perhaps legal status will be made. The fate of political candidates may be decided on this issue and laws may be passed or revoked based on politicians's perceptions of voter response to abortion legislation. The Webster decision activated abortion rights supporters because a taken-for-granted right was no longer secure; and the subsequent change in decision making locale placed efforts on behalf of abortion squarely within a grassroots activism arena. In other works, *ideologically* and *structurally,* social movement involvement becomes both more compelling and more available to greater numbers of supporters.

For over twenty years "women's issues" have been hotly debated in the legislative and judicial arenas of the United States. In considering the events of the 1980s and looking to the future of the 1990s, we can draw some conclusions about feminist issues which elicit large numbers of committed activists. First, the political environment and the social movement environment both effect and are affected by legal outcomes of controversial social movement issues. And second, in comparing women's suffrage, the Equal Rights Amendment, and reproductive freedom, the underlying essence of each is the challenge they present to traditional conceptions of womanhood and sex/gender relations. Thus, abortion has the potential suffrage and ERA had to mobilize the women's movement. Conversely, and for the same reasons, it has the potential to continue to fuel anti-feminist reaction.

Chapter 10 —————————————————————————

CONCLUSION

Some of us made it and some of us were lost to the struggle. It was a time of great hope and great expectation; it was also a time of great waste. That is history. We do not need to repeat these mistakes.

(Audre Lorde, 1984: 138)

Out of the ashes of a decade of idealism and activism, the contemporary U.S. women's movement was born. Contrary to popular belief, this movement did not evolve solely out of the New Left, civil rights, or anti-war movement. Although some feminists did move from one ideology to another, feminism was both a parallel and reaction to these movements. Similar conditions which gave rise to other protest groups led women to question their own status, both in society and in the social movement groups in which they were participating. It is a well-understood irony that, of all the movements formed in the 1960s, it was the women's movement which became one of the most powerful forces for social change. The irony, of course, is that few reports on social protest activities gave serious attention to continuing developments in the women's movement.[1] As Gloria Steinem argues, the press portrayed the 1960s as being more activist than the 1970s and 1980s when, in fact, "what was happening, by-and-large, was that men were rebelling against the draft and women were supporting them in that rebellion. The press misses much of the time that 'dropping in' is what is radical and activist for women" (1983: 7).

Laughed at and scorned in the organizing stage, even the women involved sometimes wondered how they dare address their own cause. At that time, feminists were considered weird, bourgeois, or uppity. Most certainly they were not a threat to the established order, and they were not to be taken seriously. But, something happened between the 1960s and 1980s to create a gender gap serious enough in electoral politics for prospective candidates to court the women's vote, and for conferences for and about women to draw thousands of interested participants. Indeed, feminist ideals spread throughout American society and permeated the everyday language of a whole population.

The contemporary women's movement is not simply an offshoot of other movement groups, nor did it suddenly spring from the air. Organized activity on behalf of women's rights began in the United States in the mid-1800s. From the latter part of that century throughout the first quarter of this century, the woman's movement concentrated on getting the vote, as campaigns for women's suffrage took place throughout the United States and parts of Western Europe. The resurgence of the women's movement, the second wave, built upon earlier demands and expanded them into a wide range of rights encompassing the subtle and deep-seated causes of women's subordinate position in society. In applying an historical framework, the contemporary women's movement represents a continuation of long-term developments in feminist thought and action.

There is, however, no one feminist theory or liberation group. Feminist ideology developed from several distinct philosophical belief systems; hence, the women's movement consists of simultaneous and divergent orientations. Moreover, tensions beyond intra-movement relations have created a path fraught with confrontation from interconnecting sectors of society. Indeed, the re-emergence of identity divisions in the 1980s points to the need for a more inclusive feminism. Thus, a major task for the women's movement in the 1990s is the continuing challenge to societal practices of exclusion and hierarchy based on gender, as well as those based on other social group characteristics embedded in women's lives.

Because variations in social characteristics create dissimilar needs, a "difference perspective" has offered feminism the opportunity to explore the ways difference both threatens and enriches us. But at what point does a focus on difference become destructive and demobilizing? Understanding social movement change and how issues of diversity fit into a coherent scheme of movement organizing has been a major area of inquiry in this research. Of particular interest has been the ways intra-movement alliances and divisions promote or discourage mobilization efforts, and how ideology, self-identity issues, and a changed social environment contribute to changing group relations.

SOCIAL MOVEMENT CHANGE AND SOCIAL
MOVEMENT GROUP RELATIONS

The organizing stage of the contemporary movement (1966–1975) was a dynamic period representing a rise and fall in feminist activism. At that time, many participants were unaware of the long and varied history of women's protest actions. Some thought they were the first to raise such issues—they were the "new women"—without knowing much about the generations of new women who had preceded them. When movements arise, adherents are often inclined to see themselves as the discoverers of truth. Such a tendency, however, can be lessened by an informed sense of history. In the case of the women's movement, there are lessons to be learned and a perspective to be gained in knowing the past, for this is a history that is both humbling and inspiring.

The first wave of feminist activism (1848–1920) reveals that diverse groups and actions enhance support for movement issues, a more extreme group helps make moderate groups more socially acceptable to join, the introduction of alternative tactics provides new energy, and pageantry and symbols create an emotional response. Yet, learning what worked for previous generations of women is not enough; it is also important to look at those aspects of movement organizing which create barriers to movement advance. A critical gaze over the length and breadth of the women's movement shows that women who had needs which differed from white middle-class women were often misunderstood or ignored.

An ongoing thread of discord in feminist organizing has been divisions based on race, class, ethnicity, religion, and age. During the Depression, marital status created antagonisms between women when government and business regulations were enacted to prevent married women from working. In protesting the campaign to bar married women from public employment, National Woman's Party (NWP) member Alma Lutz found "the most bitter enemies of married women workers have not been men, but a militant group of single women who are obsessed with the idea that their salvation depends upon barring married women from paid labor."[2] More recently, familial lifestyle has created divisions between employed women and full-time homemakers over public policy issues such as federally supported child care, parental leave, and abortion.

Another thread of continuity in feminist relations has been the practice of dismissing, rather than confronting, conflict. Personalizing opposing voices by labeling them aberrant results in interaction patterns which shield adversaries from seriously examining competing views. Likewise, submerging dissent avoids critical explorations of underlying feminist meaning derived from different life experiences. An example of efforts to create unity by denying difference is found in the suffrage campaign, where antagonisms between the National American Woman's Suffrage Association (NAWSA) and the NWP were articulated almost wholly in terms of strategy and tactics. Because ideological differences were rarely a part of their discourse, arguments supporting women's autonomy were not a major contribution to NAWSA's massive recruitment efforts. With the victory of suffrage, the unifying issue of the movement was gone, and the various sectors dissipated into separate issues divided by two opposing views, one calling for women's equality and the other for women's protection.

In placing this example from the early woman's movement within the theoretical framework of resource mobilization, it appears that a multi-group movement supports the activation of large numbers of people but, in so doing, runs the risk of displacing ideological commitment. On the surface, this outcome questions the benefits of coalition building with groups organized under different belief systems. At a deeper level, it suggests the importance of ideological dialogue between groups supporting the same goal. Had the various groups interacted on an ideological level, they might have reached some agreement on the dual need for women's equality and a changed social structure.

Suggesting that open dialogue might draw disparate groups together is, perhaps, naive. But, in a real sense, much of intra-movement discord is more a matter of emphasis than opposition. For instance, recent scholarship by Nancy Cott (1987) points out that differences between suffrage supporters were not played down as much as they were merged together. In the later phase of the campaign, activists of all stripe turned to expediency arguments, using whatever rationale worked at the time—sometimes arguing for the natural order of equal relations and sometimes arguing for women's moral calling. Vacillating between these two apparently contradictory views was not just a tactic to win suffrage, it was also a reflection of the fact that most suffragists tended to believe in both arguments (Cott 1987). The bind women were caught in was the still familiar one of trying to reconcile the meaning of equality in a "man-made" world.

One of the lessons to be learned from the early woman's movement is that mobilization of people is not enough; social movements must also mobilize sustaining ideas. And, while a shared goal may bring people together, an essential part of the mobilization process is a unifying ideology that keeps them together. Yet, the problem with adopting a unifying feminist ideology, then and now, is that women are affected by more than their gender status. Without challenging the world as it has been defined and addressing the differences among women, divisions in feminist thought will continue to arise.

In contrast to the suffrage movement, the organizing stage of the contemporary women's movement was characterized by open conflict in group relations. A primary concern during this period was the categorization of organizational structure, activist tactics, and interactive behavior to determine who was a "real" (i.e. radical) feminist. Activists were "identified" along a continuum of conservative to radical, which equated with definitions of good and bad or, as it turned out, as high or low-caste feminists. There are a number of problems associated with hierarchical categorization, but it is important to recognize that the adoption of such terminology serves a purpose, albeit an unacknowledged one. It is ironic that it was mainly radical feminists—those activists from the small group sector who eschewed leaders and other outward manifestations of hierarchy—who freely used ideological designations to label, and thus discredit, other feminists. Ideological purity was both a sincere application of feminist principles and a method of maintaining a superior image for activists who saw themselves as radical movement people. The outcome of discrediting labeling and non-sustaining organizational structure in the small group sector was vulnerability to dissension, schism, and decline.

In the mass movement sector, the National Organization for Women also experienced serious internal division in the mid-1970s, yet overcame a major split because of a different conception of the meaning of radicalism. For instance, even when the dissenting faction used the term radical to define itself, radical was not used specifically as a personal identification, but rather to identify new organizational strategies and "risky" tactics. Because mass movement organizers envision their efforts producing large-scale social change and because they believe the support of "the masses" is needed, identification with radicalism is downplayed in an attempt to create unity among a broad spectrum of the population. Interestingly, the goals articulated as necessary to accomplish radical social change were those both factions in NOW claimed to support. In spite of the actual non-ideological nature of the schism, both contending groups used the rhetoric of philosophical difference to present their case. Applying an ingroup/outgroup psychology, acted out as the "good group" vs. the "bad group," these definitions created unnecessarily sharp divisions. Whether substantively based or not, the intense conflict engendered over a two-year period was serious enough to destroy the organization. That it did not can be attributed to the different meaning radical had for NOW members than it had for activists in the small group sector, specifically in the separation of a personal radical identity from a visualization of radical feminist activism.

Decline in the small group sector during the 1970s does not negate the critical role these groups played in the development of the women's movement. Indeed, it was radical feminism that stretched the feminist imagination and provided the inspiration for women to become activists in their own cause. It is the nature of small groups to organize and dissolve within relatively brief periods of time; thus, the state of small groups and the changing nature of their relationship to the rest of the movement serve as indicators of the ebb and flow of movement cycles. For instance, when the anti-feminist backlash gained force and ERA became a major focus of mass movement organizing, new groups emerged to work for passage. During this period, interaction among movement sectors was characterized by a lessening of overt antagonism in intra-movement group relations. This changed interactional pattern can be directly related to the changed social and political environment activists found themselves in. Indeed, the growth of the New Right can be said to have contributed to attempts at feminist unity during the height of the ERA drive. In this sense, a movement tenuously held together was encouraged by concerted opposition to recognize common bonds.

Participant observation and interview data for this research show that, during the high activist period of the ERA campaign, differences between groups were experienced as being related more to practice than to opposing belief systems. In the pre-1975 period, groups experienced themselves as being at odds with each other, almost as in competition. By 1980, however, a variety of groups saw themselves as forming parts of the same whole and it became more acceptable to view group differences as structural necessities.

Organizations desirous of building a mass movement are limited as to the ways they can achieve their goals, because they are concerned over public opinion and societal reaction. The space created by this limitation is taken up by smaller groups with the freedom to do what might be called "outrageous" acts. Smaller groups are relatively unconcerned with public opinion; they are, in fact, protesting public opinion. Because the major functions of these groups are different—one to shake the public up, the other to incorporate the public into their sphere—this difference operates to form a more coherent and dynamic movement. Utilizing this perspective, diverse social movement groups are seen as complementary parts. Thus, in the late 1970s and early 1980s a unifying issue and a recognition of underlying values resulted in a cooperative multi-group movement. These features of movement organizing contributed to the spread of feminist ideology and facilitated the mobilization process through broad participation in the movement.

During the 1980s, however, continued economic uncertainty fueled a developing conservatism in public policy and political voting. The defeat of ERA in 1982 bequeathed a decade of accelerated resistance to feminists goals. Cultural feminism, a reassertion of the superiority of a female identity, and self-transformative experiments spread within the small group sector; at the same time, public activism declined and intra-movement divisions re-emerged. Harking back to the ideological purity days of the 1970s, declarations of who was and who was not a "real" feminist were bandied about once again. It was only at the end of this decade, when a taken-for-granted right was threatened, that mass activism had an opportunity to mobilize new constituents once again.

The 1990s confront the women's movement with continued economic insecurity and a conservative political force which can no longer emphasize anti-communism as an organizing center. Instead, we can expect to see even more emphasis on the New Right strategy of mobilizing anxiety over gender and family change. Indeed, it may be the case that the "pro-family" rhetoric in the religious right has already replaced "anti-communism as the index of Americanism" (Gordon 1990).

THE WOMEN'S MOVEMENT AS A SOCIAL MOVEMENT

Research on the women's movement shows that efforts on behalf of social transformation are waged against opposition of a most serious nature. The forces opposed to overturning the status quo are overt and subtle, and they are powerful. The history of social movements demonstrates that, for social groups to change their situation, there is a need for concerted effort with multifaceted strategies: political work and disruptive direct actions, national and grassroots organizing, mass media events and personal change efforts. Recognizing the legitimacy of diversity in social movement involvement contributes to the visibility and support of the movement. Moreover, ideological disagreement, rather than dividing the movement, can facilitate an enrichment process in movement development.

Although at first glance the women's movement appears to be an isolated case of disparate movement orientations, it is more accurate to describe it as just one example of many multi-level movements. Other social movements also reveal a variation of structures and orientations, as well as antagonistic group relations which rise and fall in accordance with social environment receptivity. For example, establishing a legal basis to end racial segregation was a crucial victory for the National Association for the Advancement of Colored People (NAACP) that led to other forms of black activism in the latter part of the 1950s and 1960s.[3] However, as the civil rights movement grew in numbers and force, the NAACP and Southern Christian Leadership Conference (SCLC) were ridiculed by newer groups; indeed, Malcolm X even accused Martin Luther King Jr of being a front for white society.

> [The White man] takes a Negro, a so-called Negro, and makes him prominent, builds him up, publicizes him, makes him a celebrity. And then he becomes a spokesman for Negroes—and a Negro leader . . . to teach you and me, just like novacaine, to suffer peacefully. Don't stop suffering—just suffer peacefully.[4]

Yet, as signs of movement disintegration became apparent, Malcolm X spoke of the need for diverse forms of activism.[5]

It is no surprise, then, to find divisions in the civil rights movement described in much the same way that feminist activists have described divisions in the women's movement.

> When we disagreed with one another about the solution to a particular problem, we were often far more vicious to each other than to the originators of our common problem. Historically, difference had been used so cruelly against us that as a people we were reluctant to tolerate any diversion from what was externally de-

fined as Blackness. In the 60s, political correctness became not a guideline for
living, but a new set of shackles. (Lorde 1984: 136, 142)

The various groups loosely making up what is known as the Left provide another
history of internecine attack and organizational splits. In the 1960s, leftist
groups spent an inordinate amount of time attacking each other. By the mid-
1970s the Left itself was in dissolution as the social environment increasingly
became more estranged from socialist ideas. The merger in the early 1980s of
the New American Movement and the Democratic Socialist Organizing Committee marked a new event in socialist history as two leftist organizations joined
together rather than split apart. Not coincidentally, this merger occurred at the
same time the New Right had become a prominent force in American political
life, and the Left had evolved into a rapidly dwindling number of activists.

Another example of the relationship between intra-group divisiveness and social change is the anti-abortion movement. In the 1980s, what appeared to be a
cohesive counter-movement became one divided by "conservative and radical"
forces. Disagreements intensified after the 1980 presidential election when Ronald Reagan, a committed anti-abortion President, became head of state. Encouraged to escalate their protest tactics, new anti-abortion leaders, calling themselves "domestic terrorists," embarked on a campaign to criticize older groups
such as the National Right to Life Committee for spending their time giving
speeches instead of doing civil disobedience (Smith 1986).

What do these examples show? They reveal cycles of intra-movement division
and intra-movement cooperation, along with cycles of movement advance and
decline—all in interaction with social environmental change. Yet, there is no
unilateral direction or consistent pattern of response to outside social forces.
Social movements both affect and are affected by changes in the economic, political, and social arenas; moreover, intra-movement factors such as membership
size, organizational structure, self-identity perceptions, ideology, and unity issues also affect the nature of that response because cultural transformation occurs in both the society and the social movement as each acts to transform the
other over time. Thus, sociological analysis of social movement change contributes to ongoing strategic and relational considerations; however, as a predictive
tool, scientific analysis of movement outcome may be only slightly better than
the crystal ball of the past or the New Age psyches of the present.

THE MEANING OF RADICAL

The most intriguing question I find this research has raised is "What is radical?"
A related question is "How does the quest for radicalism affect social movement
mobilization efforts?" This study shows patterns of change in perceptions of

what defines radicalism, the importance of this designation for individuals, and the effect this term has on interactions between different types of activists. These changes are particularly noticeable in relationship to the acceptance or rejection of the movement by the outside social/political environment.

Although there are feminists who claim the radical mantle as their own, who does the defining and what the term means is a continuing point of contention. For instance, when a letter write in *The Progressive* called for a "new militant feminist grass roots movement to augment the National Organization for Women," one respondent wrote back and asked "Where have you been all this time, Sister?" Another said:

> I have been a member of NOW for about fourteen years and an activist radical feminist for thirteen years. . . . I note that the article is advertised on the cover as "A New Feminist Direction." I find that a laugh.[6]

The long-term activists interviewed for this research resist returning to a social movement environment where radical self-definitions become a form of name calling. Moreover, the interview data show that feminists from a wide range of groups consider their goals to be radical—not because they are getting arrested by the hundreds, but because they believe they are attempting to achieve social relations that are radically different than what we have known in the past.

Perhaps radical means to achieve the changes you are trying to make.[7] If that is what defines radical, then a radical social movement is one that works at creating change even if it takes a long time, the environment is hostile, losses occur, and tasks are boring and dull. And, if that is true, most activists would probably not want to be called radical.

Activist social movements and new living experiments are exciting; participants get something out of their involvement. Achieving long-term change, though, is not always exciting. Fundamental social change rarely occurs rapidly or without great effort, and in the course of a social movement's existence there will be cycles of both intensity and stagnation. Short of revolution or catastrophic disaster, how else are whole societies to change entrenched customs and beliefs? There are benefits for social movement participants, such as the joy of committed involvement and the building of social ties; but activist efforts alone rarely lead to a changed society. For the women's movement in particular, "nonfeminist" women are an important component in achieving feminist goals. Indeed, the history of women's activism over the last 150 years might well be called the social movement of women rather than the women's movement.[8]

The hard part of dedicated social movement involvement lies in the recognition that it is the persistent tapping—sometimes a hammer, sometimes a feather—that leaves a mark. And it is through this process, a series of marks, that a new cultural reality is born.

NOTES

Introduction

1. For diverse explorations of social change and social relations, see Gerth and Mills (1958); Gusfield (1970b); Lauer (1976); Mandle (1979); Marx and Engels (1977 [1859]); Nisbet (1953); Olson (1971).

2. See, for instance, Blumer (1969, 1978); Gamson (1975, 1980); Heberle (1951); Lauer (1976); Olson (1968); Touraine (1981); Turner and Killian (1957); Wood and Jackson (1982).

3. Psychologically based explanations for social movement participation include characteristics related to an authoritarian personality (Adorno *et al.* 1950), feelings of marginality (Lasswell and Blumenstock 1939), isolation (Ernst and Loth 1952), personality peculiarities (Hoffer 1951), individual pathology (Heberle 1951), and aggressive tendencies (Dollard *et al.* 1971). Analyses on the emergence of social movements come from various mass society and cultural mileau perspectives (Kornhauser 1959; Gusfield 1962; Riesman 1961; Mills 1951, 1956); social conflict forces (Dahrendorf 1958); structural change (Smelser 1962); and relative deprivation perceptions (Davies 1962, 1971; Merton and Kitt 1950; Gurr 1970).

4. With the exception of Michels' "iron law of oligarchy," analysis of ongoing change within social movements had been virtually ignored until the 1960s and 1970s when resource mobilization theorists began studying this process. In *Political Parties*, Michels maintains that there are "oligarchic tendencies in every kind of human organization which strives for the attainment of definite ends" ([1911] 1959: 11). According to this theory, over time organizations become more conservative because leaders will put their efforts into entrenching their power and maintaining the organization rather than attaining goals. However, subsequent studies on an agrarian socialist movement (Lipset 1950) and the International Typographical Union (Lipset *et al.* 1956) question this supposition. Further, social movement researchers have argued that movement structure and ideology are offsetting factors in oligarchic tendencies (Myers 1971; Wilson 1961) and that organizations respond to the ebb and flow of sentiment in the larger society rather than a set pattern of organizational direction (Zald and Ash 1966).

5. See Andersen (1983), Banks (1981) Carden (1974), Cassell (1977), Evans (1980), Fritz (1979), Jaggar and Struhl (1978), among others.

6. Post-feminism is a term coined by the media to define the period after the defeat of ERA and the conservative political environment of the 1980s. Research for this study does not substantiate the use of this terminology when applied to activist commitment or the growth of a generalized feminist consciousness in public awareness.

7. A notable exception to this is Jo Freeman who in the early 1970s was involved in a number of diverse groups in the Chicago area. Her academically oriented book *The Politics of Women's Liberation* (1975) represents an analysis which transcends the narrow sectarian view often found in social movement literature.

8. For methodological foundations of participant observation and oral history research, see Becker and Geer (1957); Bertaux and Bertaux-Wiame (1981); Douglas (1970); Gans (1968); Kluck-hohn (1940); Thompson (1978). For discussions of experiential research and the use of data from subjective accounts," see Gouldner (1970a, b); Phillips (1971); Reinharz (1979, 1983); Stanley and Wise (1983); Znaniecki (1934).

9. By service organizations I mean the multitude of groups established since the early 1970s to serve women, e.g., rape crisis centers, battered women's shelters, bookstores, etc.

10. Specifically I would like to thank Chris Guerrero for her collection of NOW archives covering the years 1971–77; and Alan Howes for copies of NAM literature from 1973 to 1982.

11. The historical document search was facilitated by Sara Sherman of the Women's Collection at Northwestern University.

12. Joining is a misleading term as both the Congressional Union and A Group of Women were geographically limited to the Northeast. By joining I mean I was put on a mailing list and received literature.

13. Initially my attention was drawn to this fact as I read interviews done by students in my women's movement class.

14. Women's Equality Day is August 26, the anniversary of the passage of the 19th Amendment granting women the right to vote. This gathering was called by Sonia Johnson to "envision together the post-patriarchal age and to think and plan how to hasten it" (mailing dated July 1983).

15. My thanks to Washington University for the Summer Travel Award which allowed me to travel to conferences and interview sites.

Chapter I

1. Letter to Mary S. Parker, President of the Boston Female Anti-Slavery Society (quoted in Papachristou 1976: 13).

2. When *The Subjection of Women* was published, Taylor had been dead for three years. Although her name is not on this widely acclaimed work, her contribution is acknowledged by Mill, and can be found in many of their writings and letters beginning with their *Early Essays on Marriage and Divorce* (1832). Taylor was more radical than Mill and, over the years, her influence shows in his writing. See Alice Rossi's introductory essay in her edited work of Mill and Taylor *Essays on Sex Equality* (1970).

3. The Frances Wright and Angelina Grimke quotes came from "An Exhibition Commemorating the 150th Anniversary of The Anti-Slavery Conventions of American Women, 1837, 1838, 1839," The Library Company of Philadelphia, Phillip Lapsansky, Curator, March-June 1989.

4. Letter from Elizabeth Cady Stanton to Susan B. Anthony, February 19, 1854 (quoted in Flexner 1975: 84).

5. At this time Lucy Stone spoke in favor of keeping the suffrage issue for freed slaves and women together. Later, she sided with the abolitionist position of working for Black male suffrage first and women's suffrage after the achievement of the 15th Amendment. When the 15th Amendment

passed, Stone did work for women's suffrage but, with few exceptions, the abolitionists who asked women to wait their turn were not to be found in the women's suffrage struggle.

6. For precise details of events following the Civil War, see *History of Woman Suffrage, Vol. II, 1861–1876* edited by Elizabeth Cady Stanton, Susan B. Anthony, and Matilda Joslyn Gage. Between 1881 and 1922 six volumes of this history were published by women's rights activists. These sources contain minute details of year-by-year meetings, conventions, and campaigns, including speeches and articles representing the different factions within the movement.

Chapter 2

1. Quoted in Cott (1987: 66) from *The Suffragist*, November 30, 1920.

2. The first issue of *The Revolution* is telling of the National's concerns. This weekly paper, subtitled "Principle, Not Policy: Justice, Not Favors," was edited by Elizabeth Cady Stanton and Parker Pillsbury with Susan B. Anthony listed as proprietor and manager. Advocacy was stated for educated suffrage irrespective of sex or color; equal pay to women for equal work; an eight-hour day; abolition of standing armies; and the elimination of party despotisms. Utilizing the slogan, "Down with Politicians—Up with the People," they called for more organized labor, including strengthening of the Brotherhood of Labor (vol. 1, no. 1, January 8, 1868: 1; in Graphics Collection, Women's Rights-Leaders, Folder 4404, Library of Congress).

3. In 1868 Anthony and a group of working-class women formed the Working Women's Association. The Association allowed any women to join and many middle-class women did; indeed they made up half the membership. The sexism of male union officials led middle-class women to focus on working-class women's need for political power through the vote, whereas the working women were more interested in being identified as workers who were in need of economic power and labor solidarity. By the end of 1869 the organization had collapsed. See Balser (1987, Chapter 5) and DuBois (1978, Chapter 5) for a full account of this early attempt to create an organizational alliance between feminist activists and working-class women.

4. Victoria Woodhull aligned with the Stanton/Anthony faction and published articles in *The Revolution*. An ardent supporter of suffrage, she also was involved with other interests, including advocacy of a single sexual standard for both sexes. This position alarmed most women's rights activists and tainted the National for some time as being associated with "free love" (sexual freedom). By 1872 the National had lessened their involvement with Woodhull. When she ran for President of the United States on a third party ticket (the first woman to do so) and Susan B. Anthony was arrested for voting in that election, Anthony had not even voted for her, choosing the Republican candidate instead. For full details of the scandal Woodhull precipitated in revealing an adulterous affair between the president of the American Woman's Suffrage Association (Henry Ward Beecher, a well-known preacher) with one of his parishioners (Elizabeth Tilton, the wife of respected women's rights reformer, Theodore Tilton) see Flexner (1975, Chapter 10) and Papachristou (1976, Chapter 4).

5. Social purity, a polite way of saying sexual purity, was a frequent topic of discussion among reform groups in the last quarter of the nineteenth century. There was a sexual repressiveness in the social purity movement, but there was also an element of feminist thinking based on the desire to "create some limitations on men's unilateral right to define every sexual encounter" and "to support deviations from the standard act of sexual intercourse" (Gordon 1977: 119–20). Although believing in the concept of voluntary motherhood (through natural restraints), contraception was rejected by many women reformers because of their fear of the possibilities for promiscuity. The women did not really trust the men; contraception was associated with sexual immorality and the destruction of the family.

6. See Klandermans (1984) for the difference between consensus mobilization and action mobilization.

7. A term coined by William O'Neill (1969), meaning reformers who felt women were morally

superior to men and, given the vote, would create a more just society. In this view, women are seen as fundamentally different from men, possessors of nurturing qualities which lead them into work best suited for their nature, i.e. homemaking and mothering, or, if outside the home, social work and teaching.

8.   Even when suffragists attempted to serve as poll watchers, most states ruled that this task could only be performed by legal voters.

9.   The 15th Amendment had been resisted in the South by voter qualification laws and/or literacy tests. An often used restrictive voting practice was the grandfather clause which granted the vote only to those having it before the Civil War and their legal descendants.

10.   Individual states could grant suffrage to women, and throughout the late nineteenth and early twentieth centuries some did. Wyoming was the first, in 1869, when it was still a territory, coming into statehood in 1890 with equal suffrage intact. In the 1890s Western states were assisted along the equal suffrage path by the Populist Movement, which advocated extended popular participation in governmental bodies. For example, Colorado was the second state to adopt women's suffrage, doing so in 1893 when there was a Populist governor and Populist legislators controlled the senate.

11.   For instance, at the height of the ERA campaign in the 1980s the largest feminist organization, the National Organization for Women, only claimed 275,000 members. (*National NOW Times* 1982).

12.   Women's suffrage was a narrow victory. Prohibition passed by a much greater margin (45 states); only the required number of 36 states passed the 19th Amendment.

13.   Even with a lack of information, women were practicing some form of birth control as evidenced by a fertility rate at the turn of the century that was half what it had been in 1800. A declining birth rate was associated with independence for women and the demise of the family or, as President Theodore Roosevelt proclaimed in 1905, "race suicide" (Gordan 1977).

14.   When first introduced the amendment read: "Men and women shall have equal rights throughout the United States and every place subject to its jurisdiction." In the early 1940s the wording was changed to: "Equality of rights under the law shall not be denied or abridged by the United States or by any State on account of sex."

15.   Years after her own part in the conflict, Esther Peterson, the first head of the President's Commission on the Status of Women, admitted that part of her resistance to the amendment had been the way she felt about its supporters (see Zelman 1982).

Chapter 3

1.   Parts of Chapter 3 and Chapter 4 were published in Ryan (1989).

2.   The year before, in *Brown v. The Board of Education,* the Supreme Court had ruled against segregated schools.

3.   For histories and analysis of a variety of 1960s' social movement groups see, among others, Carson (1981); Draper (1965); Farmer (1985); Gitlin (1987); Isserman (1987); King (1987); McAdam (1988); Oberschall (1978); and Sale (1973).

4.   Only one member of the Commission was an ERA supporter, Margaret Rawalt, a former president of BPW and a paper member of NWP. Outnumbered, she was stymied in getting an ERA endorsement; however, it was through her efforts that the word "now" was inserted in the Commissions's statement. See Rupp and Taylor (1987) for a full account.

5.   See Robin Morgan's anthology *Sisterhood is Powerful* (1970: 512–14) for a list of NOW's Bill of Rights.

6.   The Feminists established leaderless groups, a policy of no media stars, consensus decision making, and a lot system for work assignments. Other groups incorporated some of these ideas; however, these methods were later criticized as unworkable and even repressive to individual members. See Jo Freeman (Joreen 1973); also Robin Morgan (1977).

7. Radicalesbian members came from both the women's movement and the Gay Liberation Front. Originally they called themselves The Lavender Menace, a term Betty Friedan used to describe the lesbian faction in the movement. For a copy of their position paper "The Woman Identified Woman," see Radicalesbians (1973: 240–245).

8. For more detailed descriptions of the events leading to the development of the small group sector, see Ware (1970); Hole and Levine (1971); Salper (1972); Carden (1974); Freeman (1975); Evans (1980); Deckard (1983); and Echols (1989).

9. See Morgan (1970: 521–4), "No More Miss America," for the document this group put out explaining the reasons for their protest.

10. In 1968, when Redstockings formed, it derived most of its members from the original members of New York Radical Women (Salper 1972: 173). The name Redstockings was taken from two sources: Bluestockings, a term used to describe nineteenth-century feminist writers, and Red for revolution (Redstockings 1975: 55). The book Firestone wrote was *The Dialectic of Sex: The Case for Feminist Revolution* (1970).

11. Consciousness raising is likened to the Chinese practice of "speak bitterness," which entails the sharing of personal experience. Conceptually, through this process, one comes to see that what was thought to be an individual problem is instead a social or political problem requiring a collective solution. CR groups developed the slogan "the personal is political," originally coined by Kathie Sarachild. Sarachild defined CR as a way for women to analyze their condition, develop new theory, and plan action (1978). For theoretical and personal descriptions of consciousness raising as it was developed in the late 1960s, see Sarachild (1970) and Susan (1970).

12. Interview, Ann Snitow (June 1983).

13. Interview, Deidre English (June 1983).

14. The Women's Collection at Northwestern University provided much of the information on the Chicago Women's Liberation Union. Most particularly, see "The Women's Movement in Chicago and its Future: Proposal for a Regional Conference to set up a Regional Structure" (n.a.); "The Women's Movement in Chicago and its Future" (n.a.); "Proposed Structure for a Chicago Women's Liberation Union" (n.a.); "Report on Pallatine Liberation Conference" (*The Roger Spark*, 3 (2), n.d.); "Proposed Statement of Political Principles" (n.a.); "III—The Organization" (n.a.; however, identified separately as part of a bigger work by Margaret Schmid and Shirley Starkweather, "Working Towards Women's Liberation: Analysis and Proposals"). These manuscripts are located in WEF/CWLU ORG/REG IL/Chic 1969.

15. Interview, Chris Riddeough (August 1983).

16. Radinsky and Gadlin (1969).

17. Interview, Liz Weston (April 1982).

18. From "The Impact of Feminism on Lesbianism: A Look at the Daughters of Bilitis." Washington University in St Louis, Women's Studies Colloquium, March 1982.

19. For women who had a commitment to race and class solidarity, these issues were more muted until the latter part of the 1970s and the 1980s.

Chapter 4

1. Interview, Chris Guerrero (June 1983)

2. See Echols (1989) for a concise breakdown of the varieties of radical feminism during this period. Jaggar (1983) also provides detailed descriptions of types of feminists, although Echols claims that Jaggar's analysis does not capture the more subtle nuances of radical feminism in these years.

3. Interview, Laurel Richardson (June 1983).

4.   Anonymous member of Redstockings (see, Notes from the Second Year, editor Shulamith Firestone, 1970: 63)

5.   Also, interview with Eleanor (Ellie) Smeal (September 1983).

6.   Interview, Robin Morgan (November 1983).

7.   WITCH (Women's International Terrorist Conspiracy from Hell) derived its members from the original New York Radical Women. Morgan maintains this division was a split along political lines, with radical feminists founding Redstockings (to do CR and writing) and "hip Left style" politicos founding WITCH to be an action group. See Morgan (1977) for other WITCH actions.

8.   NOW claims it does not currently keep membership profiles, but in 1974 a "Report of the Finance Vice-President to the NOW National Conference" printed the results of a survey sampling NOW members. The survey covered a range of demographic characteristics including sex, which showed males constituting 8 percent of the total membership (WEF ORG/NAT NOW (Nat) Folder 12, 1974, Women's Collection, Northwestern University).

9.   For instance, in nineteenth-century social movements, cultural taboos prohibited women and men from working together in mixed organizations.

10.   The primary motivation for founding the Caucus was to have an organization that would focus on getting women elected or appointed to office. Nonetheless, the Caucus endorses and works for men when there are no women candidates. Given the scope of the political work the Caucus does, some feminists would disagree with a policy excluding men from membership, reasoning "why not take their money if you're going to give endorsement or support?" (interview, Ellie Smeal, October 1983).

11.   However, since that time the League has admitted male members. According to a June 1985 mass mailing letter from the president, Dorothy Ridings, the League counts "approximately one-quarter of a million men and women members and supporters." See NOW ACTS, 1972, 5 (1): 7 for the League member and Steinem quotes.

12.   Interview, Joyce Trebilcot (October 1983).

13.   Interview, Mary Jean Collins (August 1983).

14.   For example, International Women's League for Peace and Freedom (IWLPF), American Legion Women's Auxiliary, Parent and Teachers Association (PTA), National Colored Parent Teachers Association, Young Women's Christian Association (YWCA), Business and Professional Women's Clubs (BPW), American Association of University Women (AAUW), and various Jewish, Black, and Catholic women's organizations were all either founded in the post-war years or saw dramatic increases in their membership numbers during the 1920s.

15.   The NWP counted 151 dues-paying members in 1923 compared with around 50,000 in 1919; NAWSA went from 2 million members to about 5 percent of that number when it became the League of Women Voters in 1920 (figures quoted in Cott 1987: 73, 86).

Chapter 5

1.   Interview, Ann Boyce (April 1983).

2.   The tendency has been for primary research to focus on only one segment of the movement or on only the early years. For instance, the books by Evans (1980) and Fritz (1979) both covered only the small group sector, the former concentrating on the roots of revolt and the latter on the early years. Deckard's 1975 book on the movement came out with two later editions; however, little new information was included in either the second or third edition. Carden's 50-page update on the movement for the Ford Foundation in 1977 concerned itself, for the most part, with changes from 1970 through the end of 1975. Buechler (1990) compares the early woman's movement with the contemporary movement, but he conceptually separates them into examples of women's *movements,* rather

than one continuous movement with shifting views and varying levels of activism which change overtime.

3. Before the 1973 Supreme Court decision legalizing abortion, NARAL, which had organized in 1969, was called the National Conference for Repeal of Abortion Laws.

4. Betty Friedan was one of the people instrumental in the formation of both NARAL and NWPC. Forty percent of the founding members of NWPC were NOW members.

5. For diverse examples of anti-feminist groups and member characteristics, see Klatch (1987), a field study of right-wing women where she found two orientations: social conservatism and laissez-faire conservatism; Marshall (1984), a chronology of anti-feminist groups' foundings; and Brady and Tedin (1976), a survey of anti-ERA activists providing both demographic characteristics and religious attitudes.

6. Most notably, *Fascinating Womanhood* (Andelin 1970) and *Total Woman* (Morgan 1973).

7. STOP ERA is an acronomyn for Stop Taking Our Privileges and Extra Responsibility Amendment (Marshall 1984b).

8. Weyrich was also instrumental in the formation of the Moral Majority in the latter part of the 1970s.

9. Individual letters were written by Bella Abzug (calling it McCarthyite); Jane Alpert (decrying the destructive attacks); and Adrienne Rich (charging the article as a salacious voyeurism of anti-feminist editors). The group letter was signed by Michele Wallace, Letty Cottin Pogrebin, Robin Morgan, Vivian Gornick, Andrea Dworkin, Phyllis Chesler, Charlotte Bunch, and Susan Brownmiller (*Village Voice,* May 28, 1979: 4–5).

10. NAM was a democratic socialist organization formed in the early 1970s. It called itself socialist feminist but differed from the women's liberation unions by being a mixed-sex group and by having an organized structure with bylaws, official leadership positions, and a national orientation. A feminist perspective was encouraged by a 50 percent female representation rule for committees, commissions, leadership positions, and chairing of plenaries at conventions. There were also informal rules such as calling on women before men at meetings or asking for women's comments first when a session was opened up for discussion. The planning for the Socialist Feminist Conference also included members of unions, particularly from the Chicago Women's Liberation Union.

11. The positive side of the conference was that it "gave me a name for what I was and put me in touch with other like minded women" (interview, Liz Weston, April 1982).

12. Papers from this conference were given to me by Liz Weston. This quote came from the keynote speaker, Barbara Dudley. Also see "Report to the Conference," *Socialist Revolution,* no. 26 (Oct-Dec), 1975: 109.

13. Interview, Chris Riddeough (August 1983). Riddeough was a long-time activist and leader in CWLU. Later she became active in NAM and she was a vice-chair of the newly formed Democratic Socialists of America (DSA). She also joined NOW and in 1982 was appointed the Action Vice-President's Assistant for Lesbian Rights.

14. Two such groups were organized in the early 1970s: the New American Movement (NAM) and the Democratic Socialist Organizing Committee (DSOC). In 1981 NAM and DSOC merged to form the Democratic Socialists of America (DSA).

15. Interview, Liz Weston, member of Buffalo DSA, former chair of NAM's Feminist Commission and Co-chair of the Women Organizing advisory board. (April 1982).

16. Interview, Naomi Ross, Illinois State NOW officer (July 1983).

17. The president is mandated to chair national conferences and conventions, but DeCrow was out of the country visiting China at the time of the bylaws convention. In social movement analysis, the changes instituted by the Caucus were fruitful in terms of what the organization needed at that time for building a mass movement. Much of the rhetoric between the Caucus and Chicago faction, however, overstated the differences between the two groups. In an overview of the Philadelphia convention, a *New York Times* article found that the goals the Caucus said they would work for—

federal legislation insuring a job for everyone, action against discrimination that would offer better job opportunities for women workers, and ratification of the ERA—were goals that the non-Caucus faction were also in favor of (*New York Times*, 28 October 1975).

18.   Previously there had been three national offices: a New York public relations office, a Washington DC legislative office, and the national executive office in Chicago. The new leadership accomplished the consolidation and move within a matter of months. Elected in October they opened the National NOW Action Center in Washington, DC, in January 1976.

19.   Barbara Timmer states that the 1978 extension march affected her to the point that she moved to Washington, DC, to become more involved. Later she ran for executive vice president of NOW and won (interview, June 1983).

20.   Interview, Linda Miller, Illinois State NOW officer (June 1983).

21.   NOW successfully defended the boycott in court after a lawsuit was instigated by the State of Missouri. John Ashcroft, then Attorney General of Missouri, filed the lawsuit which engaged much publicity and cost Missouri citizens thousands of dollars. In 1984, Ashcroft was elected Governor of the state.

22.   In a publication of *The American* (the "official organ of the American Party"), Carolyn Anderson charged that the elections had been rigged. (See the Ann Boyce quote at the beginning of this chapter for a feminist who makes the same charge against the anti-feminist movement.) Anderson called on all pro-family groups, including Pro-Life, Anti-ERA, and the Association of the W's (Women Who Want to be Women) to come to Houston for a rally to pass resolutions of their own (1977: 1).

23.   The Republican Party included the ERA in their platform in 1940, four years before the Democratic Party.

24.   The newly formed Congressional Union was a New York based group named after the original Congressional Union that was the forerunner to the National Woman's Party. The contemporary CU was primarily an organization of academic women, mostly historians from Sarah Lawrence College. They were interested in raising awareness of the suffrage struggle and honoring the militant spirit of CU and NWP leaders.

25.   Unlike the earlier NWP demonstrators, where women picketed but did not actually break any law, these activists held a sit-in at the White House driveway. There is no evidence of NWP members using chains in their suffrage demonstrations; however, militant suffragists in England did. The use of chains in the contemporary U.S. movement actually derives from the English activists. Another difference with this militant action was that the women paid the fine (mainly because they wanted to get their chains back), rather than remain in jail.

26.   This action led the new Congressional Union to have a short history. In the formation stage, the idea of reclaiming women's militant past, through both the revival of history and present-day action, was part of their agenda. A report in the first newsletter on members' experiences at an NWP convention revealed scorn for the NWP's present-day non-militant program. Nevertheless, within six months they were distancing themselves from the Sonia Johnson DC Congressional Union chapter and disavowing any connection with a February 15 Susan B. Anthony birthday action in which 24 CU women were arrested at the White House. Johnson's group broke away because of the reluctance the New York based headquarters had for actually doing civil disobedience. After the break, the DC women simply called themselves "A Group of Women." The Congressional Union dissolved within two years. (Congressional Union mailings; A Group of Women mailings; interview, Sonia Johnson, August 1983; and interview, Charlotte Bunch, June 1983.)

27.   Of the 15 states that failed to pass the ERA most were Southern, sunbelt, or rural based: Nevada, Utah, Arizona, Oklahoma, Arkansas, Louisiana, Mississippi, Alabama, Georgia, South Carolina, North Carolina, Virginia, Florida, Missouri, and Illinois. Five states passed the ERA and then voted to rescind their vote: Idaho, South Dakota, Nebraska, Kentucky, and Tennessee.

28.   Hand-out, n.d.

29.   Press release, issued by the Religious Committee for the ERA, May 18, 1981. The RCERA is a coalition of over 40 Jewish, Catholic, and Protestant organizations.

30. They were told that if they left they would not be allowed back in, so they stayed for the weekend. Information on the fasters and the Grassroots Group came from newspaper articles in the *St Louis Post Dispatch* and *St Louis Globe Democrat* (May–July 1982), hand-outs from both groups, field notes from the events, a workshop put on by representatives of the Grassroots Group at a 1984 Illinois NOW convention, and interviews with participants.

31. They sprayed the names of the Governor and anti-ERA legislators on the walls of the capitol with blood from a local slaughter house. Initially some observers thought the women had slit their wrists and hysteria reigned through the chambers as ambulances were called. The demonstrators chose to use animal blood for symbolic reasons—the slaughtering of the ERA and because "blood is what men hate; it disgusts them; it reminds them of menstruation and birth" (group interview with seven members of the Grassroots Group, June 1983; see also, Carroll 1986, and Lambrecht 1982). There was an attempt to also charge the Grassroots Group with further destruction of property. Massive doses of fertilizer had been used to kill a large patch of grass on the capitol grounds in the shape of the three letters—ERA. These charges were dropped for lack of evidence. This action was actually done by NOW members who meant to enrich (rather than kill) the grass, thereby making a bright green ERA design for the following Spring (conversation with anonymous NOW member).

32. Mailing from Sonia Johnson, June 16, 1983.

Chapter 6

1. Interview, Charlotte Bunch, theorist and activist in the women's movement (June 1983).

2. Interview with a member of a civil disobedience group, The Grassroots Group of Second Class Citizens (July 1983). Note: seven members of the Grassroots Group were interviewed simultaneously and, at their request, quotes from this interview will be anonymous.

3. Ibid.

4. Ibid.

5. Interview, quotes from three different anonymous members of the Grassroots Group.

6. Interview, anonymous member Grassroots Group.

7. Interview, Sonia Johnson, civil disobedience direct action activist, Congressional Union, A Group of Women, and Women Rising in Resistance (August 1983); and field notes of the 1981 national NOW conference.

8. The process of strategy and tactic selection is one which is open to individual chapters. National organizational decisions come out of motions passed at the yearly conference which are then passed on to a board made up of national officers and regional representatives.

9. Interview, Eleanor (Ellie) Smeal, National NOW president 1977–82, 1985–87 (two interviews in September and October 1983). Supporting Smeal's position, the history of NOW shows that the organization has, indeed, engaged in civil disobedience in the past. For example, in 1970 NOW members, including Wilma Scott Heide, the third president of NOW, disrupted a Senate Subcommittee on Constitutional Amendments demanding that they meet on ERA. Ironically, while NOW members were engaged in a civil disobedience action, the radical feminist group "The Feminists" sent the Senate Subcommittee a message denouncing ERA. They also advised other feminists "against squandering invaluable time and energy on it" (see Echols 1989: 200). Not only has NOW engaged in CD previously, but in the 1990s the organization has plans to do so in the future. At the 1991 national NOW conference, delegates voted to incorporate CD into their activist actions. Subsequently the Board developed CD guidelines, organized CD workshops, and planned a CD action focusing on Congress following the 1992 April 5th "We Won't Go Back . . . March for Women's Lives" (National Organization for Women 1991). Interestingly, other mass movement groups refused to participate in the April 5th march if there was a CD action. NOW cancelled the plans for civil disobedience and notified chapters to plan a CD action in their localities when the Supreme Court decision on the PA Abortion Control Act was announced in July 1992.

10.   Conversation, Norma Mendoza, NOW chapter president (March 1984).
11.   Interview, Sonia Johnson.
12.   Conversation, Norman Mendoza.
13.   Interview, anonymous member Grassroots Group.
14.   Ibid.
15.   Ibid.
16.   Interview, Sonia Johnson.
17.   Interview, Ellie Smeal.
18.   Speech by Ellie Smeal, University of Missouri, St. Louis, April 8, 1983.
19.   Interview, Charlotte Bunch.
20.   Interview, Barbara Timmer, National NOW vice president (June 1983).
21.   Interview, anonymous member of Grassroots Group.
22.   Interview, Ann Snitow, member of early radical feminist CR groups (June 1983).
23.   Interview, Naomi Ross, Illinois State NOW officer (July 1983).
24.   Interview, anonymous member Grassroots Group.
25.   Interview, Sonia Johnson.
26.   Interview, Carol King, Regional NOW representative and DSA member (July 1983).
27.   Interview, Joyce Trebilcot, women's studies coordinator and feminist author (October 1983).
28.   Interview, Chris Riddeough, member Chicago Women's Liberation Union, National Organization for Women, and Democratic Socialists of America (August 1983).
29.   Interview, Joyce Trebilcot.
30.   Interview, Charlotte Bunch.
31.   Interview, Ann Snitow.
32.   Interview, Sonia Johnson.
33.   Interview, Ellie Smeal.
34.   Interview, Robin Morgan, 1960s leftist, early radical feminist activist and feminist author (November 1983).
35.   Statement from a woman in the Grassroots Group. NOW members also described the futility they felt with their lobbying efforts.
36.   Interview, Ann Snitow.
37.   Interview, anonymous member Grassroots Group.
38.   Ibid.
39.   Interview, Ann Courtney, Illinois State NOW officer (July 1983).
40.   Field notes, Illinois regional workshop on NOW activism (May 1984).
41.   Field notes of a workshop presentation by Jane Wells-Schooley, National NOW officer, at a Metro-East Illinois NOW chapter, January 1978.
42.   Johnson's campaign raised $140,000, enough to qualify for federal primary matching funds (Barron 1984). However, the election itself was discouraging to feminists in general. The Democratic Party lost every state except Walter Mondale's homestate of Minnesota and the District of Columbia. Third party candidates fared worse than in any recent election. Johnson drew 72,153 votes to come in third among some dozen third party and independent candidates (St. Louis Post Dispatch, 1984).
43.   Field notes, Women's Gathering (August 1983).
44.   Interview, Eleanor Smeal.
45.   Interview, Sonia Johnson.
46.   Unfortunately, media attention for innocuous civil disobedience and street theater actions declined after the initial stage. For instance, the 1983 Gathering received an article and picture in the Washington Post. At the 1984 Gathering in St. Louis, a small write-up in the St. Louis Post Dispatch was decidedly negative, and there was no picture. Neither of these actions received much press notice which may have been related to the fact that in both of these demonstrations it was decided to end the action just before arrest. On the other hand, at a summer 1983 march connected to the Seneca

Falls Peace Encampment, 50 women were arrested and held in a school gym for several days and there was almost no media coverage of this occurrence.

Chapter 7

1. Workshop presentation on "The History of NOW" at the 1987 National NOW Conference, Philadelphia, PA.

2. Schwartz is the founder of Catalyst, an advisory organization that works with corporations to foster career development for women.

3. "Political opportunity structure" is a term used to describe how open or closed the political environment is for social movement goals (see Tarrow 1988).

Chapter 8

1. Slogan attributed to Robin Morgan (see Morgan 1977: 169 for original quote).

2. For detailed analysis of the conflicting feminist views on this issue, as well as their connections and disconnections to conservative and liberal philosophies, see West (1987) and Cottle, Searles, Berger, and Pierce (1989).

3. See Cynthia Fuchs Epstein (1988, Chapter 2) for a description of these two positions. For a breakdown by type of feminists who adopt an essentialist or nominalist perspective, see Alcoff (1988).

4. The original quote by Anatole France is: "The law in its majestic equality forbids both rich and poor alike to beg in the streets, steal bread, and sleep under bridges."

5. The following is a partial listing of some of the many diverse women's groups representing women of color: National Association of Minority Political Women, Association of Black Women in Higher Education, Arab Women's Council, MADRE/Women's Peace Network, National Institute for Women of Color, National Hook-up of Black Women, National Association of Negro Business and Professional Women's Clubs, National Black Women's Health Project, Women for Guatemala, Third World Women's Project, Trade Union Women of African Heritage, and the National Political Congress of Black Women.

6. Interview, Brenda Mamon, a volunteer at the St Louis Abused Women's Support Project and an employee of Redevelopment Opportunities for Women (May 1983).

7. Interview, Betty Lee, an activist in the Black community (May 1983).

8. Interview, Margaret Bush Wilson, chair of the NAACP (August 1983). In the interview Wilson declined to discuss the board meeting incident, citing the need to keep such matters internal to the organization; however, newspapers reported she reprimanded Hooks and then was relieved of her duties as chair because of this action. She did mention her dissatisfaction with the low number of women serving on the board of directors, especially since women make up the majority of the membership and activist workers. Out of a 64 person board, only 11 were women. Later that year she remarked in a speech that she was "stripped of her powers as chairwoman of the NAACP by the organization's board of directors because of sexism" (*St Louis Post Dispatch*, November 1983).

9. Interview, Ann Courtney, Illinois NOW president (June 1983).

10. Interview, Robin Morgan, feminist activist and author (October 1983).

11. Also, interview, Eleanor Smeal, National NOW president (October 1983).

12. Remarks by Eleanor Smeal at the 1980 National NOW conference in San Antonio, Texas. Smeal, as chair of the conference, was responding to a delegate angered over the failure of a resolution which called for NOW to organize and protest around the issue of nuclear proliferation. Con-

ference participants had voted for the organization to take an anti-nuclear stand but refused to allocate resources to do anything more (field notes: October 1980).

Chapter 9

1. See *Ms*, 1990, excerpted from *Outside the Sisterhood*, (San Francisco: Spinsters/Aunt Lute 1991).

2. The women's spirituality movement surfaced in the mid-1970s with the re-emergence of Wicca (witchcraft) and the introduction of "New Age" awareness. Some of the books published in the 1980s include: Adler (1987 revised edition); Cady, Ronan, and Taussig (1986); Christ (1987); Sjoo and Mor (1987); Spretnak (1982); Starhawk (1982); Stein (1987); Walker (1987); and Zahava (1986).

3. See Cataldo, Putter, Fireside, and Lytel (1987) for documentation of this peace camp.

4. For a full account of civil disobedience actions Johnson was involved in, see Chapter 2 of her book, *Going Out of Our Minds: The Metaphysics of Liberation* (1987). For a detailed description of the fast she organized in the Spring of 1982 in Springfield, Illinois, see Chapter 4 of the same book.

5. Campaign speech, Cathy Webb, 1985 National NOW officer election, New Orleans, LA.

6. Campaign speech, Judy Goldsmith, 1985 National NOW officer election, New Orleans, LA.

7. Campaign speech, Eleanor Smeal, 1985 National NOW officer election, New Orleans, LA.

8. Question and answer session, Eleanor Smeal, 1985 National NOW officer election, New Orleans, LA.

9. Campaign speech, Sheri O'Dell, 1985 National NOW officer election, New Orleans, LA.

10. Paper presented at the Eastern Sociological Society 59th Annual Meeting, March 17–19, 1989, Baltimore, MD, "The Women's Movement and the Political Process." Also see Freeman (1987, 1988).

11. Much of this section is taken from field notes of this conference.

12. Conversation with Eleanor Smeal after her talk "The Feminization of Power," Lafayette College, Easton, PA, February 21, 1989.

13. At the end of her talk, NOW members pledged $350,000 for her exploratory campaign (Freeman 1988; National Organization for Women 1987).

14. Field notes, August 1987.

15. Even with concentrating on particular strategies, NOW typically continues to engage in diverse forms of activism. NOW's political emphasis differs from the National Women's Political Caucus, which limits itself to the political arena and maintains that "our only road to equality for women is through the political system" and "our only effective strategy in safeguarding women's rights will be an electoral one" (NWPC mass mailing letter, Sharon Rodine, president, July 1990).

16. Park officials estimated 300,000 participants while march organizers estimated 600,000 (Toner 1989a; Bruske 1989; National Organization for Women 1989b). In the 1992 march, NOW had participants sign-in to document the half million marchers.

17. National NOW mass mailing fundraising letter, Molly Yard, president, October 1989.

18. NARAL mass mailing pledge letter, Kate Michelman, executive director, October 1989.

19. Life style politics represents a similar dynamic to being drawn to people most like yourself, and it is this concept of an ongoing, often unconscious, social-similarity-attraction that underlies the demand for affirmative action policies which exceed the limits of equal opportunity; in other words, going beyond allowing diverse people to apply for a job to monitoring whether or not they actually get hired. Another example of the similarity attraction factor is what politicians call affinity voting, i.e. people voting for someone with their own characteristics, particularly if they have little information on which to base their decision. An embarrassing incident of affinity voting was a primary

election held in Illinois in the mid-1980s where two unknown extreme right-wing candidates with American-sounding names won over party regulars with foreign sounding names.

20. A week after the House vote, the U.S. Senate approved the bill (Welch 1989), which was then sent to the White House where President Bush vetoed it.

21. NOW mass mailing "express wire," Molly Yard, president, August 1990.

22. American Civil Liberties Union (ACLU) mass mailing recruitment letter, Ira Glassner, executive director, June 1990. In this mailing, Glassner points out the seriousness of the long-term effects of these appointments since federal judgeships carry a lifetime tenure.

23. According to Faye Wattleton, President of Planned Parenthood, within one year after Webster nearly 450 state legislative bills had been introduced to restrict abortion rights (Planned Parenthood mass mailing letter, September 1990).

Chapter 10

1. It is also worth noting that social movement research has traditionally been treated in a similar vein as generic "he." Frequently titles of books and articles about social movements will switch from a universalizing concept to one or more specific movements. When this is done, it is not just as an example, but reveals that what is being studied is a particular movement. This practice was especially true of research on movement activism of the 1960s, but is still true today. For example, McAdam (1983), in "Tactical Innovation and the Pace of 'Insurgency,'" goes from a generalizing concept of movement/society interaction to a year-by-year pattern of tactical choice and social control response in the civil rights movement. To be accurate (particularly since this is the only movement examined) he should have titled his article "Tactical Innovation and the Pace of Insurgency in the Civil Rights Movement: 1955–1970." Although this appears to be an unimportant issue, the point is that when researchers talk about social movements they rarely include the women's movement and, when the women's movement is what is being studied, that information is almost always included in the title.

2. *Equal Rights,* vol. 24, no. 19, October 1938: 334, National Woman's Party, Washington, DC. See the Warsaw Collection, Women-Box 1, Folder 29, National Museum of American History, Smithsonian Institute, Washington, DC.

3. For a thorough examination of the part the NAACP played in Supreme Court decisions of the 1940s through 1954, see *Social Problems,* vol. 2, no. 4, April 1955. This entire volume is devoted to articles exploring the process leading up to public policy on desegregating public schools.

4. "Malcolm X's Address to the Grass Roots Conference," reprinted in *Lifeline,* vol. 12, Issue 1, 1986: 1–2, Black Student Union, Northern Illinois University, DeKalb, IL.

5. This more conciliatory view was expressed shortly before Malcolm X was assassinated.

6. Letters to the Editor, *The Progressive,* vol. 48, no. 5, May 1984.

7. Achieving social change is different than being successful in winning specific goals. As Pamela Oliver points out, the question of what constitutes success has to be considered in the present social movement environment of media manipulation and professionalism of movement organizers. Drawing in larger sums of money and numbers of demonstrators may well be more related to professional organizers' efforts than to citizen response (comments from Pamela Oliver, discussant, ASA session "Social Movements and Collective Behavior: Issues of Mobilization and Demobilization," Washington, DC, August 1990).

8. "Non-feminist" refers to people who do not claim the feminist label, but who do feminist work and adopt feminist attitudes. My thanks to both Susan Stall and Rebecca Bordt for discussing with me the use of this term in their research.

BIBLIOGRAPHY

Abbott, Sidney and Love, Barbara (1978 [1972]). *Sappho was a Right-On Woman: A Liberated View of Lesbianism.* New York: Stein & Day.

Addams, Jane (1917). Why women should vote. Pp. 110–129. In F. Bjorhman and A. Porritt (eds) *The Blue Book. Woman Suffrage: History, Arguments and Results.* New York. National Woman Suffrage Publishing.

Addams, Jane (1960 [1910]). *Twenty Years at Hull House.* New York: Macmillan.

Adler, Margot (1987). *Drawing Down the Moon: Witches, Druids, Goddess Worshippers, and Other Pagans in America Today,* revised ed. Boston, MA: Beacon Press.

Adorno, T. W., Levinson, D. J. and Sanford, R. N. (1950). *The Authoritarian Personality.* New York: Harper & Row.

Alcoff, Linda (1988). Cultural feminism versus post-structuralism: the identity crisis in feminist theory. *Signs: Journal of Women in Culture and Society,* 13(3): 405–36.

al-Hibri, Azizah (1983). Unveiling the hidden face of racism: the plight of Arab American women. *Women's Studies Quarterly,* 11(3): 10–11.

Andelin, Helen (1970). *Fascinating Womanhood.* New York: Bantam Books.

Andersen, Margaret (1983). *Thinking about Women: Sociological and Feminist Perspectives.* New York: Macmillan.

Anderson, Carolyn (1977). Calling all ladies: you are needed in Houston. *The American.* 7(10) October: 1–2.

Anonymous (1970). Them and Me. In S. Firestone (ed.) *Notes from the Second Year,* pp. 63–8. New York: Radical Feminist.

Associated Press [AP] (1987). NOW president, aide held in embassy protest. *Chicago Tribune,* 9 September, A6.

Associated Press [AP] (1989). Study: women's pay and poverty rise. *Philadelphia Inquirer,* 8 February, B9.

Atkinson, Ti-Grace (1974). *Amazon Odyssey.* New York: Links Books.

Axinn, June and Stern, Mark J. (1988). *Dependency and Poverty: Old Problems in a New World.* Lexington, MA: Lexington Books.

Balser, Diane (1987). *Sisterhood and Solidarity: Feminism and Labor in Modern Times.* Boston, MA: South End Press.

Banks, Olive (1981). *Faces of Feminism: A Study of Feminism as a Social Movement.* New York: St Martin's Press.

Barrientos, Tanya (1990). LA. Senate votes to ban nearly all abortions. *Philadelphia Inquirer,* 27 June, A4.

Barron, James (1984). Feminist seeks Presidency for Citizen's Party. *New York Times,* 12 August, Section 1, p. 23.

Barry, Kathleen (1988). *Susan B. Anthony: A Biography of a Singular Feminist.* New York: New York University Press.

Beck, Evelyn Torton (1983). No more masks: anti-Semitism as Jew hating. *Women's Studies Quarterly,* 3:11–14.

Becker, Howard S. and Geer, Blanche (1957). Participant observation and interviewing: a comparison. In J. Manis and B. Meltzer (eds), *Symbolic Interaction: A Reader in Social Psychology,* 3rd ed, pp. 76–82. Boston, MA: Allyn & Bacon.

Becker, Susan (1981). *The Origins of the Equal Rights Amendment: American Feminism between the Wars.* Westport, CT: Greenwood Press.

Belmont, Rosemary (1975). New Orleans: We caucused. *Electric Circle* (published by the Majority Caucus, Pittsburgh, PA), 1(1):7.

Berg, Barbara (1978). *The Remembered Gate: Origins of American Feminism.* New York: Oxford University Press.

Berheide, Catherine White (1984). Women's work in the home: seems like old times. *Marriage and Family Review,* Fall/Winter.

Berry, Mary Frances (1986). *Why ERA Failed: Politics, Women's Rights and the Amending Process of the Constitution.* Bloomington, IN: Indiana University Press.

Bertaux, D. and Bertaux-Wiame, I. (1981). Life stories in the bakers' trade. In Daniel Bertaux (ed.), *Biography and Society, the Life History Approach in the Social Sciences.* London: Sage Publications.

Bjorkman, Frances and Porritt, Annie G. (eds) (1917). *The Blue Book. Woman Suffrage: History, Arguments and Results,* revised ed. New York: National Woman Suffrage Publishing.

Blatch, Harriot Stanton and Lutz, Alma (1940). *Challenging Years: The Memoirs of Harriot Stanton Blatch.* New York: G. P. Putnam's.

Bloom, Lynn Z. (1979). Listen! Women speaking. *Frontiers: A Journal of Women Studies,* 2(2):1–2.

Blue, Woody (1989). Seneca women fear microwave zapping. *off our backs,* 19(4):24.

Bluestone, Barry and Harrison, Bennett (1982). *The Deindustrialization of America.* New York: Basic Books.

Blumer, Herbert (1969). Social movements. In B. McLaughlin (ed.), *Studies in Social Movements: A Social Psychological Perspective,* pp. 8–29. New York: The Free Press.

Blumer, Herbert (1978). Social unrest and collective protests. In Norman Denzin (ed.), *Studies in Symbolic Interaction, Vol. 1,* pp. 1–54. Greenwich, CT: JAI Press.

Boldt, David R. (1989). Pro-life, pro-choice and peanut butter-and-jelly people. *Philadelphia Inquirer,* 5 November, E7.

Boles, Janet (1979). *The Politics of the Equal Rights Amendment.* New York: Longman.

Boles, Janet (1986). The Equal Rights Amendment as a non-zero-sum game. In Joan Hoff-Wilson (ed.), *Rights of Passage: The Past and Future of the ERA,* pp. 54–62. Bloomington, IN: Indiana University Press.

Bolotin, Susan (1982). Voices from the post-feminist generation. *New York Times Magazine*, 17 October, 28–31, 103–17.

Borman, Nancy (1979). Random action: whatever happened to feminist revolution? *Village Voice*, 21 May, 107–9.

Boyd, Robert S. (1989). Census Bureau: premarital pregnancy rate rising. *Philadelphia Inquirer*, 22 June, A3.

Brady, David W. and Tedin, Kent L. (1976). Ladies in pink: religious and political ideology in the anti-ERA movement. *Social Science Quarterly*, 56(4): 564–75.

Brewer, Rose M. (1980). Black/white racial inequality in the U.S.: a speculative analysis. *Humanity and Society*, 4:211–25.

Broder, David (1989). In pushing job creation, Bush must heed departing labor chief's assessment. *Philadelphia Inquirer*, 18 January, A14.

Brownmiller, Susan (1975). Against Our Will: Men, Women, and Rape. New York: Simon & Schuster.

Bruske, Ed (1989). 300,000 march here for abortion rights. *Washington Post*, 10 April, A1.

Buechler, Steven M. (1986). Social change, movement transformation, and continuities in feminist movements: some implications of the Illinois woman suffrage movement. In Gwen Moore and Glenna Spitze (eds), *Research in Politics and Society, Vol. 2: Women and Politics*. Greenwich, CT: JAI Press.

Buechler, Steven M. (1990). *Women's Movements in the United States: Woman Suffrage, Equal Rights and Beyond*. New Brunswick, NJ: Rutgers University Press.

Buhle, Marijo and Buhle, Paul (eds) (1978). *The Concise History of Woman Suffrage: Selections from the Classic Work of Stanton, Anthony, Gage and Harper*. Urbana, IL: University of Illinois Press.

Burt, Martha R. and Pittman, Karen J. (1986). *Testing the Social Safety Net: The Impact of Changes in Support Programs during the Reagan Administration*. Washington, DC: Urban Institute Press.

Butler, Jessie Haver (1976). On the platform. In Sherna Gluck (ed.), *From Parlor to Prison: Five American Suffragists Talk about Their Lives*, pp. 61–123. New York: Vintage Books.

Cady, S., Ronan, M., and Taussig, H. (1986). *Sophia: The Future of Feminist Spirituality*. San Francisco, CA: Harper & Row.

California Majority Caucus (1975). Why members-in-trust are members of NOW. Los Angeles, CA: pamphlet published by California National Organization for Women.

Carden, Maren Lockwood (1974). *The New Feminist Movement*. New York: Russell Sage Foundation.

Carden, Maren Lockwood (1977). *Feminism in the Mid-1970s: The Non-Establishment, the Establishment and the Future. A Report to the Ford Foundation*. New York: Ford Foundation.

Carelli, Richard (1989). After much anxious waiting, abortion ruling draws near. *Philadelphia Inquirer*, 26 June, A3.

Carlson, Avis (1959). *The League of Women Voters in St. Louis: The First Forty Years, 1919–1959*. St. Louis, MO: publication of League of Women Voters.

Carroll, Berenice (1986). Direct action and constitutional rights: the case of the ERA. In Joan Hoff-Wilson (ed.), *Rights of Passage: The Past and Future of the ERA*, pp. 63–75. Bloomington, IN: Indiana University Press.

Carson, Clayborne (1981). *In Struggle: SNCC and the Black Awakening of the 1960s*. Cambridge, MA: Harvard University Press.

Cassel, Andrew (1989). An emotional issue from America's heart-land: abortion. *Philadelphia Inquirer*, 24 April A1, A8.

Cassell, Joan (1977). *A Group Called Women: Sisterhood and Symbolism in the Feminist Movement*. New York: David McKay.

Cataldo, M., Putter, R., Fireside, B., and Lytel, E. (1987). *The Women's Encampment for a Future of Peace and Justice: Images and Writings*. Philadelphia, PA: Temple University Press.

Catt, Carrie Chapman and Shuler, Nettie Rogers (1923). *Woman Suffrage and Politics: The Inner Story of the Suffrage Movement*. New York: Charles Scribner's.

Chafe, William (1972). *The American Woman: Her Changing Social, Economic, and Political Roles, 1920–1970*. New York: Oxford University Press.

Chafe William (1977). *Women and Equality*. New York: Oxford University Press.

Chafetz, Janet Saltzman and Dworkin, Anthony Gary (1986). *Female Revolt: Women's Movements in World and Historical Perspective*. Totowa, NJ: Rowman & Allanheld.

Chicago Sunday Sun Times (1971). Feminist angle. 7 March, H2.

Chow, Esther Ngan-Ling (1987). The development of feminist consciousness among Asian American women. *Gender & Society,* 1(3):284–99.

Christ, Carol P. (1987). *Laughter of Aphrodite: Reflections on a Journey to the Goddess*. San Francisco, CA: Harper & Row.

Clark, Kenneth B. (1953). The social scientist as an expert witness in civil rights litigation. *Social Problems,* 1(1):5–10.

Collins, Patricia Hill (1986). Learning from the outsider within: the sociological significance of Black feminist thought. *Social Problems,* 33(6): S14–S32.

Collins, Patricia Hill (1990). *Black Feminist Thought: Knowledge, Consciousness, and the Politics of Empowerment*. Boston, MA: Unwin Hyman.

Collins, Randall (1986). *Sociology of Marriage and the Family: Gender, Love, and Property*. Chicago, IL: Nelson-Hall.

Congressional Union (1981). Fact sheet on the Congressional Union. *Congressional Union* (Washington, DC), 1(1): 1.

Conover, Pamela Johnston and Gray, Virginia (1983). *Feminism and the New Right*. New York: Praeger.

Coser, L. A. (1969). Letter to a young sociologist. *Sociological Inquiry,* 39: 131–17.

Cott, Nancy F. (1987). *The Grounding of Modern Feminism*. New Haven, CT: Yale University Press.

Cottle, Charles E., Searles, Patricia, Berger, Ronald J., and Pierce, Beth Ann (1989). Conflicting ideologies and the politics of pornography. *Gender & Society,* 3(3): 303–33.

Crater, Flora (1976). Candidate endorsement: opinion. *Do It NOW,* 9(2): 6.

Curb, Rosemary (1987). Living as a radical. *The Women's Review of Books,* 5(1): 9.

Dahrendorf, Ralf (1958). Toward a theory of social conflict. *Journal of Conflict Resolution,* 2(2): 170–83.

Danziger, Sheldon H. and Weinberg, Daniel H. (eds) (1986). *What Works and What Doesn't*. Cambridge, MA: Harvard University Press.

Davies, James C. (1962). Toward a theory of revolution. *American Sociological Review,* 27(1): 5–19.

Davies, James C. (1967). The circumstances and causes of revolution: a review. *Journal of Conflict Resolution,* 11(2): 247–57.

Davies, James C. (1971). *When Men Revolt and Why: A Reader in Political Violence and Revolution*. New York: Free Press.

Davis, Elizabeth Gould (1971). *The First Sex*. New York: Penguin Books.

de Beavoir, Simone (1984). France: feminism—alive, well, and in constant danger. In Robin Morgan (ed.), *Sisterhood is Global: The International Women's Movement Anthology*, p. 229–35. Garden City, NY: Anchor Books.

Deckard, Barbara Sinclair (1983). *The Women's Movement: Political, Socioeconomic, and Psychological Issues*, 3rd edn. New York: Harper & Row.

DeCrow, Karen (1988). The rise and fall of the ERA. *National NOW Times,* 21(1), 15 April, 7.

Dehart-Mathews, Jane and Mathews, Donald (1986). The cultural politics of the ERA's defeat. In Joan Hoff-Wilson (ed.), *Rights of Passage: The Past and Future of the ERA*, p. 44–53. Bloomington, IN: Indiana University Press.

Deming, Barbara (1974). *We Cannot Live without Our Lives*. New York: Grossman Publishers.

Dill, Bonnie Thorton (1983). Race, class, and gender: prospects for an all-inclusive sisterhood. *Feminist Studies,* 9(1): 131–50.

Dionne Jr, E. J. (1989). Poll on abortion finds the nation is sharply divided. *New York Times,* 26 April, A1.

Dollard, J., Doob, L., Miller, N., Mowrer, O., and Sears, R. (1971). Frustration and aggression: definitions. In James C. Davies (ed.), *When Men Revolt and Why: A Reader in Political Violence and Revolution,* pp. 166–80. New York: Free Press.

Douglas, Jack D. (1970). *The Relevance of Sociology*. New York: Appleton-Century-Crofts.

Draper, Hal (1965). *Berkeley: The New Student Revolt*. New York: Grove Press.

DuBois, Ellen Carol (1978). *Feminism and Suffrage: The Emergence of an Independent Women's Movement in America 1848–1869*. Ithaca, NY: Cornell University Press.

DuBois, Ellen Carol (1981). *Elizabeth Cady Stanton, Susan B. Anthony: Correspondence, Writings, Speeches.* New York: Schocken Books.

DuBois, Ellen Carol and Gordon, Linda (1984). Seeking ecstasy on the battlefield: danger and pleasure in nineteenth century feminist sexual thought. In Carole S. Vance (ed.), *Pleasure and Danger: Exploring Female Sexuality,* pp. 31–49. Boston, MA: Routledge & Kegan Paul.

Dudley, Barbara (1975). A report to the conference. *Socialist Revolution,* 26 (Oct–Dec): 109.

Durkheim, Emile (1951). *Suicide*. New York: Free Press.

Durkheim, Emile (1964). *The Division of Labor in Society*. New York: Free Press.

Dworkin, Andrea (1979). *Pornography*. New York: Perigee Books.

Echols, Alice (1983). The New feminism of yin and yang. In Ann Snitow, Christine Stansell, and Sharon Thompson (eds), *Powers of Desire,* pp. 439–59. New York: Monthly Review Press.

Echols, Alice (1989). *Daring to Be Bad: Radical Feminism in America, 1967–1975*. Minneapolis, MN: University of Minnesota Press.

Ehrenreich, Barbara (1983). *The Hearts of Men: American Dreams and the Flight from Commitment.* Garden City, NY: Anchor Books.

Ehrenreich, Barbara (1986). Where the boys are. *Mother Jones,* 11(11): 6.

Ehrenreich, Barbara (1987). The next wave. *Ms.,* 16 (1&2): 116–68, 216–18.

Ehrenreich, Barbara and English, Deidre (1989). Blowing the whistle on the "Mommy track." *Ms.,* 18(1&2): 56–8.

Eichel, Larry (1989). New-Style Black candidates found abortion issue crucial. *Philadelphia Inquirer,* November A1.

Eisenstein, Zillah (1981). *The Radical Future of Liberal Feminism*. New York: Longman.

Ellis, Kate (1984). I'm black and blue from the Rolling Stones and I'm not sure how I feel about it: pornography and the feminist imagination. *Socialist Review,* 14(3&4): 103–25.

Endor, Karen (1989). Conference: legacies of race and ethnicity. *off our backs,* 14(6): 2–4.

Engels, Frederick 1935. *Socialism: Utopian and Scientific*. New York: International Publishers.

Epstein, Aron (1989a). Court widens right to fight affirmative action plans. *Philadelphia Inquirer,* 13 June, A1–6.

Epstein, Aron (1989b). Court narrows thrust of civil rights laws. *Philadelphia Inquirer,* 18 June, C1.

Epstein, Barbara (1988). Direct action: lesbians lead the movement. *Outlook: National Lesbian and Gay Quarterly,* 1(2): 27–32.

Epstein, Cynthia Fuchs (1975). Ten years later: perspectives on the woman's movement. *Dissent,* Spring, 169–76.

Epstein, Cynthia Fuchs (1988). *Deceptive Distinctions: Sex, Gender, and the Social Order.* New Haven, CT: Yale University Press.

Ernst, Morris and Loth, David (1952). *Report on the American Communist*. New York: Holt, Rinehart & Winston.

Essien-Udom, E. U. (1962). *Black Nationalism: A Search for an Identity in America*. Chicago, IL: University of Chicago Press.

Evans, Sara (1980). *Personal Politics: The Roots of Women's Liberation in the Civil Rights Movement and the New Left.* New York: Vintage Books.

Farmer, James (1985). *Lay Bare the Heart: An Autobiography of the Civil Rights Movement.* New York: Arbor House.

Farrell, Warren (1988). *Why Men Are the Way They Are.* New York: McGraw-Hill.

Feminists, The (1973). The feminists: a political organization to annihilate sex roles. In A. Koedt, E. Levine, and A. Rapone (eds), *Radical Feminism,* pp. 368–78. New York: Quadrangle Books.

Ferree, Myra Marx, and Hess, Beth B. (1985). *Controversy and Coalition: The New Feminist Movement.* Boston, MA: Twayne Publishers.

Ferree, Myra M. and Miller, Frederich D. (1985). Mobilization and meaning: toward an integration of social psychological and resource perspectives on social movements. *Sociological Inquiry* 55: 38–61.

Fireman, Bruce and Gamson, William. (1979). Utilitarian logic in the resource mobilization perspective. In M. Zald and J. McCarthy (eds), *The Dynamics of Social Movements,* pp 8–44. Cambridge, MA: Winthrop Publishers.

Firestone Shulamith (1970). *The Dialectic of Sex: The Case for Feminist Revolution.* New York: Bantam Books.

Fish, Virginia Kemp (1988). The women's trade union league revisited, 1903–1920. Paper presented at the Midwest Sociological Society Meeting, Minneapolis, March 23–26.

Fishman, Walda Katz (1987). The struggle for women's equality in an era of economic crisis: from the morality of reform to the science of revolution. *Humanity & Society,* 11(4): 519–32.

Fishman, Walda Katz and Fuller, Georgia E. (1981). Unraveling the right wing opposition to women's equality. Paper available from Interchange Resource Center, New York.

Fithian, Nancy (1981). Women control chain of events at E.R.A. demo. *off our backs,* 9(9), October.

Flexner, Eleanor (1975 [1959]). *Century of Struggle: The Woman's Rights Movement in the United States,* revised edn. Cambridge, MA: Belknap Press of Harvard University Press.

Ford, Royal (1990). As state official, Souter opposed unlimited abortion. *Philadelphia Inquirer* (from the *Boston Globe*), 5 August, A6.

Frankel, Sara (1988). Smart men, foolish books. *Mother Jones,* 13(9): 48–9.

Freeman, Jo (1975). *The Politics of Women's Liberation: A Case Study of an Emerging Social Movement and Its Relation to the Policy Process.* New York: Longman.

Freeman, Jo (1979). Resource mobilization and strategy: a model for analyzing social movement organization actions. In Mayer N. Zald and John D. McCarthy (eds), *The Dynamics of Social Movements,* pp. 57–189. Cambridge, MA: Winthrop.

Freeman, Jo (1986). Review of Marx-Ferree and Hess "Controversy and Coalition." *Contemporary Sociology: A Journal of Reviews,* 15(1), January.

Freeman, Jo (1987). Whom you know versus whom you represent: feminist influence in the Democratic and Republican parties. In Mary Fainsod Katzenstein and Carol McClurg Mueller (eds), *The Women's Movements of the United States and Western Europe: Consciousness, Political Opportunity, and Public Policy,* pp. 215–44. Philadelphia, PA: Temple University Press.

Freeman, Jo (1988). Women at the 1988. *off our backs,* 17(9): 4–5.

Friedan, Betty (1963). *The Feminine Mystique.* New York: Dell Publishing.

Friedan, Betty (1976). *It Changed My Life: Writings on the Women's Movement.* New York: Random House.

Friedan, Betty (1981). *The Second Stage.* New York: Summit Books.

Friedland, William H. (1969). For a sociological concept of charisma. In Barry McLaughlin (ed.), *Studies in Social Movements: A Social Psychological Perspective,* pp. 243–57. New York: Free Press.

Fritz, Leah (1979). *Dreamers and Dealers: An Intimate Appraisal of the Women's Movement.* Boston, MA: Beacon Press.

Fromm, Eric (1945). *Escape from Freedom.* New York: Rinehart.

Fuchs, Victor R. (1988). *Women's Quest for Economic Equality.* Cambridge, MA: Harvard University Press.

Gallup, George (1980). Poll finds little change in ideology of electorate. *St Louis Post Dispatch,* 13 November, A7.

Gallup (1986). Gallup opinion poll. *Newsweek,* 31 March, 51.

Gamson, William A. (1975). *The Strategy of Social Protest.* Homewood, Il: The Dorsey Press.

Gamson, William A. (1980). Understanding the careers of challenging groups: a commentary on Goldstone. *American Journal of Sociology,* 85(5): 1043–60.

Gans, Herbert J. (1968). The participant-observer as a human being: observations on the personal aspects of field work. In Howard Becker *et al.* (eds), *Institutions and the Person,* pp. 300–17. Chicago, IL: Aldine.

Garcia, Alma (1989). The development of Chicana feminist discourse, 1970–1980. *Gender & Society,* 3(2): 217–38.

Gardner, Marilyn (1988). Former US First Ladies provide launch pad for new ERA drive. *Christian Science Monitor,* 16 February, 5.

Geerken, Michael and Gove, Walter R. (1983). *At Home and at Work: The Family's Allocation of Labor.* Beverly Hills, CA: Sage Publications.

Gelb, Joyce and Palley, Marian Lief (1982). *Women and Public Policies.* Princeton, NJ: Princeton University Press.

Gerth, H. H. and Mills, C. Wright (1958). *From Max Weber: Essays in Sociology.* New York: Oxford University Press.

Gillespie, Marcia Ann (1987). My gloves are off, sisters: power, racism, and that domination thing. *Ms.,* 15(10): 19.

Gillespie, Marcia Ann (1989). Repro woman: Faye Wattleton maps strategy with Marcia Ann Gillespie. *Ms.,* 8(4) (October): 50–5.

Gilman, Charlotte Perkins (1903). *The Home: Its Work and Influence.* New York: McClure, Phillips.

Gilman, Charlotte Perkins (1935 [1898]). *Women and Economics.* New York: Harper & Row.

Gilman, Charlotte Perkins (1979 [1915]). *Herland.* New York: Pantheon.

Gimenez, Martha E. (1987). Black family: vanishing or unattainable? *Humanity & Society,* 11(4): 420–39.

Gitlin, Todd (1987). *The Sixties: Years of Hope, Days of Rage.* New York: Bantam Books.

Gluck, Sherna (1976). *From Parlor to Prison: Five American Suffragists Talk about Their Lives.* New York: Vintage Books.

Gluck, Sherna (1979). What's so special about women? Women's oral history. *Frontiers: A Journal of Women Studies,* 2nd edn, 2(2): 3–14.

Goodman, Ellen (1989). Life goes on with a celebration of the bra at 100 years. *Philadelphia Inquirer,* 7 June, All.

Goodman, Howard (1991). Abortion hostility is divisive in Wichita. *Philadelphia Inquirer,* 11 August, F1.

Gordon, Linda (1977). *Woman's Body, Woman's Right: A Social History of Birth Control in America.* New York: Penguin Books.

Gordon, Linda (1990). Losing battles. Review of "The Undeserving Poor: From the War on Poverty to the War on Welfare" by Michael B. Katz. *The Women's Review of Books,* 7(6)(March): 78.

Gordon, Suzanne (1975). DeCrow reelected. *Philadelphia Daily News,* 27 October, A3.

Gouldner, Alvin (1970a). *The Coming Crisis of Western Sociology.* New York: Basic Books.

Gouldner, Alvin (1970b). Anti-Minotaur: the myth of a value-free sociology. In Jack Douglas (ed.), *The Relevance of Sociology,* pp. 199–213. New York: Appleton-Century-Crofts.

Green, Charles (1989). After 16 years, foes of abortion hope this is their day. *Philadelphia Inquirer,* 29 June, A15.

Greenhouse, Linda (1991). 5 justices uphold U.S. rule curbing abortion advice. *New York Times,* 24 May, A1.

Griffith, Elisabeth (1984). *In Her Own Right: The Life of Elizabeth Cady Stanton.* New York: Oxford University Press.

Gurr, Ted Robert (1970). *Why Men Rebel.* Princeton, NJ: Princeton University Press.

Gusfield, Joseph R. (1962). Mass society and extremist politics. *American Sociological Review,* 27(1): 19–30.

Gusfield, Joseph R. (1970a). *Protest, Reform, and Revolt: A Reader in Social Movements.* New York: John Wiley.

Gusfield, Joseph R. (1970b). *Symbolic Crusade: Status Politics and the American Temperance Movement.* Chicago, IL: University of Illinois Press.

Hamos, Julie E. (1982). Alliances with other movements. *Aegis: Magazine on Ending Violence Against Women,* 33:36–43.

Hanisch, Carol (1978). The liberal takeover of women's liberation. In Redstockings (ed.), *Feminist Revolution,* pp. 163–7. New York: Random House.

Hansen, Karen (1986). The women's unions and the search for a political identity. *Socialist Review,* 16(2): 67–95.

Harris Survey, The (1982). Public support for ERA soars as ratification deadline nears. Press Release, 6 May, ISSN 0273-1037.

Hartmann, Susan M. (1982). *The Home Front and Beyond: American Women in the 1940s.* Boston, MA: Twayne Publishers.

Hartmann, Susan (1989). *From Margin to Mainstream: American Women and Politics since 1960.* New York: Alfred A. Knopf.

Hayge, Howard (1986). Working women with children. *Monthly Labor Review,* February.

Heberle, Rudolf (1951). *Social Movements.* New York: Appleton-Century-Crofts.

Hegger, S., Ryan, B., and Weston, E. (1983). Women, the family, and politics. *Issues in Radical Therapy,* 11(1): 14–17, 50.

Hernandez, Aileen (1971). Editorial from NOW's president. In J. Sochen (ed.), *The New Feminism in Twentieth-Century America,* pp. 176–8. Lexington, MA: D. C. Heath.

Hernton, Calvin (1985). The sexual mountain and Black women writers. *Black Scholar,* 16(4): 2–11.

Hewlett, Sylvia Ann (1986). *A Lesser Life: The Myth of Women's Liberation in America.* New York: Warner books.

Hoffer, Eric (1951). *The True Believer.* New York: Harper & Row.

Hogeland, Roland W. (1976). The female appendage: feminine life styles in America, 1820–1860. In J. Friedman and W. Shade, (eds), *Our American Sisters: Women in American Life and Thought,* 2nd ed, pp. 133–48. Boston, MA: Allyn and Bacon.

Hole, Judith and Levine, Ellen (1971). *Rebirth of Feminism.* New York: Quadrangle Books.

Hollander, Nicole (1989). Women with a past: looking back to understand feminism's future. *Mother Jones,* 14(8): 47.

hooks, bell (1981). *Ain't I a Woman: Black Women and Feminism.* Boston, MA: South End Press.

Hull, Gloria T., Scott, Patricia B., and Smith, Barbara (eds) (1982). *All the Women are White, All the Blacks are Men, But Some of Us are Brave: Black Women's Studies.* Old Westbury, NY: The Feminist Press.

Humphreys, Laud (1972). *Out of the Closets: The Sociology of Homosexual Liberation.* Englewood Cliffs, NJ: Prentice-Hall.

Hunter College Women's Studies Collective (1983). *Women's Realities, Women's Choices.* New York: Oxford University Press.

Irwin, Inez Haynes (1921). *The Story of the Woman's Party.* New York: Harcourt Brace.

Isserman, Maurice (1987). *If I Had a Hammer: The Death of the Old Left and the Birth of the New Left.* New York: Basic Books.

Jaggar, Alison M. (1983). *Feminist Politics and Human Nature.* Totowa, NJ: Rowman & Allanheld Publishers.

Jaggar, Alison and Struhl, Paula Rothenberg (1978). *Feminist Frameworks: Alternative Theoretical Accounts of the Relations between Women and Men.* New York: McGraw-Hill.

Jenkins, J. Craig (1983). Resource mobilization theory and the study of social movements. *American Review of Sociology,* 9:527–53.

Jernigan, David (1988). Why gay leaders don't last: the first ten years after Stonewall. *Out/Look: National Lesbian and Gay Quarterly,* 1(2) Summer: 33–49.

Johnson, Anjela (1988). Prepackaged spirituality. *off our backs,* 18(12): 4–5.

Johnson, Sonia (1987). *Going out of Our Minds: The Metaphysics of Liberation.* Freedom, CA: The Crossing Press.

Johnson, Sonia (1989). *Wildfire: Igniting the She/Volution.* Albuquerque, NM: Wildfire Books.

Johnston, Jill (1973). *Lesbian Nation: The Feminist Solution.* New York: Simon & Schuster.

Jonasdottir, Kristin (1988). Oligarchy and/or goal transformation: the case of the National Organization for Women. Paper presented at the Midwest Sociology Society, Minneapolis, MI.

Jones, Bev (1975). Levelling the hierarchy. *Electric Circle* (published by the Majority Caucus, Pittsburgh, PA), 1(1), August.

Jones, Beverly and Brown Judith, (1970). Toward a female liberation movement. In Leslie Tanner (ed.), *Voices from Women's Liberation,* pp. 362–415. New York: A Signet Book from NAL.

Joreen (1973). The tyranny of structurelessness. In A. Koedt, E. Levine, and A. Rapone (eds), *Radical Feminism,* pp. 285–99. New York: Quadrangle Books.

Joreen (1976). Trashing: the dark side of sisterhood. *Ms.,* 9(10): 49–98.

Katzenstein, Mary Fainsod (1987). Comparing the feminist movements of the United States and Western Europe: an overview. In Mary Fainsod Katzenstein and Carol McClurg Mueller (eds.), *The Women's Movements of the United States and Western Europe: Consciousness, Political Opportunity, and Public Policy,* pp. 3–20. Philadelphia, PA: Temple University Press.

Kessler-Harris, Alice (1975). Where are the organized women workers? *Feminist Studies,* 3(1–2): 92–110.

Kettler, Ernestine Hara (1976). In prison. In Sherna Gluck (ed.), *From Parlor to Prison: Five American Suffragists Talk about Their Lives,* pp. 227–70. New York: Vintage Books.

Kimmich, Madeleine (1985). *America's Children—Who Cares? Growing Needs and Declining Assistance in the Reagan Era.* Washington, DC: Urban Institute Press.

King, Deborah K. (1988). Multiple jeopardy, multiple consciousness: the context of a Black feminist ideology. *Signs: Journal of Women in Culture and Society,* 14(1): 42–72.

King, Mary (1987). *Freedom Song: A Personal Story of the 1960s Civil Rights Movement.* New York: William Morrow.

Kinnard, Cynthia D. (1986). *Antifeminism in American Thought: An Annotated Bibliography.* Boston, MA: G. K. Hall.

Klandermans, Bert (1984). Mobilization and participation: social psychological expansions of resource mobilization theory. *American Sociological Review* 49:583–600.

Klatch, Rebecca E. (1987). *Women of the New Right.* Philadelphia, PA: Temple University Press.

Klein, Ethel (1987). The diffusion of consciousness in the United States and Western Europe. In Mary Fainsod Katzenstein and Carol McClurg Mueller (eds), *The Women's Movements of the United States and Western Europe: Consciousness, Political Opportunity, and Public Policy,* pp. 23–43. Philadelphia, PA: Temple University Press.

Kluckhohn, Florence (1940). The participant observer technique in small communities. *American Journal of Sociology,* 46: 331–43.

Komarovsky, Mirra (1985). *Women in College*. New York: Basic Books.

Kornhauser, William (1959). *The Politics of Mass Society*. New York: Free Press.

Kraditor, Aileen S. (1968). *Up from the Pedestal: Selected Writings in the History of American Feminism*. Chicago, IL: Quadrangle Books.

Kraditor, Aileen S. (1981 [1965]). *The Ideas of the Woman Suffrage Movement 1890–1920*. New York: W. W. Norton.

Ladyslipper (1983). Herstory of women's music. Music Catalog from Ladyslipper, Inc., New York.

Lambrecht, Bill (1982). Blood spilled in Illinois capitol as curtain falls on ERA. *St Louis Post Dispatch*, 27 June, A10.

Lasswell, Harold D. and Blumenstock, Dorothy (1939). *World Revolutionary Propaganda*. New York: Alfred A. Knopf.

Latourell, Elaine (1976). Candidate endorsement: opinion. *Do It NOW*, 9(2): 2.

Lauer, Robert H. (1973). *Perspectives on Social Change*. Boston, MA: Allyn & Bacon.

Lauer, Robert H. (1976). *Social Movements and Social Change*. Carbondale, IL: Illinois University Press.

Leahy, Peter J., Snow, David A., and Worden, Steven K. (1983). The anti-abortion movement and symbolic crusades: reappraisal of a popular theory. *Alternative Lifestyles* 6(1): 27–47.

Lear, Martha Weinman (1971). The second feminist wave. In June Sochen (ed.), *The New Feminism in Twentieth-Century America*, pp. 161–72. Lexington, MA: D. C. Heath.

LeDuc, Daniel (1989). Some leaders urge GOP to ease abortion stance. *Philadelphia Inquirer*, 16 November, B5.

Leidner, Robin (1991). Stretching the boundaries of liberalism: democratic innovation in a feminist organization. *Signs: Journal of Women in Culture and Society*, 16(2): 263–89.

Lemons, J. Stanley (1973). *The Woman Citizen: Social Feminism in the 1920s*. Chicago, IL: University of Illinois Press.

Leon, Barbara (1978). Separate to integrate. In Redstockings (ed.), *Feminist Revolution*, pp. 152–7. New York: Random House.

Lerner, Gerda (1977). *The Female Experience: An American Documentary*. Indianapolis, IN: Bobbs-Merrill Publishing.

Levine, Suzanne and Lyons, Harriet (eds) (1980). *The Decade of Women: A Ms. History of the Seventies in Words and Pictures*. New York: Paragon Books.

Lewin, Miriam and Tragos, Lilli (1987). Has the feminist movement influenced adolescent sex role attitudes? A reassessment after a quarter century. *Sex Roles*, 3–4: 125–35.

Lewis, James I. (1985). Race, gender and cultural identity. *Subject to Change*, 2(3): 31–4.

Liebman, Robert C. and Wuthnow, Robert (eds.), (1983). *The New Christian Right: Mobilization and Legitimation*. Hawthorne, NY: Aldine.

Lipset, Seymour Martin (1950). *Agrarian Socialism*. Berkeley, CA: University of California Press.

Lipset, S. M., Trow, M., and Coleman, J. (1956). *Union Democracy: The Internal Politics of the International Typographical Union*. Glencoe, IL: Free Press.

Listen Real Loud (1986). Leau Tutu: literacy first goal of domestic workers in South Africa. *Listen Real Loud: News of Women's Liberation Worldwide*, Nationwide Women's Program of the American Friends Service Committee, 7(1&2): 1.

Lofland, John (1979). White-hot mobilization: strategies of a millenarian movement. In M. M. Zald and J. D. McCarthy (eds.), *The Dynamics of Social Movements*, pp. 157–66. Cambridge, MA: Winthrop Publishers.

Lorde, Audre (1984). *Sister Outsider*. Trumansburg, NH: The Crossing Press.

Luker, Kristin (1984). *Abortion and the Politics of Motherhood*. Berkeley, CA: University of California Press.

Luker, Kristin (1986). Losers in a zero-sum game. *New York Times Book Review*, 17 October, 7.

Luker, Kristin (1989). Motherhood and morality in America. In Arlene Skolnick and Jerome Skolnick (eds), *Family in Transition*, 6th edn, pp. 534–52. Glenview, IL: Scott, Foresman.

Lyman, Rick (1989). Pro-choice group crosses line of civil disobedience. *Philadelphia Inquirer*, 13 April, A3.

McAdam, Doug (1983). Tactical innovation and the pace of insurgency. *American Sociological Review*, 48(6): 735–54.

McAdam, Doug (1988). *Freedom Summer*. New York: Oxford University Press.

McCarthy, John and Zald, Mayer (1977). Resource mobilization and social movements: a partial theory. *American Journal of Sociology*, 82(6): 1212–41.

Macdonald, Barbara (1990). Politics of aging: I'm *not* your mother. *Ms.*, Premier Issue, July/August, 56–8.

MacKinnon, Catharine A. (1987). *Feminism Unmodified: Discourses on Life and Law*. Cambridge, MA: Harvard University Press.

MacKinnon, Catherine A. (1990). Liberalism and the death of feminism pp. 3–13 in D. Leidholdt and J. Raymond. (eds) *The Sexual Liberals and the Attack on feminism*. New York: Pergamon.

McLanahan, Sara S., Sorensen, Annemette, and Watson, Dorothy (1989). Sex differences in poverty, 1950–1980. *Signs: Journal of Women in Culture and Society*, 15, Autumn, 101–22.

McPhail, Clark (1983). Collective behavior: traditional conceptions and alternatives. Paper presented at the Annual Meeting of the American Sociological Association, Detroit, MI, August 31–September 4.

Mainardi, Patricia (1978). The marriage question. In Redstockings (ed.), *Feminist Revolution*, pp. 120–2. New York: Random House.

Majority Caucus (1975). Out of the mainstream, into the revolution. Conference booklet prepared by South Hills (PA) NOW, Majority Caucus Committee, National Organization for Women.

Mandle, Joan (1979). *Women and Social Change in America*. Princeton, NJ: Princeton Book Co.

Mann, Judy (1982). Here to stay. *Washington Post*, 24 March, A3.

Mannheim, Karl (1940). *Man and Society in an Age of Reconstruction*. London: Routledge & Kegan Paul.

Mansbridge, Jane J. (1986). *Why We Lost the ERA*. Chicago, IL: University of Chicago Press.

Marshall, Susan E. (1984). Keep us on the pedestal: women against feminism in twentieth-century America. In Jo Freeman (ed.), *Women: A Feminist Perspective*, 3d ed., pp. 568–81. PaloAlto, CA: Mayfield Publishing Co.

Marshall, Susan E. (1986). In defense of separate spheres: class and status politics in the antisuffrage movement. *Social Forces*, 65 (Dec): 327–51.

Marshall, Susan E. (1990). Equity issues and Black-White differences in women's ERA support. *Social Science Quarterly*, 71 (June): 290–314.

Martin, Wendy (1972). *The American Sisterhood: Writings of the Feminist Movement from Colonial Times to the Present*. New York: Harper & Row.

Marx, Gary T. (1979). External efforts to damage or facilitate social movements: some patterns, explanations, outcomes, and complications. In Mayer Zald and John McCarthy (eds), *The Dynamics of Social Movements*, pp. 94–125. Cambridge, MA: Winthrop Publishers.

Marx, Karl and Engels, Friedrich (1977 [1859]). Class struggle and the change from feudalism to capitalism. In Dennis Wrong and Harry Gracey (eds), *Readings in Introductory Sociology*, 3rd edn, pp. 140–9. New York: Macmillan.

Mason, Karen Oppenheim and Lu, Yu-Hsia (1988). Attitudes toward women's familial roles: changes in the United States, 1977–1985. *Gender & Society*, 2(1): 39–57.

Mayo, Edith and Frye, Jerry K. (1986). The ERA: postmortem of a failure in political communication. In Joan Hoff-Wilson (ed.), *Rights of Passage: The Past and Future of the ERA*, pp. 76–89. Bloomington, IN: Indiana University Press.

Mednick, Martha T. (1989). Single mothers: a review and critique of current research. In Arlene S. Skolnick and Jerome H. Skolnick (eds), *Family in Transition*, pp. 441–56. Glenview, IL: Scott, Foresman.

Merton, Robert K. (1957). *Social Theory and Social Structure*. Glencoe, IL: Free Press.

Merton, R. K. and Kitt, A. S. (1950). Contributions to the theory of reference group behavior. In R. K. Merton and P. F. Lazarsfeld (eds), *Continuities in Social Research: Studies in the Scope and Method of the American Soldier*. Glencoe, IL: Free Press.

Michels, Robert (1959 [1911]). *Political Parties*. New York: Dover Publication.

Mill, J. S. (1970). The subjection of women. In Alice Rossi (ed.) *Essays on Sex Equality by John Stuart Mill and Harriet Taylor Mill*. Chicago: University of Chicago Press.

Mills, C. Wright (1956). *White Collar*. New York: Oxford University Press.

Mills, C. Wright (1956). *The Power Elite*. New York: Oxford University Press.

Mills, C. Wright (1959). *The Sociological Imagination*. New York: Grove Press.

Misztal, Bronislaw (1982). Participation theory: the meaning of participation in contemporary sociological theory. From a Sociology Colloquium, Washington University, St Louis, MO, 8 February.

Molatch, Harvey (1979). Media and movements. In Mayer Zald and John McCarthy (eds), *The Dynamics of Social Movements*, pp. 71–93. Cambridge, MA: Winthrop Publishers.

Moraga, Cherrie and Anzaldua, Gloria (eds) (1981). *This Bridge Called My Back: Writings by Radical Women of Color*. Watertown, MA: Persephone Press.

Morgan, Marybelle (1973). *Total Women*. New Jersey: Fleming H. Revell.

Morgan, Robin (ed.) (1970). *Sisterhood is Powerful: An Anthology of Writings from the Women's Liberation Movement*. New York: Vintage Books.

Morgan, Robin (1977). *Going Too Far: The Personal Chronicle of a Feminist*. New York: Random House.

Morgan, Robin (1984). *Sisterhood is Global: The International Women's Movement Anthology*. Garden City, NY: Anchor Press/Doubleday.

Ms. (1983). Why the ERA failed. *Ms.*, 11(7): 37.

Mueller, Carol McClurg (1987). Collective consciousness, identity transformation, and the rise of women in public office in the United States. In Mary Fainsod Katzenstein and Carol McClurg Mueller (eds), *The Women's Movements of the United States and Western Europe: Consciousness, Political Opportunity, and Public Policy*, pp. 89–108. Philadelphia, PA: Temple University Press.

Mueller, Carol and Dimieri, Thomas (1982). The structure of belief systems among contending ERA activists. *Social Forces*, 60(3).

Murray, Charles (1984). *Losing Ground: American Social Policy, 1950–80*. New York: Basic Books.

Myers, Frank (1971). Civil disobediance and organizational change: the British Committee of 100. *Political Science Quarterly*, 86: 92–112.

Myhre, Donna and Capps, Mary (1981). Conferences we have known. *Aegis: Magazine on Ending Violence against Women*, Summer, 35.

National Commission on the Observance of International Women's Year (1978). The spirit of Houston: The first National Women's Conference. *Official Report to the President, the Congress, and the People of the United States*. Washington, DC, March.

National Committee on Pay Equity (1988). Slight earnings gains by women of color, yearly Census Bureau data indicates. *National Committee on Pay Equity Newsnotes*, 9(2).

National Organization for Women (1974). You can't stop now. *Souvenir Journal from the 7th National NOW Conference*, 25–27 May, Houston, TX.

National Organization for Women (1975). National NOW unifies. *Do It NOW* 8(3): 1.

National Organization for Women (1976). Election results. *Do It NOW* 9(2): 27.

National Organization for Women (1982). A salute to NOW president Ellie Smeal, 1977–1982. *National NOW Times*, 9(8): 3.

National Organization for Women (1985). Smeal elected NOW president. *National NOW Times*, 18(5): 1.

National Organization for Women (1987). Molly Yard elected NOW president, Schroeder campaign gets huge boost. *National NOW Times*, 20(3): 1.

National Organization for Women (1988). Proposed by-laws amendments to be presented to the 1988 National NOW conference. *National NOW Times*, 20:13.

National Organization for Women (1989a). ERA is No. 1 in House. *National NOW Times*, 21(5): 3.

National Organization for Women (1989b). 600,000 march for abortion rights. *National NOW Times*, 21(1): 1.

National Organization for Women (1991). NOW CD guidelines passed. *National NOW Times*, 24(2): 4.

New York Times (1975). NOW elects new officers pledged to expand group's activism. 28 October L15.

Newsweek (1986). Too late for Prince Charming. 2 June, 54–5.

Nisbet, Robert (1953). *The Quest for Community*. New York: Oxford University Press.

Oakley, Ann (1981). Interviewing women: a contradiction in terms. In Helen Roberts (ed.), *Doing Feminist Research*, pp. 30–61. London: Routledge & Kegan Paul.

Oberschall, Anthony (1973). *Social Conflict and Social Movements*. Englewood Cliffs, NJ: Prentice-Hall.

Oberschall, Anthony (1978). The decline of the 1960s social movements. *Research in Social Movements, Conflicts and Change*, 1: 257–89.

off our backs (1988). Letters to the editor in Utopia. 18(2): 25.

off our backs (1991). NWSA staff resigns. 21(1): 6.

Oliver, Pamela (1983). Discussant, Social movements and collective behavior, American Sociological Association Meetings, Detroit, MI, August 31–September 4.

Olson, Mancur (1968). *The Logic of Collective Action*. New York: Schocken.

Olson, Mancur (1971). Rapid growth as a destabilizing force. In James C. Davies (ed.), *When Men Revolt and Why: A Reader in Political Violence and Revolution*, pp. 215–27. New York: Free Press.

On the Issues (1988). The making of a radical feminist: a different perspective on Andrea Dworkin in an intimate, candid interview. *On the Issues: The Journal of Substance for Progressive Women*, 9: 4–5, 16–18.

O'Neill, William L. (1969). *Everyone Was Brave: The Rise and Fall of Feminism in America*. Chicago, IL: Quadrangle Books.

O'Neill, William L. (1989). *Feminism in America: A History*, revised ed. New Brunswick, NJ: Transaction Books.

O'Reilly, Jane (1983). Watch on the right: the big-time players behind the small-town image. *Ms.*, 10(1): 37–9.

Paley, Grace (1988). We're talking to each other more and more. *off our backs*, 18(4): 4–5.

Palmer, Phyllis Marynick (1983). White women/Black women: the dualism of female identity and experience in the United States. *Feminist Studies*, 9(1): 151–70.

Palmer, Phyllis and Skolnick, Joan (1983). *The Emerging Woman*. Washington, DC: Educational TV and Film Center.

Pane, Carol Williams (1973). Consciousness raising: a dead end? In A. Koedt, E. Levine and A. Rapone (eds), *Radical Feminism*, pp. 282–4. New York: Quadrangle Books.

Paolantonio. S. A. (989). Governor seat won in 3d try. *Philadelphia Inquirer*, 18 November, A1.

Papachristou, Judith (1976). *Women Together*. New York: Alfred A. Knopf.

Peck, Mary Gray (1944). *Carrie Chapman Catt: A Biography*. New York: H. W. Wilson.

Perkins, Bill and Arenth, Betty (1981). 1981 NOW convention. *Women Organizing*, Socialist Feminist Commission of the New American Movement, 9, Winter.

Phillips, Bernard (1971). *Knowledge from What: Theories and Methods in Social Research*. New York: Rand McNally.

Phillips, Don (1989). House eases abortions for poor. *Philadelphia Inquirer*, 13 October, A1.

Pleck, Elizabeth (1983). Notes on the defeat of the ERA. *Working Paper No. 103*, Wellesley College Center for Research on Women.

Plutzer, Eric and Ryan, Barbara (1987). Notifying husbands about an abortion: an empirical look at constitutional and policy dilemmas. *Sociology and Social Research*, 71(3): 183–9.

Pollitt, Katha (1986). Being wedded is not always bliss. *The Nation*, 20 September, 239–42.

Pombeiro, Beth Gillin (1975). NOW takes a turn toward all women, not just members. *Philadelphia Inquirer*, 28 October, A3.

Poole, Keith T. and Zeigler, L. Harmon (1981). The diffusion of feminist ideology. *Political Behavior*, 3(3): 229–56.

Pratt, Minnie Bruce (1984). Who am I if I'm not my father's daughter? *Ms.*, 12(8): 72–3.

Purdy, Matthew (1989). Put back on the defensive, pro-choice groups mobilize. *Philadelphia Inquirer*, 9 July, A1, A10.

Radford-Hill, Sheila (1986). Considering feminism as a model for social change. In Teresa de Lauretis (ed.), *Feminist Studies/Critical Studies*, pp. 157–72. Bloomington, IN: Indiana University Press.

Radicalesbians (1973). The woman identified woman. In A. Koedt, E. Levine and A. Rapone (eds), *Radical Feminism*, pp. 240–5. New York: Quadrangle Books.

Radinsky, Terry and Gadlin, Lucy (1969). Towards a revolutionary women's union: a strategic perspective. Unpublished paper, from the Women's Collection at Northwestern University, Folder 19.

Redstockings of the Women's Liberation Movement (1978). *Feminist Revolution: An Abridged Edition with Additional Writings*. New York: Random House.

Reinharz, Shulamit (1979). *On Becoming a Social Scientist: From Survey Research and Participant Observation to Experiential Analysis*. San Francisco, CA: Jossey-Bass.

Reinharz, Shulamit (1983). Experiential analysis: a contribution to feminist research. In Gloria Bowles and Renate Duelli Klein (eds), *Theories of Women's Studies*, pp. 162–91. London: Routledge & Kegan Paul.

Renzetti, Claire M. (1987). New wave or second stage? Attitudes of college women toward feminism. *Sex Roles*, 16: 265–77.

Reskin, Barbara F. (1988). Bringing the men back in: sex differentiation and the devaluation of women's work. *Gender & Society*, 2(1): 58–81.

Rew (1989). Jane: the abortion service transformed into feminist practice. *off our backs*, 14(9): 17.

Rich, Adrienne (1979). *On Lies, Secrets, and Silence: Selected Prose 1966–1978*. New York: W. W. Norton.

Rich, Adrienne (1980). Compulsory heterosexuality and lesbian existence. *Signs: Journal of Women in Culture and Society*, 5(4): 631–60.

Richardson, Laurel Walum (1981). *The Dynamics of Sex and Gender: A Sociological Perspective*, 2nd ed. Boston, MA: Houghton Mifflin.

Riesman, David, with Nathan Glazer and Reuel Denney (1961 [1950]). *The Lonely Crowd*, abridged ed. New Haven, CT: Yale University Press.

Rosenberg, Rosalind (1982). *Beyond Separate Spheres: Intellectual Roots of Modern Feminism*. New Haven: Yale University Press.

Rosenfelt, Deborah and Stacey, Judith (1987). Second thoughts on the second wave. *Feminist Studies*, 13(2): 341–61.

Ross, Luana (1989). Special report: midyear, 1989. Mailing insert with *SWS Network News*, Sociologists for Women in Society, 7(3): p. 6–7.

Rossi, Alice (ed.) (1970). *Essays on Sex Equality: John Stuart Mill and Harriet Taylor Mill.* Chicago, IL: University of Chicago Press.

Rossi, Alice (ed.) (1973). *The Feminist Papers: From Adams to de Beauvoir.* New York: Bantam Books.

Roth, Julius A. (1988). To the Editor. *Gender & Society,* 2(2): 243.

Rothenberg, Paula (1989). The hand that pushes the rock. *The Women's Review of Books,* 7(5): 18.

Rothman, Barbara Katz (1989). Women as fathers: motherhood and child care under a modified patriarchy. *Gender & Society,* 3(1): 89–104.

Rothschild-Whitt, Joyce (1979). The collectivist organization: an alternative to rational-bureaucratic models. *American Sociological Review,* 44:509–27.

Rupp, Leila J. and Taylor, Verta (1987). *Survival in the Doldrums: The American Women's Rights Movement,* 1945–1960. New York: Oxford University Press.

Ryan, Barbara (1982). Thorstein Veblen: a new perspective. *Mid-American Review of Sociology,* 7(2): 29–47.

Ryan, Barbara (1989). Ideological purity and feminism: the U.S. women's movement from 1966 to 1975. *Gender & Society,* 3(2): 239–57.

Ryan, Barbara and Plutzer, Eric (1989). When married women have abortions: spousal notification and marital interaction. *Journal of Marriage and the Family,* 51(1): 41–50.

St Louis Post Dispatch (1983). Mrs Wilson accuses NAACP of sexism. 27 November, A1.

St Loius Post Dispatch (1984). Minor parties big losers in election. 23 December, A6.

St Loius Post Dispatch (1985). Smeal elected NOW head again. 22 July, A6.

Sale, Kirkpatrick (1973). *SDS.* New York: Vintage Books.

Salper, Roberta (1972). The development of the American women's liberation movement, 1967–1971. In Robert Salper (ed.), *Female Liberation: History and Current Politics,* pp. 169–84. New York: Alfred A. Knopf.

Sarachild, Kathie (1970). A program for feminist consciousness raising. In S. Firestone (ed.) *Notes from the Second Year,* a journal of writings from the women's liberation movement. New York: Radical Feminist.

Sarachild, Kathie (1978). The power of history. In Redstockings (ed.), *Feminist Revolution,* pp. 13–43. New York: Random House.

Sargent, Lydia (1981). *Women and Revolution: A Discussion of the Unhappy Marriage of Marxism and Feminism.* Boston, MA: South End Press.

Scanlan, Christopher (1989). Buoyed abortion-rights groups discover new political clout. *Philadelphia Inquirer,* 13 October, A1.

Schattschneider, Elmer Eric (1960). *The Semisoverign People.* New York: Holt: Rinehart & Winston.

Schechter, Susan (1982). Speaking to the battered women's movement. *Aegis: Magazine on Ending Violence against Women,* 33 (Winter): 36–43.

Schmich, Mary T. (1988). Women talk of past but look to future: ERA on back burner but still warm. *Chicago Tribune,* 14 February, A3.

Schmid, Margaret and Starkweather, Shirley (1969). Working towards women's liberation: analysis and proposals. Unpublished paper.

Schwartz, Felice N. (1989). Management women and the new facts of life. *Harvard Business Review,* Jan–Feb: 65–76.

Scott, Anne Firor (1984). *Making the Invisible Woman Visible.* Chicago, IL: University of Illinois Press.

Segal, Lynne (1987). *Is the Future Female? Troubled Thoughts on Contemporary Feminism.* New York: Peter Bedrick Books.

Sellen, Betty-Carol and Young, Patricia A. (1987). *Feminists, Pornography, & the Law: An Annotated Bibliography of Conflict, 1970–1986.* Hamden, CT: Library Professional Publications.

Shanahan, Eileen (1975). Lawyer re-elected president of NOW. *New York Times,* 27 October, Section 1, p. 8.

Shelley, Martha (1970). Notes of a radical lesbian. In Robin Morgan (ed.) *Sisterhood is Powerful: an Anthology of Writings from the Women's Liberation Movement,* pp. 306–11. New York: Vintage Books.

Shostak Arthur B. and Gary McLouth with Lynn Seng (1984). *Men and Abortion: Lessons, Losses and Love.* New York: Praeger.

Showalter, Elaine (ed.) (1978). *These Modern Women: Autobiographical Essays from the Twenties.* Old Westbury, NY: The Feminist Press.

Simmel, Georg (1971). *Georg Simmel: On Individuality and Social Forms. Selected Writings and Introduction by Donald Levine.* Chicago, Il: University of Chicago Press.

Simpson, Peggy (1988). Child care: all talk, no action. *Ms.,* 17(6): 81.

Simpson, Peggy (1989). Big movement on campus. *Ms.,* 17(12): 74.

Sjoo, Monica and Mor, Barbara (1987). *The Great Cosmic Mother: Rediscovering the Religion of the Earth.* Sna Francisco, CA: Harper & Row.

Skocpol, Theda (1979). *States and Social Revolutions: A Comparative Analysis of France, Russia, and China.* New York: Cambridge University Press.

Smeal, Eleanor (1975). The National story: St Louis we stood fast. *Electric Circle* (published by the Majority Caucus), 1(1): 5.

Smeal, Ellie (1987). The ERA: should we eat our words? *Ms.,* 16(1&2): 170, 218.

Smelser, Neil (1962). *Theory of Collective Behavior.* New York: Free Press.

Smith, Barbara (1982). Review of "Ain't I a Woman: Black Women and Feminism" by bell hooks. *The New Women's Times Feminist Review,* 9(24).

Smith, Barbara (ed.) (1983). *Home Girls: A Black Feminist Anthology.* New York: Kitchen Table Press.

Smith, Bill (1986). The abortion wars: part one. *St Louis Post Dispatch,* 13 July, A5.

Smith, Gerrit (1968 [1855]). Correspondence between Gerrit Smith and Elizabeth Cady Stanton. In Aileen Kraditor (ed.), *Up from the Pedestal: Selected Writings in the History of American Feminism,* pp. 125–9. New York: Quadrangle Books.

Snitow, Ann (1985). Retrenchment versus transformation: the politics of the antipornography movement. In Varda Burstyn (ed.), *Women against Censorship,* pp. 107–29. Vancouver, British Columbia: Douglas & McIntyre.

Southern, David (1981). An American dilemma: Gunnar Myrdal and the civil rights cases, 1944–1954. *Journal of the History of Sociology,* 3(2): 81–107.

Spokeswoman, The (1974a). New AT&T agreement gives $30-million to women and minorities. 5(1): 1.

Spokeswoman, The (1974b). Sisterhood is powerful: fund destroyed by suit. 5(4): 4.

Spokeswoman, The (1974c). Economy poses major challenge for women. 5(6): 1–3.

Spokeswoman, The (1975). Special report: NOW and the women's movement. 6(6): 1–5.

Spretnak, Charlene (ed.) (1982). *The Politics of Women's Spirituality: Essays on the Rise of Spiritual Power within the Feminist Movement.* Garden City, NY: Anchor/Doubleday.

Staggenborg, Suzanne (1987). Life-style preferences and social movement recruitment: illustrations from the abortion conflict. *Social Science Quarterly,* 68(4): 779–97.

Staggenborg, Suzanne (1989). Stability and innovation in the women's movement: a comparison of two movement organizations. *Social Problems,* 36(1): 75–92.

Stanley, Liz and Wise, Sue (1983). *Breaking Out: Feminist Consciousness and Feminist Research.* London: Routledge & Kegan Paul.

Stanton, Elizabeth Cady (1968 [1855]). Correspondence between Gerrit Smith and Elizabeth Cady Stanton. In Aileen Kraditor (ed.), *Up from the Pedestal: Selected Writings in the History of American Feminism,* pp. 129–31. New York: Quadrangle.

Stanton, Elizabeth Cady, Anthony, Susan B., and Gage, Matilda Joslyn (1881). *History of Woman Suffrage, Vol. 11, 1861–1876.* Rochester, NY: Charles Mann.

Stanton, Theodore and Blatch, Harriot Stanton (1922). *Elizabeth Cady Stanton: As Revealed in Her Letters, Diary and Reminiscences, Vol. 1.* New York: Harper & Brothers.

Starhawk (1982). *Dreaming the Dark: Magic, Sex & Politics.* Boston, MA: Beacon Press.

Stein, Diane (1987). *The Women's Spirituality Book.* St Paul, MN: Llewellyn Publications.

Stein, Harry (1988). *One of the Guys: The Wising up of an American Man.* New York: Simon & Schuster.

Steinem, Gloria (1983). Women grow more radical with age. *Women's Political Times,* 7(4).

Steinem, Gloria, with Joanne Edgar and Mary Thom (1983). Post-ERA politics: losing a battle but winning the war. *Ms.,* 22(7): 35–7.

Stevens, Doris (1920). *Jailed for Freedom.* New York: Boni & Liveright.

Susan, Barbara (1970). About my consciousness raising. In Leslie Tanner (ed.), *Voices from Women's Liberation,* pp. 238–43. New York: Signet Books.

Sturgis, Susanne J. (1989). New Age fills a need. *off our backs,* 14(2): 17–18.

Tarrow, Sidney (1988). National politics and collective action: recent theory and research in Western Europe and the United States. *Annual Review of Sociology,* 14: 421–40.

Tavris, D., with A. I. Baumgartner (1983). How would your life be different? *Redbook,* February, 92–5.

Tax, Meredith (1989). March to a crossroads on abortion. *The Nation,* 8 May, 630–3.

Taylor, Barbara (1979). The men are as bad as their masters . . . : socialism, feminism and sexual antagonism in the London tailoring trade in the 1830s. *Feminist Studies,* 5(1): 7–40.

Taylor, Verta (1986, 1989). The future of feminism in the 1980s: a social movement analysis. In L. Richardson and V. Taylor (eds), *Feminist Frontiers: Rethinking Sex, Gender, and Society,* pp. 434–51. Reading, MA: Addison-Wesley.

Taylor, Verta (1989). Sisterhood, solidarity, and modern feminism. *Gender & Society,* 3(2): 277–86.

Terry, Don (1991). For judge in abortion furor, unusual acts in turbulent times. *New York Times,* 10 August, A4.

Tilly, Charles (1978). *From Mobilization to Revolution.* Reading, MA: Addison-Wesley.

Tilly, Charles (1983). Symbols and interaction in collective behavior. Paper presented at the Annual Meeting of the American Sociological Association, Detroit, MI, August 31–September 4.

Thompson, Paul (1978). *The Voice of the Past: Oral History.* New York: Oxford University Press.

Thorne, Barrie (1975). Protest and the problem of credibility: uses of knowledge and risk-taking in the draft-resistance movement of the 1960s *Social Problems* 23: 111–23.

Toner, Robin (1989a). Right to abortion draws thousands to capital rally. *New York Times,* 10 April, A1.

Toner Robin (1989b). Abortion marchers gather in capital. *New York Times,* April 9, A28.

Touraine, Alain (1981). *The Voice and the Eye: An Analysis of Social Movements.* Cambridge, England: Cambridge University Press.

Tribe, Lawrence H. (1991). "Natural law" and the nominee. *New York Times,* 15 July, Op-Ed section.

Turley, Donna (1986). The Feminist debate on pornography: an unorthodox interpretation. *Socialist Review,* 16(3&4): 81–96.

Turner, Ralph (1983). Figure and ground in the analysis of social movements. *Symbolic Interaction,* 6(2): 175–81.

Turner, Ralph and Killian, Lewis (1957). *Collective Behavior.* Englewood Cliffs, NJ: Prentice-Hall.

Ullmann, Owen (1990). Souter filed brief in '76 on abortion: document opposed Medicaid payment. *Philadelphia Inquirer* (Inquirer Washington Bureau), 31 July, A3.

Valentine, Paul W. (1989). 80 abortion foes arrested in clash at College Park Clinic. *Washington Post,* 30 April, D1.

Van Gelder, Lindsy (1989). It's not nice to mess with Mother Nature. *Ms.,* 17(7&8): 60–3.

Vance, Carole S. (ed.) (1984). *Pleasure and Danger: Exploring Female Sexuality.* Boston, MA: Routledge & Kegan Paul.

Veblen, Thorstein (1973 [1899]). *The Theory of the Leisure Class.* New York: Mentor Books.

Walker, Barbara (1987). *The Skeptical Feminist: Discovering the Virgin, Mother and Crone.* San Francisco, CA: Harper & Row.

Ware, Cellestine (1970). *Woman Power.* New York: Tower Books.

Ware, Susan (1981). *Beyond Suffrage, Women in the New Deal.* Cambridge, MA: Harvard University Press.

Ware Susan (1982). *Holding Their Own: American Women in the 1930s.* Boston, MA: Twayne Publishers.

Warren, Ellen (1989). Bush downplays abortion's political heft. *Phildelphia Inquirer,* 8 November, A3.

Webb, Kathy and Bacon, Lynn (1985). Chronology of major events in NOW's history. *National NOW Times,* 6(2): 4.

Weber, Max. (1977). *Protestantism and the Rise of Modern Capitalism.* In D. Wrong and H. Gracey (eds), *Readings in Introductory Sociology,* 3rd edn, pp. 149–61. New York: Macmillan.

Weinstein, James (1967). *The Decline of Socialism in America, 1912–1925.* New York: Vintage Books, a division of Random House.

Weiss, Michael J. (1989). Equal rights: not for women only. *Glamour,* March, 276–7, 317–22.

Weitzman, Lenore J. (1985). *The Divorce Revolution: The Unexpected Social and Economic Consequences for Women and Children in America.* New York: Free Press.

Welch, William M. (1989). Candidates ease abortion views. *Philadelphia Inquirer,* 10 December, A6.

West, Robin (1987). The feminist-conservative anti-pornography alliance and the 1986 Attorney General's Commission on Pornography Report. *American Bar Foundation Research Journal,* 1987(4): 681–711.

Westcott, Diane (1982). Blacks in the 1970's: did they scale the job ladder? *Monthly Labor Review,* 105: 29–38.

Whitaker, Jan (1984). Nationalism during the Progressive Era. Unpublished paper.

Whitehurst, Carol (1977). *Women in America: The Oppressed Majority.* Snata Monica, CA: Goodyear Publishing.

Wilkins, Roy (1955). The role of the National Association for the Advancement of Colored People in the desegregation process. *Social Problems,* 2(4): 201–4.

Willis, Ellen (1983). Feminism, moralism, and pornography. In Ann Snitow, Christine Stansell, and Sharon Thompson (eds), *Powers of Desire,* pp. 460–7. New York: Monthly Review Press.

Wilson, Bryan (1961). *Sects and Societies.* London: Heinemann.

Wilson, William Julius and Neckerman, Kathryn (1989). Poverty and family structure: the widening gap between evidence and public policy issues. In Arlene S. Skolnick and Jerome H. Skolnick (eds), *Family in Transition,* 6th edn, pp. 504–21. Glenview, IL: Scott, Foresman.

Winnow, Jackie (1989). Lesbians working on AIDS: assessing the impact on health care for women. *Outlook: National Lesbian and Gay Quarterly,* 2(1): 10–18.

Wood, James L. and Jackson, Maurice (1982). *Social Movements: Development, Participation, and Dynamics.* Belmont, CA: Wadsworth.

Woolf, Virginia (1966 [1938]). *Three Guineas.* New York: Harcourt Brace.

Yates, Jenny (1989). Tools for change. *off our backs,* 14(2): 17–19.

Yost, Paula (1989). Battle lines are drawn on abortion. *Philadelphia Inquirer,* 5 July, A1.

Zahava, Irene (ed.) (1986). *Hear the Silence: Stories by Women of Myth, Magic and Renewal.* Trumansburg, NY: The Crossing Press.

Zald, Mayer M. and Ash, Roberta (1966). Social movement organizations: growth, decay and change. *Social Forces,* 44(3): 327–40.

Zald, Mayer M. and McCarthy, John D. (eds) (1979). *The Dynamics of Social Movements, Resource Mobilization, Social Control and Tactics*. Cambridge, MA: Winthrop.

Zald, Mayer M. and McCarthy, John D. (1987). *Social Movements in an Organizational Society: Collected Essays*. New Brunswick, NJ: Transaction Books.

Zausner, Robert (1989). Why has Pa. seized initiative on abortion? *Philadelphia Inquirer*, 5 November, E1, E5.

Zelman, Patricia (1982). *Women, Work, and National Policy: The Kennedy-Johnson Years*. Ann Arbor, MI: UMI Research Press.

Zinn, Maxine Baca, Cannon, Lynn Weber, Higginbotham, Elizabeth, and Dill, Bonnie Thornton (1986). The costs of exclusionary practices in women's studies. *Signs: Journal of Women in Culture and Society*, 11(1): 290–303.

Znaniecki, Florain (1934). *The Method of Sociology*. New York: Farrar, Straus & Girous.

Zurcher, Louis A. and Snow, David A. (1981). Collective behavior: social movements. In Morris Rosenberg and Ralph H. Turner (eds), *Social Psychology: Sociological Perspectives*, pp. 447–82. New York: Basic Books.

INDEX

Abbott, Sidney, 45
Abolitionism, 14 16, 19 20
Abortion, 68, 100, 144–52
Addams, Jane, 23, 24, 26, 35
Affirmative action, 100, 121
AIDS, 139
Ailes, Roger, 149
al-Hibri, Azizah, 133
American Anti-Slavery Society, 14
American Federation of Labor (AFL), 25
American Journal of Sociology (*AJS*), 24
American Woman Suffrage Association
  (*American*), 20, 21–22, 32
Anthony, Susan B.
  arrest for voting, 165n4
  Civil War, 19
  dress reform, 18
  early women's rights meetings, 16
  suffrage movement, 9, 20, 23
Anti-abortion movement, 160
Anti-feminism
  backlash in 1970s, 3, 56, 68
  ERA and New Right, 69
  racist, classist, and homophobic ideology,
    131
  Reagan and Bush administrations, 101
  sexual difference, 118
  traditional family model, 103

Anti-Semitism, 128
Anti-suffrage movement, 33–34
Asian-Americans, 127
Atkinson, Ti-Grace, 44, 50, 62
AT&T, 68

Backlash (*See* Anti-feminism)
Barnett, Ida B. Wells, 26
Beauvoir, Simone de, 12, 135
Beck, Evelyn Torton, 128
Belmont, Alma, 35–36
Berry, Mary Frances, 107, 108
Birth control, 33, 165n5, 166n13
Blacks, 26, 125–26, 127, 128 (*See also* Race;
  Racism)
Blackwell, Henry, 15, 20
Blackwell, Samuel, 15
Blatch, Harriot Stanton, 28, 36
Bloomer, Amelia, 14, 17
Bolotin, Susan, 110
Bork, Robert, 151
Brewer, Rose, 129
Brown, Antoinette, 14
Brown, Rita Mae, 44
Brownmiller, Susan, 114
Bunch, Charlotte, 84
Burns, Lucy, 28
Bush, George, 100, 101, 148–49

Business and Professional Women (BPW), 37
Butler, Jessie Harver, 22

Calvinism, 12–13
Carden, Maren Lockwood, 66
Carmichael, Stokely, 46
Cassell, Joan, 40
Catt, Carrie Chapman, 30, 36
Censorship, 115–16
Chafetz, Janet Saltzman, 66–67
Chicago Women's Liberation Union, 5, 48, 71,
    150
Child care, 105–106, 120
Chow, Ester, 127
Civil disobedience, 76–77, 79, 171n9
Civil rights, 42, 61, 142–43, 159–60
Civil Rights Act of 1964, 42, 43
Civil War, 19
Class
    affirmative action and pay equity, 121–22
    child care, 120
    early women's movement and labor issues,
        26, 165n3
    early women's movement and reform
        societies, 11–12
    interactive effects of gender and race, 128–30
    as issue in contemporary women's
        movement, 124–32
    NOW membership, 82
    popular support for feminist goals in 1980s,
        110–11
    socialist feminism, 48
Cleveland, Grover, 26
Club Woman's Movement, 26
Coalition building, 27–28
Collins-Robson, Mary Jean, 71
Colorado, 166n10
Congress, 35, 136
Congressional Union (CU), 28–29, 170n24, 25
Consciousness raising, 11–12, 47, 89, 167n11
Consensus, 56, 94
Conservatives, 22–26, 62, 68, 99–102, 115
    (See also New Right)
Constitution, 19–20, 30, 31, 34, 164–65n5
    (See also Supreme Court)
Consumer League, 24
Contraception, 33, 165n5, 166n13
Cott, Nancy, 156
Courtney, Ann, 91
Craven, Liz, 49
Cultural feminism, 55

Daughters of Bilitis (DOB), 49
Davis, Elizabeth Gould, 51
DeCrow, Karen, 71–73, 107
Democratic Party, 93, 142–43, 149
Depression, Great, 36, 155
Dill, Bonnie Thornton, 125–26
Divorce, 101–102
Dole, Robert, 106
Dress reform, 17–18
DuBois, Carol Ellen, 16
Dworkin, Andrea, 114–15, 116–17
Dworkin, Anthony Gary, 66–67

Eagle Forum, 69
Eastman, Crystal, 35
Echols, Alice, 51, 117
Economics, 68–69, 101–102
Education, 13–14, 23–24
Ehrenreich, Barbara, 103, 106
England, 28
English, Deidre, 106
Environmentalism, 137
Equal Employment Opportunity Commission
    (EEOC), 44
Equal Pay Act of 1963, 42, 121
Equal Rights Amendment (ERA)
    assessment of past in 1980s, 106–108
    defeat and feminist organizations, 77, 158
    early women's rights movement, 34, 37
    last stages of campaign, 79–80
    NOW campaign, 73–75
    passage by Congress, 68, 69
    success from failed campaign, 108–12
    women's movement and mobilizing issues
        after, 135–52
    wording, 166n14
Equity, 119–24 (See also Pay equity)
Essentialism, 118, 119
Evangelism, 12, 13
Expressive/interactive system, 91–96

Factionalism, 61
Family, 36, 42, 103–105
Farrell, Warren, 105
Fathers' rights groups, 147
Feldman, Maxine, 67
Feminism
    considerations of practice in 1980s, 90–91
    current challenges, 132–34
    defectors from cause, 105–106
    defining in early 1980s, 83–88

Feminism *contd.*
    factors contributing to changing views,
      88–90
    ideological classifications, 2
    ideology and methodology, 6
    ideology and schisms, 54–64
    popular support for goals in 1980s, 109–12
    pornography debate, 114–17
    re-emergence in 1960s, 41–44
    small group sector, 49–51
    women of color, 125–28
Feminist Anti-Censorship Taskforce (FACT),
    115–16
Feminist Revolution, 69–70
The Feminists, 50, 51
Ferraro, Geraldine, 93
Ferree, Myra Marx, 66, 67
Firestone, Shulamith, 46, 49
Flexner, Eleanor, 22
Fourier, Charles, 133
Frankel, Sara, 105
Freeman, Jo, 40–41, 62, 67, 90, 142
Friedan, Betty, 42, 45, 61
Fritz, Leah, 40
Frye, Jerry K., 108

Gamson, William, 53
Garabillo, Toni, 105
Gay Liberation Front, 50
Gay Liberation Movement, 61
Gender, 103–105, 117–19, 128–30
General Federation of Women's Clubs, 26
Gilman, Charlotte Perkins, 24
Goldsmith, Judy, 141
Government, 42–44
A Grassroots Group of Second Class Citizens,
    77, 171n31
Greenham Common Women's Peace Camp,
    138
Griffith, Martha, 43
Grimke, Angelina and Sarah, 15
Group relations, 156–58

Hanisch, Carol, 57
Hansen, Karen, 70
Heritage Foundation, 68
Hess, Beth B., 66, 67
Hewlett, Sylvia, 105
Hill, Anita, 151
Hispanics, 127

History, 155
Homeless, 101–102
hooks, bell, 132

Identity, 63–64
Ideology
    changing orientations of women's movement
      in 1980s, 79–97
    classifications and contemporary women's
      movement, 2
    definitions of feminism in 1980s, 89–90
    early women's movement, 12, 37–38
    methodology, 6
    resource mobilization research, 4
    schisms in contemporary women's
      movement, 54–64
    social movement change and group relations,
      155–58
Illinois, 7, 35, 76
Immigration, 27
Internationalism, 36
International Women's Year Conference
    (IWY), 75
Interviews, 5–6, 6–7

Jenkins, J. Craig, 95
Jewish women, 128
Johnson, Anjela, 138
Johnson, Lyndon, 43
Johnson, Sonia
    civil disobedience, 76, 81, 82
    definition of feminism, 85, 87
    Democratic Party, 93
    feminist alternatives, 77
    interview selection, 7
    personal and fundamental social change, 96
    post-ERA activism, 139–40
    presidential campaign, 92, 172n42
    on war against women, 83
    Women's Equality Day, 164n14
Johnston, Jill, 51
Jones, Beverly, 57–58

Kelley, Florence, 25
Kennedy, Anthony, 100, 151
Kennedy, John F., 42, 43
King, Carole, 85
King, Martin Luther, Jr., 42, 159
Kinnard, Cynthia, 111
Knights of Labor, 25

Labor issues, 24–26, 37, 103–105, 165n3 (*See also* Pay equity; Wage discrimination)
Leadership, 94
League of Women Voters, 34, 37, 59, 67, 168n11
Legal Defense and Education Fund (LDEF), 67–68
Lesbianism, 44–45, 49–51, 83, 139
Liberal feminism, 2, 5
Life style politics, 174–75n19
Lobbying, 88
Lorde, Audre, 127
Louisiana, 149
Love, Barbara, 45
Luker, Kristin, 108, 146–47
Lutz, Alma, 155

MacKinnon, Catherine, 115, 119
Mainardi, Pat, 57
Malcolm X, 159
Mansbridge, Jane, 108
Marxism, 48, 49 (*See also* Socialist feminism)
Maternity leave policy, 120
Matriarchy, 126
Mayo, Edith, 108
Media, 153–54, 172–73n46
Methodology, 4–6
Michelman, Kate, 146
Militancy, 32, 170n25
Mill, John Stuart, 11
Miller, Elizabeth Smith, 18
Mobilization (*See* Resource mobilization)
Mommy track, 106
Morgan, Robin, 58, 131, 134
Mormon Church, 76
Motherhood, 147
Motivation, 93
Mott, James, 15, 17
Mott, Lucretia, 14–15
Music, women's, 67

National Abortion Rights Action League (NARAL), 146
National American Woman's Suffrage Association (National), 30, 32, 155–56
National Association for the Advancement of Colored People (NAACP), 126, 159, 173n8
National Congress for Men, 147
National Consumers' League, 24–25
National Organization for Women (NOW)
    civil disobedience, 81–82, 171n9

defining of issues, 44–46
diverse forms of activism, 174n15
early group leaders, 54
ERA campaign, 73–75
formation, 44
group relations, 157
groups studied, 5
image as conservative organization, 82–83
internal challenges in 1970s, 71–73
mass movement sector and party politics, 141–44
membership, 168n8
nuclear proliferation, 173–74n12
as reform organization, 40
small group sector, 46–51
women's movement in 1970s, 67–69
National Right to Life movement, 68
National Woman's Party (NWP), 29–30, 32, 37, 38, 43, 155–56
National Woman Suffrage Association (NAWSA), 20, 21–22, 22–23, 32
National Women's Music Festival, 67
National Women's Political Caucus (NWPC), 5, 59, 143, 168n10, 169–70n17, 174n15
National Women's Studies Association (NWSA), 132
Nevada, 151
New Age, 138, 139
New American Movement (NAM), 5, 71, 169n10
New Jersey, 69
New Right, 69, 74, 158, 160 (*See also* Conservatives)
New York, 69
New York Radical Women (NYRW), 46
Nineteenth Amendment, 31, 34
Nominalism, 118
Non-feminism, 175n8

Oberlin College, 13–14
Occupational status, 122
Oligarchy, 163n4
Oregon, 151

Palmer, Phyllis Marynick, 130
Parental leave, 121
Parks, Rosa, 42
Patriarchy, 140
Paul, Alice, 28, 35, 74
Pay equity, 121–23 (*See also* Wage discrimination)

Peace, 137, 138–39, 173–74n12
Pennsylvania, 149
Perfectionism, 13
Peterson, Esther, 42–43, 166n15
Philanthropy, 11–12
Planned Parenthood v. Danforth, 147
Politicos (*See* Socialist feminism)
Politics, 91–96, 140–44, 148–50, 154, 174–
    75n19 (*See also* Suffrage movement)
Populist Movement, 166n10
Pornography, 114–17, 119
Postfeminism, 136, 164
Poverty, 101–102, 124–25, 130
Power, 83
Pratt, Minnie Bruce, 128
President's Commission on the Status of
    Women (PCSW), 43
Prisons, 30
Progressive Action Caucus (PAC), 143
Progressive era, 22–26
Prohibition, 27

Quakerism, 12, 13

Race, 26, 120, 128–30 (*See also* Blacks;
    Racism)
Racism, 100, 124–32, 130–32
Radicalesbian, 167n7
Radical feminism, 5, 47–49, 55, 58, 69–70,
    117
Radicalism, 160–61
Reagan administration, 99–112
Reckitt, Lois, 105
Redstockings, 69–70, 167n10
Reform societies, 11–12
Religion, 12–13
Religious Committee for the ERA (RCERA), 76
Republican Party, 75, 142–43, 148–49
Reskin, Barbara, 122–23
Resource mobilization, 3–4, 156
The Revolution, 20, 165n2
Reynolds, William Bradford, 100
Richardson, Laurel, 56–57
Riddeough, Chris, 7, 71, 86, 169n13
Robert, Sylvia, 68
Roe v. Wade, 68
Ross, Luana, 129
Ross, Naomi, 84–85
Roth, Julius, 120
Rothman, Barbara Katz, 147, 148
RU486, 150

Salem Ohio Women's Rights Convention, 16
Sanger, Margaret, 33
Sanitary Commission, 19
Sargeant, Mary Lee, 92–93
Schneiderman, Rose, 25
Schroeder, Patricia, 143
Schwartz, Felice, 106
Self-definition, 63–64
Seneca Falls Woman's Rights Convention, 11,
    16–17
Seneca Women's Peace Encampment, 138–39
Separatism, 51, 59–60, 140
Service work, 91–92
Settlement house movement, 23
Sexism, 100
Sexual difference, 117–19, 123
Sexuality, 114, 116
Simmel, Georg, 53
Small group sectors, 46–51, 137–40, 157
Smeal, Eleanor
    civil disobedience, 76, 81
    ERA and politics, 75, 141–42
    goals of NOW, 87–88
    interview selection, 6–7
    leadership of NOW, 73, 74
    political activism, 95–96
    on women and power, 83
    women as priority, 133
Smith, Barbara, 128, 132
Snitow, Ann, 47, 84, 117
Snow, David A., 75
Socialism, 160
Socialist feminism, 5, 47–49, 55, 59, 70–
    71, 87
Socialist Workers' Party, 56
Social movements
    change and group relations, 155–58
    coalition building, 27–28
    demobilizing effect of theory as ideology,
        60–61
    meaning of radicalism, 160–61
    oligarchic tendencies, 163n4
    resource mobilization framework, 3–4
    sexism in research, 175n1
    social change, 31–37
    studies of contemporary women's movement,
        1–3
    women's movement as, 159–60
    women's movement from 1975 to 1982,
        65–77
Social purity movement, 165n5

Social services, 101
Sociology, 24
Souter, David H., 150–51
Southern Christian Leadership Conference
    (SCLC), 159
Spirituality, 137–40, 174n2
Stanton, Elizabeth Cady
    Civil War, 19
    dress reform, 18, 31
    education, 13
    relationship with Susan B. Anthony, 16
    suffrage movement, 10, 20, 22–23
    temperance and women's rights, 14, 15
Stanton, Henry, 15
Stein, Harry, 105
Steinem, Gloria, 41, 59, 153
Stone, Lucy, 13–14, 15, 19, 20, 164–65n5
Strategy, 95–96
Structure, 93–94
Student Nonviolent Coordinating Committee
    (SNCC), 46
Suffrage movement
    coalition building, 27–28
    conservatism in progressive era, 22–26
    continuity of women's movement, 135–36
    ideology, 37–38, 155–56
    individual states, 166n10
    new forces and new methods, 28–31
    overview, 9–10, 21–22
    social change and social movement, 31–37
Sununu, John, 151
Supreme Court, 68, 100, 145, 146, 150–51
Symbolization, 4

Tactics, 96
Taft, Jessie, 24
Tavris, Carol, 110
Taylor, Harriet, 11, 17
Taylor, Verta, 66
Temperance, 14, 23, 27
Theory, 3–4, 60–64
Thomas, Clarence, 151
Timmer, Barbara, 84
Trashing, 62
Trebilcot, Joyce, 85–86
Troy Female Seminary, 13
Truth, Sojourner, 17

Unemployment, 129–30
Unions, 25

United Auto Workers Women's Commission,
    44
United Feminist Action Campaign (UFAC), 143
Universities, 23–24
University of Chicago, 24

Vance, Carole, 115
Veblen, Thorstein, 13, 122
Violence, 114–15

Wage discrimination, 25, 43, 129 (See also Pay
    equity)
Wald, Lillian, 26
Wattleton, Faye, 148
Weeks v. Southern Bell Telephone Company, 68
Weld, Theodore, 15
Weyrich, Paul, 68
Willard, Emma, 13, 16
Willard, Frances, 23
Willis, Ellen, 117
Wilson, Margaret Bush, 126, 173n8
Winnow, Jackie, 139
Wollstonecraft, Mary, 10
The Woman's Journal, 20
Woman's Party, 29
Women's Christian Temperance Union
    (WCTU), 23
Women's Equality Day, 164n14
Women's Equity Action League (WEAL), 44
Women's Gatherings, 95
Women's International Terrorist Conspiracy
    from Hell (WITCH), 168n7
Women's Loyal National League, 19
Women's movement. (See also Feminism;
    Suffrage movement)
    contemporary
        defining issues in NOW, 44–46
        ideology and activism in 1980s, 79–97
        mobilizing issues after ERA, 135–52
        overview, 40–41, 153–54
        Reagan years, 99–112
        re-emergence, 41–44
        small group sector, 46–51
        as social movement, 159–60
        studies of and social movements, 1–3
        transformation from 1975 to 1982, 65–77
    early woman's rights movement
        factors contributing to demise of in
            1920s, 64
        failure to address sex/gender differences,

Women's movement *contd.*
    120
    organization, 16–20
    origins, 10–16
    overview, 9–10
Women Rising in Resistance, 95, 137
Women's Strike for Equality, 50
Women's Studies, 123
Women's Trade Union League, 26
Woodhull, Victoria, 165n4

Work (*See* Labor issues)
Working Women's Association, 165n3
World Anti-Slavery Convention, 15
World War I, 29
Wright, Frances, 15
Wyoming, 166n10

Yard, Molly, 143, 146, 151

Zurcher, Louis A., 75